PLANNING FOR A NATION OF CITIES

edited by *Sam Bass Warner, Jr.*

THE M.I.T. PRESS
Massachusetts Institute of Technology
Cambridge, Massachusetts, and London, England

First M.I.T. Press Paperback Edition, August 1966
Second Paperback Printing, April 1967
Third Paperback Printing, October 1969

SBN 262 23021 6 (hardcover)
SBN 262 73013 8 (paperback)

Library of Congress Catalog Card Number 66-21355
Printed in the United States of America

PREFACE

Amid America's network of rapidly changing cities, thousands of scattered institutions are practicing some form of city planning. Social agencies, planning boards, special-purpose authorities, city, state, and federal governments — all are engaged in shaping the multitude of urban environments of the United States. Yet the total effort falls far short of what can be demanded from everyday professional competence, reasonable applications of funds, and commonplace democratic aspirations. This gap between what a thoughtful citizen is entitled to expect from urban planning and public policy, and the contemporary performance of American cities is the subject of this book of essays.

In a democratic society, the goal of planning is not to promote one particular style of urban living, rather the goal of planning is to create humane environments which will widen the choices open to individual city dwellers and which will enrich the many cultural styles that now exist.

Current American urban environments considerably restrict individual choice, and they foster a good deal of self-destructive behavior in all cultural styles. Racial prejudice degrades one whole set of life styles, while poverty degrades many others. Together prejudice and poverty drag down every city in the nation. Lack of public resources and programs narrows the choices and potentials of middle-class life. At the upper extreme, the habits of wealthy Americans resemble escape from a hostile world more than broad mastery of the possibilities of urban living.

At present, American society influences the way people live in three strong ways: by the kinds of jobs cities offer, by the kinds of physical settings cities possess, and by the public services cities furnish. National and metropolitan employment are not generally dealt with as ingredients of urban planning, yet they are the first subjects that must be mastered if physical planning and public services are to be complementary. The world of urban work not only determines the personal income of city dwellers, it also is a major determinant of urban styles of life. For these reasons, this book has been organized with one section on urban work in addition to sections on physical planning and public services.

Today the range of urban events is enormous; it varies in size from the behavior of the street and the neighborhood to the terms of national business and international trade. Generally the larger events impinge upon the smaller, as in the case of a national corporation's opening or closing a factory in a city. Nevertheless, local government can significantly ease or exacerbate the conditions under which its citizens must make their lives. One of the purposes of this book is to show the interconnections between large-scale and local events in a wide variety of planning issues.

Part I, "The Federal Responsibility," deals with the general social, economic, and administrative problems that confront any attempt to deal with cities at their national scale; Part II,

"Work and the Quality of Urban Life," shows how much of the familiar strengths and weaknesses of American cities arises out of day-to-day social and economic interactions; Part III, "Responsive Physical Planning," takes up some of the consequences of the goal of trying to plan physical environments for the variety of urban publics which exist in America and to design and administer at the many scales which urban design problems must be worked; Part IV, "Responsive Urban Services," uses education and social welfare as two cases where masses of citizens must be served on an individual basis by local institutions.

The 1964 Bicentennial of the City of St. Louis provided the occasion for the research and writing of this book. Its essays, and the conference for which they were first prepared, were Washington University's part in the celebration of the city's bicentennial. The entire project was most generously supported by the St. Louis Regional Planning and Construction Foundation and Washington University.

Research was begun informally with a seminar of the Washington University urban faculty guided by Wilbur Thompson. Later, outside scholars were invited to join the work of the St. Louis group. On April 21 through 23, 1964, we all came together for the Bicentennial Conference on Planning for the Quality of Urban Life. In addition to the contributors to this volume, the following participants at the conference aided our progress with their discussion and criticism of the work: The Honorable Jack Bronston, Chairman, New York State Senate Educational Planning Committee; Dr. Leonard J. Duhl, Chief, Office of Planning, National Institute of Mental Health; Dr. Hylan G. Lewis, Professor of Sociology and Director of Community Research Projects, Howard University; and Professors Harold J. Barnett, Lattie F. Coor, Robert F. Dannenbrink, Roger Mongomery, and Irvin Sobel of Washington University.

It was the intention of the group when it first gathered to use the occasion of the anniversary of one of the nation's largest cities to take a long view into America's urban future. Utopian criticism and vision were to be encouraged. The discussions of the conference, and the essays of this book, however, remain strongly rooted in the present concerns of American cities. If we have failed in our distant vision, may I remind the reader that the first summer of our labors was heralded by the Harlem Negro riots and the opening of President Johnson's "War on Poverty," the second summer closed with the Watts, California, riots and the establishment of a cabinet post for Housing and Urban Development. A high-temperature urban foreground!

Sam Bass Warner, Jr.

Institute for Urban and Regional Studies
Washington University
St. Louis, Missouri
November 1, 1965

CONTENTS

PART I

THE FEDERAL RESPONSIBILITY

ONE *NATIONAL PLANNING FOR HEALTHY CITIES: TWO CHALLENGES TO AFFLUENCE* 3
Gunnar Myrdal

TWO *THE PUBLIC AND PRIVATE RATIONALE FOR A NATIONAL URBAN POLICY* 23
John W. Dyckman

THREE *URBAN CONSTRAINTS AND FEDERAL POLICY* 43
Sam Bass Warner, Jr.

FOUR *FEDERAL RESOURCES AND URBAN NEEDS* 61
Murray L. Weidenbaum

PART II

WORK AND THE QUALITY OF URBAN LIFE

FIVE *THE ROLE OF WORK IN A MOBILE SOCIETY* 81
Marc A. Fried

SIX *WORK AND IDENTITY IN THE LOWER CLASS* 105
Lee Rainwater

SEVEN *TOMORROW'S WORKERS: THE PROSPECTS FOR THE URBAN LABOR FORCE* 124
Stanley Lebergott

PART III

RESPONSIVE PHYSICAL PLANNING

EIGHT *SUBURBS, SUBCULTURES, AND THE URBAN FUTURE* 143
Bennett M. Berger

NINE *THE RISING DEMAND FOR URBAN AMENITIES* 163
Jean Gottmann

TEN *A PLANNING INVENTORY FOR THE METROPOLIS* 179
Joseph R. Passonneau

ELEVEN *REGIONAL PLANNING IN BRITAIN* 193
John R. James

TWELVE *A LEGAL STRATEGY FOR URBAN DEVELOPMENT* 209
Daniel R. Mandelker

PART IV

RESPONSIVE URBAN SERVICES

THIRTEEN *TOWARD A FRAMEWORK FOR URBAN PUBLIC MANAGEMENT* 229
Wilbur R. Thompson

FOURTEEN *URBAN EDUCATION IN LONG-TERM CRISIS* 246
Judson T. Shaplin

FIFTEEN *URBAN POLITICS AND EDUCATION* 268
Robert H. Salisbury

SIXTEEN *THE REINSTITUTIONALIZATION OF SOCIAL WELFARE* 285
Ralph E. Pumphrey

INDEX 299

THE FEDERAL RESPONSIBILITY

CHAPTER ONE

NATIONAL PLANNING FOR HEALTHY CITIES: TWO CHALLENGES TO AFFLUENCE

Gunnar Myrdal

Urban planning depends for its success upon a supporting national structure of economic and social policies. One part of this structure must be federal programs to sustain full employment and rapid growth of the economy. A second part of this structure must be a whole set of federally guided attacks on the inherited patterns of poverty and segregation which now degrade American cities.

I

My title suggests that fundamental planning for the growth and health of a nation of cities can be most effectively pursued at the level of national or federal policy making. A crucial fact emerges from many chapters of this book: if we rely entirely on policies induced at the local level, planning for the quality of urban life will become an almost hopeless task. In many fields, indeed, we should have to expect a worsening of the present situation. Reaching our goal will require changes in what I call "national parameters," or fundamental determi-

Gunnar Myrdal is a Professor of Economics and Director of the Institute for International Economic Studies, Stockholm. He is well known to American readers as the author of *An American Dilemma* (1944), and *Challenge to Affluence* (1962).

nants of national growth. One such set of parameters I will allude to in terms of the unconditional war on poverty against the conditions of residential segregation and against the associated vicious circle of underemployment, asocial behavior, and unequal standards in schools, housing, and community facilities. Closely related to this set of national parameters is another set, which I will discuss in terms of sustained economic growth. The rate of economic growth has, both directly and indirectly, the most important effects on the poverty problem in American cities, and on planning for the regeneration of those cities. Taken together, national planning to intensify the war on poverty and to assure sustained economic growth are two challenges to American affluence of the greatest significance.

II

For a person with my particular background it is perhaps natural at this point to stress again that American metropolitan areas, in their development toward an inegalitarian residential segregation, are living out old traditions in a country that originally had Negro slavery and that until comparatively recently had mass immigration which in later periods came mostly from Southern and Eastern Europe. As a nation, Americans have become accustomed to having large, culturally and economically unassimilated enclaves of disadvantaged people in their midst. Thus patterns of segregation developed as a part of the social heritage of Americans. It was natural to keep a social distance from such people and thus to feel less concerned when they suffered.

But to put the blame entirely on this subjective factor of attitudes does not give anything resembling a full explanation. First, when people in the enclaves of the poor showed traits of inferiority, this in turn justified and fortified prejudice. Moreover, systems of institutional factors strengthened prejudices by circular causation. These included, for instance, restrictive housing covenants — which for decades were given legal sanction, and even now operate in practice even without such sanction — certain aspects of zoning ordinances, etc. For decades even the federal housing agencies were not active in breaking down residential segregation, but rather had an influence in the opposite direction by either leaving the matter to local authorities or setting up such conditions for mortgage insurance that virtually necessitated segregation. Even when more recently these policies have been reversed — particularly in regard to Negro-white relations — these changed policies have been made effective only for new projects, with the result that today eighty percent of public housing is still segregated.

The motivational basis of this institutionalized residential segregation is in turn strengthened, as intrusion from a lower stratum is experienced as a threat to the private economy of the individual who fears a decrease in value of his property. Meanwhile, the resulting overcrowding of slums, the lower standards of the schools, and, more generally, poverty and all that poverty implies give more impetus to the vicious circle of prejudice.

The slum inhabitants are, of course, not the only ones who suffer. The slums develop like a cancer growth around the heart of the city, clog plans for urban renewal, and hasten decay even of adjacent areas; they also often prevent construction of high-speed highways or the use of land for parks, etc. If, in order to accomplish these projects, the inhabitants are evicted from their houses, they will turn other areas into slum districts. The slums are, in any event, tending to increase because of immigration to the cities of ever more very poor people and because of the high natural population increase.

What is the background of inegalitarian residential segregation and institutionalized poverty? The social tourist sees immediately that urban areas in the United States, more than in other rich countries, have become spatially segregated along lines determined not by income class differences alone but also by racial, ethnic, and, to some extent, religious and cultural differences. This, of course, has its roots in the less homogeneous character of the American nation, even after decades and generations of national integration.

The social tourist also comes to know, almost from immediate observation, that there is a correlation between the economic and the other differences. Some racial and ethnic groups are on the average very much poorer, as for instance the Negroes, as well as many other groups. It should always be remembered, however, when the nation is taken as a whole, that Negroes make up only one third or one fourth of the poor in America, depending on where the poverty line is drawn. Indeed, a large part of the poor is of "old American" stock without any ethnic stigma. In the big cities, however, Negroes — and in some of them also other minority ethnic groups — constitute a much larger part of the really poor.

In general terms, as we all know, the pattern of residential segregation works itself out in the following way. The majority of urban Americans who are well off in differing degrees and who, according to the ideological preferences in this country, all refer to themselves as "middle class" — a fact confirmed by opinion polls for several decades — live in their own well-kept areas: in the inner city, if any such areas are left and not in the process of too rapid deterioration, but increasingly in the suburbs. Occasionally publicity has been given to people in this middle class seeking to return to the inner city, but, statistically speaking, there has, as a general rule, been a continual net migration from the inner cities. As a matter of fact, much work and employment also moves that way, and not just retail trade.

Meanwhile, Negroes and other nonwhite people who are mostly very poor, and also other members of what I call the American "underclass," continue to live in slum districts of the inner city or in districts that soon become slum districts as more of the "underclass" moves there.

As the American population is becoming increasingly urbanized — in 1970 two out of three Americans will live in the metropolitan areas and at the end of the century perhaps four out of five — the suburbs are increasing in area and population. At the same time, the slums in the inner cities are also rapidly increasing both in population and in area. For various reasons which have been analyzed by several authors of these chapters

— the variety of job opportunities, more generous relief administration, and so on — the cities, and particularly the big cities, continue to attract poor and culturally disadvantaged people from the countryside.

Life in the suburbs undoubtedly has its problems. But the really serious problems related to the quality of urban life concern, of course, the inner city and, more particularly, the poor people in the slums; and it is around their problems that many of the chapters that follow are centered. Not one of the authors suggests that this misery is caused by inherited traits. The fact that the inhabitants of the slums usually show certain characteritics which are a disadvantage in the American competitive social and economic system, and even that they manifest a relatively higher proportion of asocial behavior, is commonly considered a result of environment in the widest sense. This, however, is also "inherited," though in another sense than the biological. It is a heritage of the conditions under which they live and have lived for a long time.

By various economic and social processes, the pattern of residential segregation of the poorer groups in the cities has itself contributed to the preservation of their low status by keeping down not only their incomes but their levels of culture in the broadest meaning. When the Supreme Court, in ordering the abolition of school segregation for Negro children and youth, took its stand on the thesis that "separate cannot be equal," the judges expressed a truth with much wider application than to the white–Negro relationship.

It is thus also apparent that in the urban areas of the United States this residential segregation has been permitted to reflect itself in extremely large quality differences, not only in regard to the physical structure and maintenance of streets, roads, parks, playgrounds, and houses, but also in regard to all sorts of community amenities and social institutions. Not only the school buildings, for instance, but also the standards of teaching in the schools are inferior in the areas where the poor and disadvantaged live. Under the pressure of the swelling population of children in the slums of most big cities — and in spite of courageous efforts to prevent it—schools have often actually been deteriorating in recent years, in contrast to majority America where there has been such a spectacular and continuing advance.

III

This vicious circle that leads to the deterioration of the old cities can only be broken by policies. And the policies must be of a rather radical nature. Of the greatest importance will be policies on the national level. In this section I shall discuss the unconditional war on poverty, and I shall present an approach through this means to the problems of the decay and waste of lives and property in the inner cities.

If we should accept the present trends of the American economy and the present federal policies, not very much could be done on the local or even the state level. Efforts to break down the basic residential segregation that implies keeping the poor enclosed in overcrowded slum areas meet strong vested interests. Even insofar as the poor actually come to move outside the old borders of segregation under the pressure of the population increase in the slums, this move regularly means only bigger slums that soon become equally overcrowded. The poor cannot afford a much higher housing standard. This does not mean that it would not ordinarily be a good thing if there were less resistance to enlarging these areas where they have to live.

The setting and enforcing of uniform standards in regard to all community amenities, from the provision of streets, parks, and playgrounds and their upkeep to the building of schools and the improvement of the level of teaching, would seem to be appropriate local policy. The need for "enforcible uniform standards" of administration and services is stressed in several chapters of this book.

It is also shown, however, that what would often be needed, at least in a transitional period, would be discrimination in reverse. To lift the level of teaching of the children in the slums, for example, we would need specially trained elite teachers who in our type of society should have higher wages than those having the easier and more pleasant tasks of educating the children of the majority of Americans outside the slums. And to compensate for the many disabilities of children from very poor homes, a number of special institutions and social activities related to the schools are needed.

To have any effectiveness, uniform standards for what the community is providing would need to be set and enforced in urban communities, including both the rich and the poor residential districts in a metropolitan area. In the present situation, however, a metropolitan area as recognized by the Census Bureau may contain a hundred or more governmental units with power to tax and to spend. This jurisdictional division is, in fact, nothing but a legalized superstructure of the inegalitarian residential segregation.

The opinion that we need much larger jurisdictional units is stressed in other chapters as a necessary condition for progress in improving our cities. It must seem doubtful, however, whether a development in that direction could be expected to come as the result of a rational conclusion by the citizens in a metropolitan area that such a change is practical and fair. The people in the suburbs would feel an economic interest not to become joined with other and poorer communities. It is, of course, a fact that the ordinary dwellers in the suburbs have chosen to live there, partly in order to have pleasant, clean surroundings and, not least, to have good schools for their children without paying too high taxes.

There are thus overwhelmingly forceful vested interests for preserving the division of local government in functionally irrational, small jurisdictional units and in not setting and enforcing uniform standards. These vested interests are set upon preserving the present residential segregation that is the framework within which the decay of the old inner cities developed. The architect and engineer will remain as powerless as the school reformer, not only because so much more than the reconstruction of the physical structure is needed, but also — apart from this factor that I shall discuss later — because saving the old cities from deterioration implies tremendous expenditures that cannot be financed except in the setting of a much larger unit.

But even if we had arrived at the functionally more rational, consolidated jurisdictional, administrative, and political units, could it realistically be expected that they would be effective in setting the uniform standards, the need for which I mentioned previously, and vote the taxes that would have to be spent in order to give reality to these standards? How could the richer inhabitants — who if the unit were made big enough would be in a majority — be enthusiastic about joining in sharing the costs?

One fact stressed in various contexts in several essays is that an attack merely on the physical structure of cities does not accomplish much. The architect and the engineer, aided by the social reformer, may do a beautiful job of constructing an entirely new city, usually a suburb. During my traveling in the United States I have seen admirable examples of their efforts in many parts of America. Homes, parks, playgrounds, streets, and all sorts of community services, including shopping centers, can be built and organized in a functional way since there is no historical legacy preventing perfectly rational solutions. By selecting the clientele, the pattern of segregation on racial and ethnic grounds can also be avoided, even if these new settlements provide no place for the really poor and disadvantaged, who cannot pay the costs. These experiments show us what a pleasant, functionally rational, effective, democratic, and economic urban life we should be able to create today, if we were not frustrated by the legacy of the deteriorating physical structure of the cities and, specifically, by its human content of very poor and disadvantaged people in the slums, the people from whom others preserve a distance, even to the extent of remaining unconcerned about their conditions of life.

If we could forget about these very poor people, if we could assume that they disappeared as they were cleared out of the slums, city renewal would nevertheless be a very expensive affair, implying huge investments, though all worth undertaking. But these people do not disappear; and wherever they move they are poor, and, because of their poverty and all that poverty implies, particularly where it has become a permanent condition, they will create new slums. In addition, the great need is to make it possible for them to lift themselves out of poverty, human misery, and low economic productivity and, primarily, to motivate them to do it.

Since the consequences of their weaknesses imply a tremendous drag on the economic progress of the nation, the unconditional war against poverty has the character of a national investment that in time should prove more profitable to the nation than an equal investment in plants and machinery. About this I have no misgivings, though it would take me too long to develop this theme in the present context. In countries more advanced as welfare states than the United States, for instance Norway, there are studies proving the favorable national income effect of welfare policies.

In this connection there are a few specific points that I should make, as they have direct relevance for the ensuing chapters. My first observation is that the war against poverty can be effectively pursued only by national policies, whereas, as I have pointed out, policy efforts at the local level are apt to be frustrated by vested interests and insufficient financial resources. This has, incidentally, implications far outside the problem of slums. The American citizen is generally a much more broadminded individual, prepared to act more in line with the American ideals when he acts on the national level. Consequently, much more can be accomplished, and with broader support, at this level.

My second point is that while this war against poverty must almost by necessity be waged on the national level and be a matter for the federal government, particularly in regard to its financing, the actual effectuation and administration of many, though by far not all, of the reforms — for instance, the improvement of education for the poor — must in this large and diversified country come to be a state and, even more a local responsibility. But even if the federal government should be prepared to appropriate funds according to some formula to state and local governments without tying them to a specific purpose, I believe it is incredible that it would not set certain conditions — or later find it necessary to set such conditions. Among such conditions would be the request for consolidation of local government in larger and functionally more effective units and for the enforcement of unified minimum standards.

As the unconditional war against poverty gets under way and really comes to grips with the problem, this would then solve the problem that I do not believe will be solved by local initiative: enlarging the administrative units and enforcing uniform standards. We have already seen this beginning to happen in several fields, for instance when the Federal government has given financial support for transportation. The most conspicuous federal actions in this direction have, of course, recently been directed toward preventing discrimination against Negroes. But as federal involvement in welfare policies increases, I believe we will see additional setting of standards to be enforced by consolidating local government. This, together with the financial contribution, will open up new possibilities for the city planners and the reformers generally.

These changes will undoubtedly raise much controversy concerning centralization of controls. I will confess that my own mind is a little split on this issue. I am enough of a Jeffersonian Democrat to see value in having responsible independent local administrations and not having everything settled in Washington. The ideal that we might approach as the goal of development would be a rational compromise where we would get the functionally rational, consolidated local governments as well as uniformity of standards that prevent the too low standards for the poor, but where nevertheless much freedom, particularly for experimentation and improvement, would be protected once reasonably high minimum standards are met.

My third point, which has been implied in what I have

already said, is that this unconditional war against poverty, to be successful, requires much greater efforts and expenditure than have until now been commonly recognized. For the time being, the war against poverty has mainly had the character of a moral and intellectual catharsis in the body politic, which has, as yet, resulted only in some rather minor and sometimes spurious reform activities. I believe, however, that this catharsis will continue and develop momentum. New statistical investigations, a multitude of projects coming out of the mill of many departments in Washington, conferences, books, articles, speeches, and policy declarations are like drops in a rapidly swelling, mighty flood.

As a background to what is now on the verge of happening, we should recall that very generally economic and social policies in the United States have had a perverse tendency to aid the not-so-poor, while leaving the really poor to destitution which is mitigated to some extent by state, local and private charity in one form or another. This is true about taxation, which is regressive up to a rather high level; agricultural policy, which has not helped the poor farmer or the farm laborer very much; housing policies, which have often favored middle-class groups; minimum-wage legislation, which has left the very poorest groups without protection against exploitation, and so on. It is also true of the various forms of social security, whose benefits are dependent upon regular employment or other specific eligibility requirements.

This tendency is, of course, not unrelated to the fact that what I have called the American "underclass" has been the world's least revolutionary proletariat. The poor have traditionally remained silent. They have not organized themselves for effective action. The trade unions, for instance, include not much more than a fourth of the labor force. Poor people have not participated much in voting or at any rate have not used their voting strength as a force to defend their interests. This is true even when they have not been prevented from registering, as have a large part of the Negro people in the South. The momentum of the moral and intellectual catharsis that

I mentioned will be strengthened when not only the Negroes —who have now risen in rebellion and whose right to vote in the South will be protected by new federal legislation—but also other members of the "underclass" increase their political participation, particularly by voting.

As the war against poverty develops, changes in the direction of giving the poor a better deal will come up in the whole range of the policy fields I mentioned. In fact, we have already seen this beginning to happen; modest changes in this direction have already occurred. Taking the longer view, I believe these policy changes will accumulate and there will evolve a major alteration of the income distribution—a factor that is at the very root of the problem dealt with in this book. In regard to Social Security, I believe that, in time, health facilities will have to be provided on a national level for all, as in England or Sweden. In historical perspective, the Medicare reform, as many of its opponents have pointed out, will be seen only as a step in this direction. Old-age pensions will be given to all people over a certain age; likewise, income compensation will be given to handicapped and widowed, etc. Gradually, America will liberate itself from the pattern it borrowed from the time of Lloyd George and Bismarck when the social problem was looked upon as "a labor question." More and more social insurance will be financed on a regular tax basis, as the present financial basis cannot carry it when it is enlarged in these ways.

The United States has been late to recognize the relation between poverty and number of children. The Report of the President's Economic Council reveals a recent study showing that if one fifth of the nation is counted as falling under the poverty line, this fifth contains one fourth of the children. This is a very serious situation. I believe that it will soon stand out as an obvious and generally recognized obligation that much more will have to be done in the interest of the children and the families with children. Part of the aid might be given in the form of family allowances worked into the Social Security system. At the same time, the rising feeling of a special obligation to the children will give powerful support to all the efforts to improve schools and make them and other supporting agencies the vehicles for giving children services and goods so to speak in kind. Such improvements will, wholly or partly, substitute for cash aid. The problem of providing decent housing for poor families will also be considered much more as a part of the need to protect the children and the families with children.

This movement will imply gradually larger increases in federal expenditures. In my view they will soon swallow up any federal budget surpluses that otherwise are bound to accrue even if the growth of the economy were only modest, as federal taxes are progressive; it is quite likely that in time these expenditure increases will require higher federal tax rates. To the state and local governments these policies will, first, improve the general welfare situation — as when the aged and the handicapped are given stable incomes on a national basis without restriction — and, second, mean federal aid for various projects which will spur the local and state government to more preventive and prophylactic social policies, particularly in regard to children and the young. The climate of hopelessness that often now surrounds local welfare policies, and, indeed, even regular school policies, will have improved.

When I foresee this radical change of attitude toward the poverty problem in national policies, it is partly because I reckon with a continuation and an intensification of the rationalistic and at the same time deeply humanitarian public discussion that has an educational influence. People will be drawn out of their indifference. Partly, it is because I foresee that in this social process not only the Negroes but all poverty-stricken groups will increasingly stand up for their interests. The majority outside this group will also learn pragmatically that society can afford to do much more in this direction and that such expenditures are, indeed, good investments. Partly, it is because I reckon with a speedier economic growth in the future — a point I shall elaborate more fully in Section IV — which will make it even more apparent to everyone that policies can then be financed and, indeed, that they will support a more rapid economic growth. Partly, I also reckon with the fact that the American nation and particularly its majority of economically secure people with good jobs and incomes are proud. I do not find it likely that they will be satisfied for a very long time with a situation where, among the rich countries, their country has the highest unemployment rate, the biggest and most horrible slums with the dirtiest streets and subways, and is most niggardly to its aged, its handicapped, and its needy children.

After having expressed this optimistic faith about the future development of the war against poverty, I want to add, however, as a fourth point that eradication of poverty and all that poverty implies — in the way of destruction and frustration of human values and economic productivity — will have to include policy efforts on a broad front, undertaken simultaneously and carried on for a long time. Even if wisely directed and courageously speeded up, the time period before these investments give their full yield is long. Poverty, when it has been permitted to develop and become a permanent situation as it has in the American city slums, is a complex and stratified social situation. A change of one factor or a few factors — even the most important, like, for instance, employment opportunities and housing — will not rapidly change the total situation; education is fighting environmental factors that are partly frustrating its effects. If in this essay I may speak in popular and loose terms, I might be permitted to use the term "slum-mindedness," which explains, for instance, the experience many cities have had where the provision of new houses does not always prevent their inhabitants from rapidly turning the districts into new slums. The specific difficulties the school reformer meets, even when he succeeds in including a great number of parallel remedial and compensatory activities besides the formal schooling, testify to the same initial difficulty inherent in the impoverished culture of the slums and the deficiencies in human motivation.

These difficulties are the legacy of having permitted poverty to exist and exert its all-permeating influence on the poor for a long time until it became institutionalized in our residentially segregated cities, maintained by vested interest. In the final analysis the existence of these special difficulties is the true indictment of American cities as they have evolved in a process of development where prejudices, exclusiveness, and indifference have determined private and community behavior. The resulting segregation of the poor and the vested interests maintaining it have further strengthened the prejudices, the exclusiveness and the indifference.

IV

In this section I shall address myself to the second of the two challenges to American affluence, the challenge to plan for sustained and rapid economic growth, which is so importantly related to the challenge of planning for the elimination of poverty in all its forms. Economic growth is, of course, mainly outside the effective influence of local or even state government. But it can be influenced by policies at the federal level. The rate of economic growth is, in my view, the most important national parameter to city planning.

Let me start out by pointing to the fact that, since the end of the eight years of the Eisenhower era, during which the United States remained in what is now clearly seen to be a state of relative economic stagnation, this country has now for more than four years had an annual growth in its Gross National Product of about five percent, that is, about double what it was before. The present business boom's most remarkable feature is, perhaps, not its unprecedented durability but the fact that even in its fifth year of growth it is so balanced. Both the administration and most business people, therefore, foresee a continuation of the boom. Even in the longer run growth prospects look assuring.

Having reached that point, I believe I should remind you that the population increase is comparatively rapid in the United States, about 1.7 percent annually. If we calculated economic growth per head, which is a more rational procedure and one which we constantly use when we are discussing economic development in underdeveloped countries, the growth rate for the United States is not very high even now.

Indeed, in comparison with the countries most similar to the United States, for example Sweden, we have to subtract more than one percent from the GNP as our population increase is only 0.5 percent annually. This observation is important because it gives a more accurate picture of the relative economic stagnation during the Eisenhower era, as well as moderating considerably the claims of rapid economic growth in the Kennedy-Johnson era. As I will argue a little later, there are reasons to speed up economic growth in the United States and, as I see it, it is also practically possible to do so.

But let me first enumerate the various ways in which a more rapid economic growth has importance for the problems we will be discussing in the book. First, it will increase the federal tax yields and do this more than proportionally. This increase should make it easier to get support for the huge expenditures needed for the reforms that would mean an intensified war against poverty. Larger tax yields would also make possible more federal aid to state and local government, which would have the same effect. Second, the more rapid economic growth would reflect itself in rising levels of business and income everywhere in the country and thus raise the base for taxation and the willingness to support higher taxes for greater expenditure in the states and the local units of government. Third, the most important consequence of a more rapid rise in the GNP would be a direct effect on the employment opportunities.

It is in the last respect that it becomes clear that economic progress is not fast enough. The unemployment rate has not decreased more than from above six percent to under five percent during the boom of the last four years. Added to this is the fact that we are just now passing a corner in the growth curve of the labor force: from now on it will increase about fifty percent faster than in recent years — by one and a half million workers per year instead of about one million. The conclusion is that, even if the present rate of economic growth is steadily maintained, we should not expect the unemployment rate to go down; the most probable thing is that it would begin to increase again.

The present unemployment rate in the United States has certain characteristics that are apt to present particularly grave problems for cities. Unemployment is much higher among teen-agers, around fifteen percent in the whole country, a rate that will now probably increase if the economic growth rate is not raised, because so much of the increase in the labor force is concentrated in the younger age groups. This must mean an intensified strain on the morale in the school system in the slums. So does the fact that nonwhite workers, who are handicapped in education and also meet discrimination in the labor market, usually show more than double the unemployment rate of white workers. I am here quoting national figures, but figures for individual cities would often be even more discouraging.

Moreover, in recent years it has been increasingly realized that the unemployment figures do not tell the whole story by far as they do not include all those who occupy an abnormal situation in the labor market. We have first to add the partially unemployed and all those who have stopped counting themselves as participants in the labor market because they do not think there are any jobs for them to secure. Some become unemployable. In addition, we have all those who are "underemployed" in the sense that as employed or self-employed they have a very low productivity and low incomes. Together these other categories of underutilized labor may account for many more than those reported as unemployed.

Let me now first say that by far the greatest single factor that could improve the quality of urban life — the subject that concerns us in this book — would be an increase in the scarcity of labor. Such a change would give employment and incomes to more people; the unemployed are a hard core of the poor. Also young people would not be in the same danger of becoming unemployables and perhaps, asocial. Scarcity of labor would, moreover, tend to draw into more productive work many of the underemployed, whose employment is often very much a "disguised unemployment." A chief cause of demoralization in schools would have disappeared. Employers, big and small, would be in the situation where they would be motivated to give workers, particularly young workers, opportunity and training. Any public training and retraining program would work much more efficiently, as there would be more certainty that there is a job at the end of the road. Indeed, every single one of the policies — federal, state, and local — and the new institutions that will be suggested in the essays that follow, would have greater possibilities of success. Making labor scarce is alpha and omega of any scheme to eradicate poverty.

This implies that the level of unemployment in the United States has a considerable elasticity or flexibility; employment can increase much more than reported unemployment figures reveal. Also the quality of the unemployed and underemployed, which we discuss in terms of "structural unemployment," is flexible: scarcity of labor will itself call into action training facilities and improve very much the effectiveness of those training and retraining facilities that exist. Indeed, scarcity of labor promises in time to change the whole climate in which poor people live. Only a full employment economy is a healthy society.

There is no mystery about the policies needed to speed up economic growth. I might only, in passing, mention that the increase of expenditures in the war against poverty is of a nature to increase total demand and so spur economic growth. So far I do not believe that there is much possibility of disagreement among economists. I believe that most economists would also agree with me that the popular excitement about automation and the rapid population increase in America as chief forces leading to unemployment is exaggerated or mistaken.

There is a transititional stage, however, where a continually high level of unemployment and underemployment for a long time past has created a difference between the quality of the labor supply and the labor demanded. Part of this discrepancy will be cured automatically by the greater efficiency, given a greater scarcity of labor, of all the policies to educate, train, and retrain workers. For the rest there is the additional possibility of changing the direction of the labor demand by speeding up construction work that needs relatively less well-trained workers and by undertaking other activities of a similar kind.

The more serious reason for controversy among economists is whether a much higher level of employment would, or would not, lead to inflation. On this point I would first refer to the great elasticity in the labor supply which I mentioned; this elasticity would reflect itself in the unemployment rate not going down so fast as it is supposed to when employment is increasing. Policies specifically directed towards mobilizing the various types of "disguised unemployment" and raising their quality, would, of course, increase still more the space for speeding up economic growth without creating imbalance in the price and cost structure in the economy.

But besides this I should not conceal from my readers the fact that, in view of the immensely wholesome social and economic effects of making labor scarce, I would be prepared to accept a measure of economic planning in order to keep the economy balanced, in spite of approaching full employment. This over-all economic planning might even have to imply a certain participation by the government in the setting of wages and prices. On the whole, not much more over-all economic planning would be needed than the American people are now becoming accustomed to and are prepared to accept in the Kennedy-Johnson era. Neither should I conceal from my readers, however, that I now tread controversial ground where many of my colleagues, whose judgment I appreciate highly, are not, or not yet, prepared to follow me.

Let me conclude by saying that I predict that even if the demand for a faster growth of the American economy is not yet being raised with much force from any quarter, it will be raised with force if and when the unemployment rate starts its upward trend again.

V

And so only a few concluding remarks. I see a danger that the intellectual and moral leaders of America will not set their sights high enough. America has so long lived with rather abominable conditions for a minority of its people that many do not see the possibility of doing much about it. It is true that the difficulties of rapid reform — or even of preventing a further deterioration — are immense on the local level, as is illustrated in many of the chapters in this volume. Only on the national level is there much of an opening for radical reform.

The challenge is met on the national level by the declaration of unconditional war against poverty. As this war is really gaining momentum it will give much greater opportunities to constructive policies on the local level. Most important is, however, the speeding up of economic growth and the creation of scarce labor. The policies needed for this purpose are unconventional in America, where public opinion has been under the influence of what the late President Kennedy referred to as "myths" — built up, as we should know, as rationale for *laissez-faire* policies. President Johnson talks about "irrational preconceptions." But as the American people gain experience with these policies and see that the economy does not go bankrupt, they will be prepared to go even further.

Basically, I am an optimist about America, and, more particularly, an optimist in regard to the problems discussed in these essays, many of which seem so intractable when dealt with without taking into account the national parameters and the great changes which these parameters will undergo in the years to come. I believe we are entering a dynamic phase of American history — economically, socially, intellectually, and morally — and it would be a pity if members of the academic profession such as these writers here represented did not become more of a leading sector in this rapidly accelerating historical process.

CHAPTER TWO

THE PUBLIC AND PRIVATE RATIONALE FOR A NATIONAL URBAN POLICY

John W. Dyckman

In order to prevent the continued conflicts and disorders between a highly organized and centralized national economy and a highly disorganized and decentralized management of American cities, the federal government will have to establish a national urban and regional development policy. This long-range goal must be supported by a number of immediate short-term efforts to equalize the levels of efficiency and service which now produce strong inequalities within and among metropolitan regions.

I. Introduction

Metropolitan planning and metropolitan decision-making interest us because they are conspicuous testimonials of lag, the primitive biplanes of a jet age. The growth of organization of our world economy in the past thirty years has outmoded our thinking about the city. If a National Resources Planning Board were reconstituted today to up-date the urbanism report of thirty years ago, the author would need to assign the urban

John W. Dyckman is Chairman of the Center for Planning and Development Research, Institute of Urban and Regional Development at the University of California, Berkeley, and author of *Capital Requirements for Urban Development and Renewal* (1961).

centers to a national and international system, rather than to the older regional systems.

The process of organization has proceeded so swiftly that we are hard pressed to prevent rapid obsolescence of our favorite concepts. Only thirty years ago, the labor force of the United States was largely unorganized. The participants in the organizing drives of the thirties considered their thinking to be advanced, for they were recognizing the industrial reality of their time, and the end of craft dominance. But within the last fifteen years, we have seen industrial organization itself take new forms. The issues of the labor movement of the thirties have largely been bypassed by automation of manufacturing, growth of the service industries, and the Negro revolution. Issues have shifted from recognition of bargaining rights to jobs, education, and political equality. The radical union positions of the thirties now seem conservative.

We have moved from an era of great rural-urban differences to one in which the greatest social and economic differences may be found within the city itself. The cities in turn have tended to grow together in large supercity systems. These in turn are linked in a national jet airport network, in which the smaller city airports feed the regional jet ports. The latter are linked in a world system. Corporate mergers and reorganization have produced new international giants, usually headquartered in New York.

Some people have begun to call these developments the "postindustrial society." [1] In this world, our revolutionary institution, comparable with the Congress of Industrial Organizations in the thirties, may be the development of new levels of "local" government. The changes in the functional interchanges between cities and within cities impose strains on the present organization.

For postindustrial society is exclusive, rejecting older businesses and corporations and excluding an army of untrained

[1] The term seems to have been used at almost the same time by many writers, including Roderick Seidenberg, Daniel Bell, and some of the "Triple Revolution" observers.

from participation in the inner society. These untrained continue to inhabit the central ghettos of the metropolitan areas, and their numbers grow rapidly. The decision-makers of the central cities are increasingly dependent on the untrained for political support, and on the elite for economic well-being. The postindustrial technicians of the elite group, however, favor rationality in local government and metropolitan-wide decisions. At the same time, the suburbs are competing with the central cities in the very services which are highly valued by the elite and relatively low-valued by the untrained, using effective alterations of the public product mix to attract residents. The reinforced differences between cities and their suburbs in the composition of population and the mix of public services, as well as the physical differences in age of stock, etc., lead to different goals and strategies for each. The exacerbation of differences between cities and suburbs makes technically rational solutions for metropolitan areas less accessible. It is not surprising that there is no single objective welfare function for metropolitan areas.

Private metropolitan area decision-making has far outstripped public metropolitan decision-making. In the public sphere, the only acceptable welfare functions are very general, and agreement typically breaks down at the operational level. Local sovereignty is so stubbornly defended that political scientists widely despair of the possibility of directly reconstituting local authority. Adherents of local government are reluctant to transfer decision prerogatives to higher governmental levels. At these levels, they are reminded, governmental actions are frequently bureaucratic, dominated by single agency goals or narrow cost-efficiency considerations.

The great expansion of government functions and programs in this decade has dramatized the poor functional fit between economic and political activities and the spatial decision units. Our economy is international, our chief political units increasingly national, and the local service base divided on interest lines. With the exception of the one-class enclaves created on the peripheries of our cities, political units tend to be composed of groups of diverse functional interests, whose basic allegiances and important memberships may be outside the political boundaries of the city.[2] The United States structure of economic and political influence is being defended in Vietnam. The revolution in the south of the United States is being made, in large part, outside the home territory, with organizers and funds from the North. The business and professional classes that once were active in local politics tend increasingly to belong to national communities of cosmopolitan, mobile people.

The tasks of government need to be resorted and redefined, both spatially and functionally. In bureaucracies, functions and programs grow by accretion. Old programs, which have become disfunctional, are rarely removed, as the history of the United States Department of Agriculture demonstrates. The extension of governmental concern beyond existing agency boundaries, into issues of poverty, the mental health of the aged, the training of preschool children and the aesthetics and amenities of outdoor recreation and urban environments has caused unfamiliar programs to be added to old offices, and new agencies to be created where no convenient one existed. Further, this expansion of public concern has created programs which overlap existing agencies and leave a residue of confusion of responsibility, and much working at cross-purposes. To add to the confusion, the broad "human resource" programs require national policies in areas where no such policies have been articulated. Thus we have training and education programs without a national policy on the mobility of labor to match skills to jobs, and programs for areas of deprivation in central cities without a policy about the national distribution of problems and opportunities. Finally, many of the impacts of government programs are unforeseen. This is a symptom of our general inability to identify the point of leverage which government can utilize effectively in achieving programs ends. And

[2] John W. Dyckman, "Changing Uses of the City," *Daedalus*, Winter, 1961; Melvin Webber, et al., "The Urban Place and the Non-Place Urban Realm," *Explorations into Urban Structure*, University of Pennsylvania Press, 1964, p. 220; John Friedmann and John Miller, "The Urban Realm; A New Concept for Urban Living," *AIP Journal* (October, 1965).

the incentives necessary for engineering social and cultural change cannot be skillfully managed when the points of decision in these changes are obscure.

II. What Issues Are Decided at the Various Levels of Social Organization?

The most important city-forming decisions in American life are expenditure decisions made by business executives, government officials, and household heads. In our mixed system, there is a slightly different calculus for business and political decisions, expenditures by public and private agencies on current and capital account, and investments in physical assets and human resources. The political markets are organized spatially—and the interpenetration of government by business and other interests varies with the level of government. But the main issues for urban policy in America arise from business location and expansion decisions, from residence choices by households, from governmental deployment of capital investment and provision of local services, and from voters' behavior in choosing representatives and endorsing or rejecting bond issues, etc.

Our cities are social artifacts, and are subject to varying degrees of public control. For example, the decisions of business men to locate plants or to expand production are dictated by considerations of profitability which are in turn affected by the locational choices of households who will constitute their customers and their labor supply; by local governments whose cooperation may be necessary to secure permission for the desired use of the land, or to provide local accessibility; by state governments which may license or tax the business operation; and by the federal government, whose fiscal policies may govern the availability of capital and the prospects of the economy, and whose specific tax policies, such as its treatment of capital gains, may be decisive in the profitability of the move. The federal government has entered some business location decisions directly, through the direction of military and aerospace contracts, and other decisions indirectly, through support of research facilities which subsequently spawn new businesses. But the federal government has no industrial location policy as such. The industrial location policies of states are frankly promotional, and often ineffective. At the metropolitan level, communities may engage in competition for industries by making available and servicing favorable sites; the policy in this case is crude mercantilism.

Public capital investment in established metropolitan areas in the United States may range from a quarter to a third of the total capital outlay in the area.[3] Governmental capital expenditures such as those on highways, dams, irrigation systems, etc., tend to be funneled through state government agencies, even where the sources of the funds are federal. These expenditures have, for some time, been the single most important instrument for state governments to direct, alter, or otherwise affect the character of urbanization within their boundaries. The massive federal interstate highway program, for example, has been administered by state highway departments, and the alignments and improvements which are so critical to the life and death of small communities have been mediated by these state agencies.

The package of decisions affecting human resources and organization also is city-forming, but its mechanisms are less well understood. State action to assure metropolitan cooperation in a bridge or tunnel or transit system connecting two or more political jurisdictions is commonplace, but metropolitan coordination of the welfare programs, job placements, and low-cost housing supply which attract and hold migrant service workers and "problem families" is rare. As a nation, we are just beginning to be self-conscious in our application of investment in human resources. While the resource aspects of public education are sometimes overrated those of related social services are

[3] William L. C. Wheaton, "Agents of Change in Urban Expansion," in *Explorations into Urban Structure*, M. M. Webber, et al., University of Pennsylvania Press, 1964, pp. 166, Table 1., for the Philadelphia area experience, 1957–1960. In the highly urbanized, rapidly growing state of California, the public share may be even larger.

ignored. The traditions of welfare service are custodial. The bureaucratic suppliers see their services as duties to be imposed on wards as often as commodities to be sold to customers or services offered to clients.[4] The basis for this outlook — when it does not stem directly from social condemnation of the recipients — is the conviction that the passive masses must be recruited for consumption of meritorious goods in the best interests of the whole community. The federal, state, and local agencies which administer the various health and welfare programs are prone to a high degree of professional compartmentalization. A given agency has as its reference group its counterpart agency at another governmental level, rather than a community of clients. Thus the social structure of the supplying agencies impedes the application of a comprehensive "human resource" approach to urban problems.

Some economists[5] distinguish between public goods which are collectively consumed, such as national defense, and other public goods whose consumption is encouraged for social and economic reasons, but which are differentially consumed by different users. Education is an example of the latter. In the American economy pure public goods tend to be provided at the federal level. National defense, and the subsidized portion of the postal service, are consumed in amounts, and in a manner prescribed by, the Congress and the federal agencies.

Merit goods, on the other hand, are consumed in markedly different amounts by the various states, counties, and municipal governments. The split between the items in the community package of merit goods, as well as the absolute amount of the support, can be used to differentiate communities. Rich states may spend three to four times as much per capita on education or other public services as do the poorer states. At the same time, certain suburban communities may spend eighty percent of locally collected taxes on schools, as compared with forty percent or less in large central cities.

[4] Martin Rein, "The Social Service Crisis," *Trans-Action*, 1 (May, 1964).

[5] Cf. Richard H. Musgrave, *Theory of Public Finance* (New York: McGraw-Hill Book Company, 1959).

Merit goods are, therefore, responsive to local markets. One of the challenges to metropolitan decision-making is that of equalizing opportunity to consume merit goods within the metropolitan region. State equalization procedures and allocation formulas are often designed, in an approximative way, to produce this effect.

Within metropolitan areas, however, there is virtually no equalization procedure at work. In this sense, the metropolitan area remains one of the last outposts of competition in the area of public service. The competition is limited by state and federal constraints and standards, and by higher-level equalization procedures, but a substantial margin of differentiation remains. Except for extralegal, informal discriminatory practices, e.g., the neglect of housekeeping services such as garbage collection in certain neighborhoods, this differentiation in public product is carried on *between* communities.

The competition between communities within metropolitan areas is an impediment to the metropolitan provision of purely public goods.[6] One might argue that air and water pollution have much the same characteristics as national defense. That is, they are more nearly equally consumed by all members of the community, and reduction in these losses do not unduly favor any class of consumers. It is therefore somewhat ironic that air and water pollution controls are applied differentially, at great variation in local cost, within metropolitan areas.

If Hammond and other lakeside communities in Indiana continue to discharge sewage into Lake Michigan, saving themselves certain treatment costs, the Chicago bathers will be losers from the ensuing pollution. If such practices were everywhere outlawed in the interest of reducing pollution danger (a national "defense" principle), Chicago, with its greater lake front area and beaches, would be the larger gainer. At present there is no effective machinery to enforce an arbitration of these matters. Presumably, Chicago could compensate Hammond

[6] There is, in my opinion, no such thing as a *pure* public good; this is a matter of degree.

for the cost of additional facilities, alternative systems, and treatment. But the metropolitan areas in the United States rarely have the power to enforce such solutions.

In summary, it is my belief that (1) economic growth and development is not controllable by local metropolitan decision makers, but is profoundly influenced by federal government policies, direct and indirect; (2) governmental programs, in both capital investment and human resource investment, are administered by allied state and local bureaucracies along departmental and professional rather than community lines; and (3) the pressure for metropolitan decision-making and planning can find no outlets in conventional political markets, but is forced upon resistant clients by the circumstances of heavy "externalities."

In the host of generalizations assembled above, I have painted a picture of the complex ecology of urban policies, and the functional specializations of different policy agents. The tradition of rationalism calls for some coordination of these interests and activities, for rationalism is favorable to unitary schemes. The rationalist would impose his crude and limited rationality on the bargains struck in the political markets.

III. The Case for Public Program Coordination

Part of the tension in local decision-making arises from the fact that American local government is extremely decentralized and putatively independent of federal influence, at the same time that the American economy is extraordinarily centralized and concentrated. As a result, national firms pursue national strategies which occasionally upset local strategies and thwart local goals. At the same time, the top leadership in the national corporations and economic groups has relatively weak local ties. The local interest is left to a segment of the economic community that has old family ties, accidental dependence on local markets or resources, or whose local investments are a large portion of the total economy of the area. These members of the economic community, along with the locally oriented political leaders, provide the major inputs in the hypothetical community power structure.

Federal programs have exacerbated the tensions between the inner city and its outer ring which have been made acute by the concentration of low-income groups in the inner ring and the metropolitan business decision makers in the outer ring. The building of express highways radiating out from the city, and connection of the radials by belt expressways, in both the interstate and state systems, has opened new prime commercial locations, reduced the collector advantage of the inner city, and has shifted patterns of retailing. Downtown department stores and other retail outlets have been hard hit. The Federal Housing Administration has provided generous financing, with high mortgages and low downpayments, for building in new subdivisions outside the central city, at the same time that its policies have remained conservative and discouraging to rebuilding and rehabilitation in the inner core. The HHFA recently proposed to grant loans and other assistance to new planned developments outside the cities for the construction of utility services. The Council of Mayors of the large cities is understandably cool to what it views as discriminatory behavior favoring suburbs over cities.

At times, the programs of different Federal agencies or offices appear to work at cross purposes. The 1949 Housing Act created an apparatus and program for urban redevelopment, but it also provided for generous financing for new house building — in the case of the Veterans Administration program, at loans so generous as to virtually eliminate downpayments. Since the new building took place on open land, usually well outside the cities, where the combination of cheap land cost and low downpayments provided housing at prices more than competitive with that available under subsidized private development in the central cities, the effect was to drain off some of the potential demand for the latter. At times, the Federal Reserve has pursued tight-money policies in the face of efforts of the FHA to stimulate activity and reduce interest rates by insurance programs.[7] Imperfect communication and coordination between Federal agencies, independent pursuit of agency goals, inconsistencies in legislative programs, and the lack of an articulated urban policy have contributed to metropolitan disorder.

In the absence of federal or state urban policy positions, individual agencies dealing with facilities with great spillover effects are not constrained with any metropolitan welfare guides. The Port of New York Authority's transportation planning demonstrates difficulties that can result from pursuit of the single-agency interest. The Port Authority builds and operates tunnels and bridges connecting parts of the metropolitan area with Manhattan. As operator of these crossings, it has an interest in fostering automobile travel which will swell its revenues. Though Manhattan Island may be choked with commuter vehicles, and effectively sterilized for private automobile use by its own residents, the Port Authority continues to pour cars into the city and steadfastly declines to operate mass transit or to reduce its competition with the rail commuters.

The great growth market of American manufacturing in the period 1950–1960 arose from government purchases of military and aerospace hardware and research products. A large part of this market was localized in the West Coast and Southwest areas of the United States. In a decade in which manufacturing employment for the whole nation virtually stabilized, new industries, manufacturing growth, and rapid central city growth was highly concentrated in a few centers of the far West and Southwest. The decisions which led to these local effects were "political," in the sense that the federal demand is politically determined. But the political rationale behind these decisions is somewhat obscure.

The only well-articulated national program for regional development is that contained in the Appalachia Bill. The latter program, however, emphasizes public works, and not federal

[7] For a fuller discussion of this point, see J. W. Dyckman, "National Planning for Urban Renewal" in the *Journal of the American Institute of Planners*, February, 1960.

purchases of manufacturing or research output. And at the same time that federal purchases have speeded urban growth in California and the Gulf Coast,[8] the federal government, operating through a separate agency (Housing and Home Finance), seeks to stimulate the revitalization of the downtown area of old manufacturing cities in the Northeast, whose traditional economic base is declining.

Should federal investment, over a variety of agency responsibilities, be geared to regional development or equalization? A massive public housing program in the Southeast might permit the assembly of cheap labor for the itinerant factories fleeing the older industrial centers of the North. (There is some evidence that the use by the South of federal public housing programs has indeed helped its industrialization, even though these programs are financially limited.) Should economic programs be accompanied by social and political programs, and will this require increased interagency cooperation? Without social and political revolution, Negroes are unlikely to remain in the South. With such developments, the migration flow might eventually be reversed. In the meantime, the cost of development failures in the South is felt in the social welfare programs in Northern cities that receive the migrants from the Southern economies. Economists have long pointed out that the agricultural assistance programs which developed from small beginnings in the thirties into a major subsidy burden have not only failed to keep population on the land, but have speeded up the exodus. The cost, in economic efficiency, of keeping people on the land might well have exceeded the cost of absorption of migrants into the cities, but the distribution of cost and benefits has been unjustifiable on welfare economics grounds.

The consequences of conflict between governments, cumbersome evolution of agencies, separate principalities and islands of financial power, absentee ownership, blockages in inter-

[8] John W. Dyckman, and Richard Burton, "The Role of Defense Expenditures in Forecasts of California's Economic Growth," *The Western Economic Journal*, 3 (Spring, 1965), 133–141.

governmental channels of communication and support, and other structural impediments to maximizing metropolitan welfare are to be found in the erratic pattern of services in metropolitan areas. Wheaton has observed that "Highways are provided in billion-dollar packages, but transit is neglected, schools are built by the thousands but libraries and parks are ignored, new hospitals crowd the urban landscape while overflowing septic tanks and inadequate sewerage systems pollute the suburban landscape."[9] Students of public administration have focused on bureaucratic competition, and conflict between bureaucrats and politicians. To these difficulties we may add the class conflicts between and within urban communities, the growing gulf between national economic power and local political interests, and the weaknesses and limitations of bureaucratic rationality.

It is unlikely, in the big cities at least, that there would be a single civic strategy, even in fiscal matters. Rather, various self-serving strategies are likely to emerge in any heterogeneous city. This is equivalent to arguing that unlike the more homogeneous suburb, the city does not have an objective welfare function to maximize. The interests of genuinely conflicting groups in the city impede its construction. Political mechanisms rather than rational ones probably must guide the pluralistic interests of the cities. The decision mode of city government is bargaining. Bargains are made with and between aldermen, bargains are made with business and money centers on the one hand and government on the other. And allocations in the interests of geographical areas or wards are made according to traditional rules. Coming to terms with the business interests, or with a single dominant interest, has entered the jargon of the public administration and planning fields as accommodating to the "power structure."

Except for its control of the press and of national and local campaign contributions, the business power structure may be

[9] W. L. C. Wheaton, "Metropolitan Political Structure and Planning," Conference on the Metropolitan Future, University of California at Berkeley, September 26–27, 1963.

something of a paper tiger in the arena of local political decision. But the power of the profit motive and market opportunity is a force with which all local politics must reckon. The free flow of private money, and the impediments to flows of public money act to produce many of the inequities in distribution of public services between the suburbs and the central cities. Given the freedom to pursue the self-interest which our society affords, efficiency-oriented systems, like the market, tend to drive out other allocative systems, such as those political systems based on equity principles. Local politicians confronted with the market choices of economically able households who vote with their feet and march to the suburbs, must appeal to state and federal agencies who have some power to alter the market terms by altering the availability of credit, raising interest rates, taxing capital gains, etc. At present, federal government decisions in these areas are not guided by a national urban policy.

IV. Conclusion: Toward Coherent Urban Policy

If the present state of urban development in the United States is the outcome of competitive processes in economic and political markets, constrained by unstable political bargains, local governments are impeded in their struggle to control urban processes by their dependence on negative sanctions, such as zoning, by inconsistencies in our legal and administrative structures, and by historical accidents of their own domain, which insure that they will be badly fitted to the extent of the markets which they seek to influence. Local planners are further handicapped by their mythology, which rests on half-truths—e.g., that size is a measure of welfare, that blight is infectious, that scientific institutes insure economic development, and that education yields monotonically increasing returns. The locals are among the last to recognize the advantages of a national urban policy which would define the conditions of regional and local competition, and set the limits on that competition.

In the short run, important improvements in the substantive rationality of decisions at the metropolitan level can be made (*a*) by rationalizing present national and state urban policies, (*b*) by improving the planning guidance of these policies, (*c*) by stressing programs which are aimed at bringing the democratic realities into closer accord with the requirements of our ideology in particular, by stressing equalization of access to the advanced technological society and by reducing those inequalities which are most destructive of community, (*d*) by fashioning those ad hoc instruments which are necessary to meet immediate physical and economic obstacles and which have freedom of action and instrumental rationality denied to the established institutions.

The recent creation of a Cabinet office of Housing and Urban Development has edged the nation closer to a national urban policy by establishing an office with a vested interest in such policy. But the Phoenix of a national urban policy will not arise from the ashes of the HHFA—it must be formed with the cooperation of a host of other federal agencies. An urban policy must more clearly articulate the objectives of national housing policy, particularly with respect to building in new areas and old cities. A national urban policy must also articulate the federal stance toward the relative roles of mass transit, highway systems, and alternative technologies in the urban transportation scene. It must consider the deployment of educational resources in equalizing conditions in the working force between regions, and between small and large cities. It must face the issues of migration, economic opportunity, and regional growth. In short, though it is politically difficult, such policy should face the issue of national distribution of population. A national urban policy is inseparable from a national manpower policy.

Our federal system and the ground rules of our Congress militate against coherent policies and program planning on a wide range of issues. These circumstances place a greater burden of leadership upon the executive branch and add responsibility to the Cabinet representative in the federal government. It is at this level that one must make the case for basic federal fiscal planning in those tax policies so critical to urban development. The Council of Economic Advisors would need to introduce regional and urban accounts into its economic calculations. Regional labor market boards, on the Swedish model, might be set up with the cooperation of Commerce, Labor, and Health, Education, and Welfare. These boards might advise on local fiscal conditions, industrial location, labor mobility, retraining programs and a host of other human resource development issues. The poverty program, if it is to be meaningful, ought to be directed at eliminating rather than ameliorating poverty. If it is to take the former course, it would become an integral part of national urban and manpower policies.

At the state level, equally with the federal, there is need for the articulation of an urban policy. The states are in an especially good position to provide leadership in land development, water and air pollution, highways, and other metropolitan issues which cross city lines. Since civil subdivisions of the state exist at the sufferance of the state constitution, the state's organizational role in metropolitan affairs can be decisive. There is some hope that the Supreme Court's position on representation (one man equals one vote), with its requirement of reapportionment of state legislatures may break down the traditional rural–urban split in many of our states and force the legislatures to more open recognition of metropolitan and urban problems. Since the suburbs have grown more rapidly in recent times than central cities or rural areas, reapportionment of legislatures is bound to touch sensitive growth issues in metropolitan areas.

Existing federal programs, such as highways, and proposed programs such as the "clean air" program operate through state agencies. Metropolitan areas, waterways, atmospheric basins, and other functional areas overlap state lines. The federal government must play a role in coordinating the activities of states which are involved in these overspills. Where uniform regulations and requirements of coordination and cooperation are imposed by the federal government, these restraints will be accepted by local decision-makers. Once part of the environment of decision-making, federal directors will play a powerful, if silent, coordinative role.

The federal requirements for coherent local planning now attached to the highway, outdoor recreation and community renewal programs might be expanded into full-fledged federal support for metropolitan planning. Individual federal agencies, notably the HHFA and the Bureau of Public Roads, recognize the functional indivisibility of metropolitan areas and attempt to secure a modicum of coherence in those local programs which they finance by requiring a metropolitan perspective in the local planning. But these direct, bureaucratic methods of administrative requirements are easily circumvented. More promising are indirect methods which create local institutions with a vested metropolitan outlook. Among the potentially most important of these creations are metropolitan information centers, or data banks. To insure a metropolitan regional perspective these might be set up by the states, with interstate compacts where necessary (approximately one fourth of the metropolitan population lives in urban regions that span state lines). These metropolitan agencies could serve many important functions.

At the beginning, their emphasis would be heavily on the provision of information and area-wide intelligence systems. We have long needed metropolitan income and product accounts; capital accounts are lacking on every level, and income accounting principles might well be expanded to embrace social and human resources.[10] The metropolitan planning agency might house the Regional Manpower Board recommended above, and serve as the regional repository for employment and labor statistics, as well as for Commerce Department building permit data, special census tabulations, and a wealth of other administratively generated information. Created by the states,

[10] Harvey S. Perloff, and Lowden Wingo, Jr., "Planning and Development of Metropolitan Affairs," *Journal of the American Institute of Planners*, 28 (May, 1962), 67–90.

these agencies could move from information handling to intelligence functions, and to the task of devising operational targets for the implementation of state urban policies. With this activity, the metropolitan planning agency could approach the "policies plan" which would bridge local physical plans with regional or state development policies.

> The policies plan would express in one place the social, economic physical and political policies intended to guide the evolution of the particular area of governmental jurisdiction. It would contain physical plans coordinating spatial relationships, schedules coordinating time relationships, budgets, coordinating financial relationships, and narrative texts and tables describing and coordinating proposed activity programs. Maps, schedules, and texts also would set forth the physical, economic and social facts, assumptions, and goals underlying the governmental policies.[11]

In the areas of transportation planning, air and water pollution, open space and conservation, the plans might have great impact. If an accepted metropolitan planning agency were to come forward at this moment with a plan for the development and conservation of San Francisco Bay, it could quickly become a rallying point for all those groups which are concerned with the spoilation of the Bay but uncertain of the equity and appropriateness of individual restrictions.

The apparatus of metropolitan planning will need to find some method of reflecting functional interest which does not result in the domination of metropolitan planning by one or two central cities, or by a dominant financial or industrial group. If this difficulty can be resolved, the planning bodies may provide a bridge to the reconstitution of metropolitan government. In the meantime, their coordinating and intelligence activities are a necessary link between federal and state policies and local action.

The third program for immediate implementation should be aimed at the reduction of the class differences which now split metropolitan areas. There is a plethora of high priority

[11] Henry Fagin, "Organizing and Carrying Out Planning Activities Within Urban Government," *Journal of the American Institute of Planners*, 25 (August, 1959), 109–114.

items in this category. Foremost on the list is destruction of the barrier which contains nonwhite population in the inner ring of the metropolitan area. Federal and state policies and all available levers must be used to open suburban areas to nonwhites.

Urban renewal must be modified to remove its present stigma of "Negro clearance." Rehabilitation, with consideration of special assistance to minority group capital as well as individuals, may become first priority. Operating programs will take precedence over capital improvement. The full range of possibilities of the Poverty Bill and other such legislation must be integrated with metropolitan strategies which are frankly aimed at destroying the restrictive boundaries which have been erected in metropolitan areas. At the same time, an effort should be made to circumvent awkward programs, such as the bussing of school children for substantial distances to achieve integration. An end to the more repressive and custodial aspects of welfare payments, public housing and other subsidized services is overdue. Direct income payments, tax relief and other devices could, if skillfully used, reduce the special status of dependency and the special disabilities of relief which now worsen class divisions. However interpreted, these latter constitute a major bar to substantive rationality in metropolitan area decisions.

A fourth set of short-run steps are frankly of an emergency nature. These would be designed to set up machinery to meet presently critical problems such as the operation of metropolitan transit systems and the control of metropolitan land developments. Despite the difficulties posed by special authorities, we are likely to need additional ad hoc corporate agencies to deal with these problems. Creation of such an agency to deal with commuter movements in the New York metropolitan area, for example, is almost certainly in the offing. The problem of land control in metropolitan areas could best be addressed by the formation of state or metropolitan land development agencies which would act to purchase land directly in the public interest. Indeed, such agencies are likely to be necessary if we are to avoid chaos in the purchasing policies and ad hoc arrangements resulting from the Open Space Bill and other available legislation. Only with the action of public corporations, with clearly defined public responsibilities can we avoid the dangerous transfer of public funds to private beneficiaries inherent in the presently proposed "New Towns" legislation.[12]

An important feature in the chartering of such agencies in the future should be the restriction of the life of the agency. Corporations created for these special purposes should have fixed life, renewable at the option of the legislature.

Limitations on the life of these agencies should be based on the frank recognition of the desirability of direct governmental assumption of the responsibility of the agencies at a future date. An effort should be made to prevent the capture of these agencies by a single operating interest and to reduce the danger of fostering the growth of a bureaucratic empire.

A major purpose of these short-run solutions is the transformation of individual ad hoc interests into some larger community interest. This unitary bias is fraught with difficulty. It is urged, however, on the conviction that some such action is needed to guide any proposals to improve competitive mechanisms, countervailing power bargains, and other pluralistic determinants of community decision. For the nagging concerns of equity and efficiency, particularly the former, require a substantial reframing of the terms and rules of competition between regions, metropolitan areas, and between central cities and suburbs. The implementation of these goals requires the sacrifice of sovereignty over existing political and bureaucratic empires. Only the invocation of a national interest and the formulation of a national policy can secure these sacrifices.

[12] John W. Dyckman, "Land Control in California," prepared for the Governor's Advisory Commission on Housing, State of California, Arthur D. Little, Inc. 1962.

CHAPTER THREE

URBAN CONSTRAINTS AND FEDERAL POLICY

Sam Bass Warner, Jr.

Throughout the twentieth century, the dynamism of the American network of metropolises has overreached any federal ability for national planning. At the same time the inherent weaknesses of state and local government have repeatedly handicapped the large and growing federal grants-in-aid programs. Professor Warner suggests a set of federal policies which would be consistent with these historical constraints.

Traditionally, America assigns the tasks that it has the greatest difficulty in performing to its weakest institutions and to its least skilled personnel. Caring for people with all their variety of backgrounds and needs, looking after the weak and the troublesome, managing all sorts of commonplace affairs which are too public and too expensive for private enterprise and too complex for mass production, these are the odd lots and remainders of American culture. These are the subjects of urban management and planning.

Our urban institutions, public and private, are and always have been the agencies that inherited all the problems big government and big business couldn't or wouldn't deal with. To

Sam Bass Warner, Jr., is an Associate Professor of History at Washington University, and formerly a research associate at the Joint Center for Urban Studies of the Massachusetts Institute of Technology and Harvard University. He is the author of *Streetcar Suburbs* (1962).

the city schools fell the task of educating waves of ignorant or illiterate rural immigrants who had not been educated in the country. At the same time, the city system attempted to offer, without charge, high culture to the children of established city dwellers. Similarly, city hospitals and clinics have tried to be both charities for the poverty stricken and practitioners of the most advanced medical service and technique. The lack of resources for servicing multiple publics has compromised many urban programs, and, especially in the case of police and elective government, city services have been torn by class, ethnic, racial, and religious conflicts as well.

Finally, difficult allocation problems have been the regular business of city government. Public works departments, water commissions, zoning boards, and planning offices have long had to deal, although often without much careful policy, with the problems of allocating the limited supply of urban space among such conflicting users as railroads, superhighways, department stores, office buildings, steam laundries, corner candy stores, apartment houses, and single-family suburban homes. To a large extent the physical form of the American metropolis today is the product of half a century of these municipal agencies' administrative practices. In sum, the uncongenial (for Americans) work of rendering personal service to all kinds of people, the complex task of allocating the limited space of cities, and the hard job of moderating at close range social, economic, and political conflict falls upon the public and private municipal institutions of the nation. The variety of goods and services which these institutions attempt to provide exceeds the range of most business corporations, while the need for talent, judgment, and power in the exercise of these responsibilities far exceeds the resources which these institutions have ever been able to muster.

The current revival of interest in urban problems announces that once again a vocal generation of American city dwellers has become dissatisfied with the contemporary patchwork of municipal services and allocations. Once again new standards are going to be applied to these weak institutions that have been compromising among the conflicting demands made upon them and coping with the limited public and private resources at their disposal.

The novelty of the present situation lies not in the demand for reform, American cities are traditionally the nation's most voracious consumers of reform energy, but rather the novelty lies in the attempt to use the federal government more directly than ever before in supervising and financing urban services and allocations. For example, under the poverty program the federal government is attempting to reorganize some of the institutional structure of local social agenices in order to raise the quality of urban social welfare services. Under the interstate highway program, the federal government is demanding metropolitan plans in order to encourage more open and hopefully more rational allocations of metropolitan land.

From the historian's point of view, the need for richer, more powerful, and more skillful urban institutions has been apparent for at least half a century. The question of the moment is, thus, not whether the federal government should or should not enter more vigorously into the field of urban affairs. The serious question today is, how can the federal government choose an urban strategy which will save its programs and its administration from all the weaknesses and failures which have characterized urban services and allocations for the past fifty years?

Any reasonably effective federal urban policy must be built upon an understanding of two major historical trends and upon an understanding of the conflict between these trends and the goal of planning more humane urban environments.

First, America is and has been for at least half a century a nation of metropolises. The number of these large cities, their individual size and arrangement, and their relationships among themselves have been continually changing. Federal urban policy must, therefore, be able to deal with large networks of cities, heavy migrations of people, and unceasing economic shifts.

Second, the desire to help city dwellers in their immediate small environments requires that many federal urban policies be administered by local institutions. But local government institutions whether they be state or municipal, are and have been for many years very peculiar organizations. They have dealt best in servicing real estate, worst in serving people. Today they cannot easily be adapted to many of the environmental goals of modern urban planning.

The National Network of Metropolises

In considering possible federal policies, one must never lose sight of a few imperatives imposed by the behavior of our metropolises themselves: the total number of metropolitan areas in the United States is large and growing rapidly. Most of the present metropolises are and have been growing steadily for sixty years; most have been growing more rapidly than the nation as a whole; and many have been growing at spectacular paces. Even those metropolises of rather average growth, like the old Atlantic and Midwestern cities, exhibit tremendous change; rearrangements within their metropolitan areas have swept up enormous waves of people and have consumed vast quantities of capital.

The sheer scale, complexity, and dynamism of the American urban network forecloses any delicately tuned planning policy. Although some urban problems like slums and rural immigrants have a long history, the urban setting for these problems changes so rapidly that any policy which was intelligently fitted to the conditions of 1900 (as some, like public baths, streetcar parks, and Latin High Schools, were) was soon swamped by the dynamism of the changes that lay ahead.

In every decade since 1900 new cities have joined the national metropolitan network and a few have even lost population and dropped out. In 1900 there were fifty-one metropolises, in 1930 one hundred and fourteen, in 1960 one hundred and seventy-six. (See Table 1.) Now there are 214. It seems highly improbable that any government administrator could have picked the new metropolises and predicted the varying rates of growth of all the United States' large cities for any extended period

TABLE 1 America's 176 Metropolises by Period

	Population in 1900	Population in 1960
51 Metropolises 1900	24,457,824	76,512,944
19 " 1910	2,086,712	8,989,392
23 " 1920	1,082,297	7,742,216
21 " 1930	1,161,120	6,288,135
10 " 1940	511,851	2,410,580
21 " 1950	870,727	4,199,972
31 " 1960	965,983	4,741,449
176 Total Population All Metropolises	31,856,514	110,884,688
% Total U.S. Population	41.9%	62.1%
51 Metropolises 1900	24,457,824	76,512,944
% Total U.S. Population	32.2%	42.9%
73 Metropolises 1910–1940	5,561,980	25,430,323
% Total U.S. Population	7.3%	14.2%
52 Metropolises 1950–1960	1,836,710	8,941,421
% Total U.S. Population	2.4%	5.0%

Note:
The metropolises of this table are the "Principal Standard Metropolitan Statistical Areas" of Donald J. Bogue's study for the Housing and Home Finance Agency, *Population Growth in Standard Metropolitan Statistical Areas 1900–1950* (Washington, 1953). These metropolises are urban areas with a central city of at least 50,000 inhabitants and a total population of 100,000 and more. There are a few urban areas with smaller multiple cores that meet the more inclusive census definition of an S.M.S.A. Bogue's figures were corrected for boundary changes listed in Bureau of the Budget, Office of Statistical Standards, *Standard Metropolitan Statistical Areas* (Washington, 1964). The United States population is that of the coterminus area.

of time. Changes in the structure of old cities like New York outdistanced the predictions of extremely careful studies of the 1920's; could a national bureau have estimated that, during the lifetime of bridges and roadbeds it was planning and financing, forty-one of the nation's metropolises would grow at less than the national rate of population growth? In short, massive though American metropolises may appear to be, the whole network of American metropolises is and always has been subject to rapid shifts and many variations.

This sixty-year performance of the national urban network constrains federal policy in two ways. First, plans that attempt to nail down the present arrangement of cities are bound to fail or to create disorder. At the very least the national urban program must respect the fliuid dimensions of the urban network. It must accept continuing rearrangements which come from the growth of new metropolises, and it must accept continuing rearrangements which come from changes in the configuration and rates of growth of individual cities. Second, both the number of cities and the number of people affected by federal urban planning are so large that the government cannot hope to supervise a host of detailed small-scale programs if it wants to foster high-quality projects that are responsive to changing conditions in our cities.

It is not difficult to construct a paradigm which would fulfill these constraints. This ideal federal program would have two parts corresponding to the two constraints. To cope with the changing network of cities the federal government by its regulatory and public works powers would endeavor to create national minimum standards for open space, clean water and air, and a grid of transport and power services such that the firms and citizens of the United States could move about the landscape in any urban configuration they wished. No further supervision would be required, no special advantages would accrue to one city as opposed to another. To assure individual safety in the midst of such continuous change, the federal government would institute a guaranteed minimum income policy for all citizens. By guaranteeing a minimum income individuals could move about the country freely and all the present cumbersome, variable, and expensive machinery for welfare and health services could be turned over to the private market for management with a minimum of federal regulation required.

The simplicity, adaptability, and undoubted efficiency of such a federal policy makes it terribly attractive. Its nice harmony with the historical performance of the national urban network suggests that at the very least large elements of the paradigm ought to be included in any formulation of federal urban policy.

Small-Scale Urban Environments

Unfortunately for the simplicity of federal urban programming, much of what we know to be essential ingredients of human life exist in small-scale settings within metropolitan regions. The scale of intense experience of most individuals is limited to the family, the school, the work group, the house, the street, the office, the shop or mill, the shopping center, the neighborhood, and the hospital. In short, most people's lives are lived out at the scale of state and local government institutions.

Since the Great Depression, the federal government has attempted to deal with small-scale environments by seeking local or state institutions to manage federal grants-in-aid programs. The continuing weakness of state and local government, however, makes this a doubtful strategy. The problem is a historical one.

In the early twentieth-century American local government experienced a brief moment of revival. Before World War I the core municipalities of the fifty-one metropolises of the United States flourished, and so did their problems. Yet because large portions of middle-class Americans still worked or lived in the core cities and because these municipalities were relatively rich, the problems generated imaginative and effective reforms and experiments. Accelerated residential and industrial suburbanization since the twenties has drained the tax wealth and middle-class voters from these municipalities. The combined loss of economic resources and balanced electorates has proved a heavy blow to municipal management, both in the new suburbs and the old core cities. Mere consolidation, however, will not necessarily revive creative local government.

The long concentration of state and local government upon servicing real estate and helping unproductive and unwanted citizens has warped the state and local institutional performance. These two specialties are considerably removed from the dominant twentieth-century currents and enthusiasms of American society. As a result they have isolated state and local governments and crippled their ability to get the money, the talent, and the legislation the proper exercise of their responsibilities demanded. Measured by historic expenditure patterns, the states have concentrated upon roads, hospitals, and school aid; the cities have concentrated upon streets, utilities, hospitals, schools, and police and fire protection.

Since state and city hospitals served poor people (the unwanted and the unproductive), their programs had to be restricted to low-per-unit cost, mass production methods. Despite occasional exceptional leaders the pressure of legislatures and taxpayers kept this segment of state and municipal civil service minimum-standard oriented. So too with public education. Throughout the twentieth century school teachers have constituted the largest body of civil servants in the nation. Like those in health services they have always operated under pressure for minimum standard, mass production methods. As to the police, a traditional American hostility to policemen kept that civil service to low wages and low performance.

Services to real estate could not redress the quality balance. Large public works have generally been contracted out to private bidders, thereby preventing the growth of creative state and municipal design, engineering, and construction staffs. Routine highway and utility maintenance and municipal fire protection, all of which service the productive world of adults, have often been well performed, but cannot by themselves generate an imaginative civil service. The total effect of the concentration of state and local government upon a few major functions thus has meant a relentless selection away from imagination and an unremitting pressure to keep down creativity whenever it appeared in the civil service. One need not add the frustrations and distortions of graft and the conflicts of petty interest groups to prove the case for low-level performance in state and municipal government.

The federal government was dragged into urban problems in the early nineteen thirties. The Great Depression had bankrupted American cities when they attempted to meet their traditional duties for poor relief. By 1933 state finances were also collapsing under the municipal and rural unemployment burden.

The federal government responded with a whole series of directly administered emergency projects, and then later enacted a number of permanent grants-in-aid programs. (See Table 2.) To staff these new projects, the federal government had to draw up leadership from state and local government thereby further weakening the meager resources of these or-

TABLE 2 Summary of Federal Grants-in-Aid Programs 1936–1960

	1936	1940	1946	1950	1960
Grants for Health, Education, Vocational Rehabilitation, Welfare, Employment Security:			(in millions of dollars)		
Health	4.4	21.9	71.2	123.8	254.7
Education	31.9	43.6	50.6	69.7	417.9
Vocational Rehabilitation	1.4	2.1	10.8	24.7	48.6
Welfare					
Public Assistance	28.4	271.1	439.1	1,123.4	2,058.9
Other Programs	32.8	65.5	67.4	158.8	527.3
Employment Security Administration	3.1	119.9	54.5	214.5	317.2
Subtotal	$101.9	524.2	843.7	1,715.2	3,624.5
% of Total Federal Grants-in-Aid	10.0%	54.2%	82.2%	77.7%	53.0%
Grants for the Physical Environment:					
Promotion of Agriculture	5.0	6.8	14.0	13.6	33.6
Preservation of Natural Resources	2.0	2.5	7.2	17.1	66.1
Public Works	681.6	269.1	1.7	0.4	—
Urban Renewal	—	—	—	—	104.4
Highways	224.1	164.5	74.5	428.8	2,941.7
Airports	—	—	—	32.8	57.1
Civil Defense	—	—	52.6	—	4.9
Disaster Relief	—	—	—	0.3	1.5
Subtotal	$912.7	443.0	150.0	492.8	3,212.0
% of Total Federal Grants-in-Aid	90.0%	45.8%	17.8%	22.3%	47.0%
Total Federal Grants-in-Aid Programs	$1,014.7	967.0	843.7	2,208.0	6,836.6

SOURCE: Department of Health, Education, and Welfare, *Trends*, 1962, pp. 108, 114; totals sometimes don't add exactly due to rounding.

ganizations. The early large-scale relief projects struggled against the inherent weakness of America's municipal and state civil service, and much of the confusion of the 1933–1935 New Deal programs came from the lack of sufficient local bureaucracy to carry them out.

Over the years the New Deal put into practice on a national level most of the earlier experiments of local and state government, but because of constitutional limitations the New Dealers had to finance their programs by grants-in-aid to the states, and to administer them by federal supervision of state and local civil servants. The result has been to immerse the federal government in local government and to draw its domestic programs down into the marsh of state and local civil service.

Since World War II, two events have further perturbed federal domestic policy. First, the concentration of the federal government and the national electorate upon defense, international affairs, and space exploration has withdrawn much public attention from the disorders of domestic government and pushed administrative talent ever farther from the concerns of local affairs. Second, elaborating knowledge of public health and natural resource conservation and heightened educational, welfare, and urban building standards have forced the federal government to attempt the supervision of local and state civil servants in ever larger and more sophisticated programs. The weaknesses of this historic patchwork of federal responses to state and local fiscal shortages and local problems are the confusions of today's metropolitan government.

A Federal Urban Strategy

The size and dynamism of the national metropolitan network, the mire of the present grants-in-aid system, and the needs for small-scale planning all point toward a functional orientation for federal urban policy. Such an orientation requires changes of two kinds: first, a considerable disengagement of federal programs from detailed supervision of state and local civil service; second, a concentration of federal effort on those programs which it could manage itself and which would substantially ease the general destructive qualities of the present dynamic shifts in the national metropolitan network. Both sets of federal policy changes start with a recognition of the enormous size and dynamism of the national network of cities. Both accept the logical proposition and historical lesson that most of the small-scale problems of urban life cannot be dealt with effectively through the national administration, whether these problems be ubiquitous or not. The goal of both changes in federal orientation would be to encourage wherever possible the growth of strong state and municipal institutions which could plan and execute the kind of complex and sophisticated tasks demanded in planning human environments. The goal of both changes would also be for the federal government to maintain national conditions that would allow all cities to experiment, grow, and change without doing great damage to their residents or each other.

These changes in federal domestic policy orientation would direct its urban policy into four kinds of programs: expansion of federal public works and commercial regulation, introduction of a minimum national personal income, coercion for metropolitan local government reorganization, and the establishment of permanent federal urban experimental institutions.

Public Works and Commercial Regulation

In its traditional national role the federal government possesses numerous regulatory powers and construction responsibilities for the maintenance of the regional network of metropolises. The goal of these powers and responsibilities should be to provide adequate water, air, transport, power, and communications for every city in the United States. To fulfill this program, the federal government will have to enter vigorously into the construction of dams, sewage treatment plants, power lines, highways, and open spaces. Less of this work should be contracted out than in the past so that the federal civil service can develop strong design, engineering, and construction staffs. For example, the federal government relied upon the individual state highway departments for design of its intercity U.S. Routes. In all the years from 1916 until the end of World War II the country received but two well-designed modern highways, the Merritt Parkway in Connecticut and the Taconic in New York. (The Pennsylvania Turnpike was severely under-designed.) When the mammoth interstate highway program was launched fifteen years ago, no design organization existed anywhere in the country which could realize the potential of this enormous new road program. Unless much of this work is done by the federal government itself the experimentation necessary for improvements in these fields will not come rapidly enough to keep pace with the increasing resource needs of a nation of cities. Moreover, the trade, natural resource, and communications regulations of the federal government will have to be similarly oriented toward the metropolitan network. The working definition of rational planning and administration should be to maintain a setting that favors the rapid change in locations of people and economic processes throughout the metropolitan society.

The task will not be an easy one. For instance, to coordinate the construction policies of the Corps of Engineers and the Department of the Interior and then to see that this construction fits well with the regulatory policies of the Interstate Commerce Commission, the Federal Trade Commission, and the Interior Department will require a whole bureau of Solomons. This essential business of federal planning and coordination has been neglected since World War II in large measure because of the popular and presidential fixation on the Cold War.

Minimum Personal Income

Many of the problems of today's metropolitan environments arise because there are too many poor people living in American cities. One cannot enforce a strict housing code because the increased rents of conforming landlords would force the poor out of their tenancies; one cannot build good public housing because it must appear and be less satisfactory than lower-middle-class housing; one cannot give good service in public and private hospitals because the poor can't pay the necessary fees; one cannot maintain a variety of cultural, recreational, and park services to match the variety of urban publics because substantial fees would have to be charged; one cannot require school children to purchase paperbacks even though the authorities cannot supply enough texts. The entire list of present municipal services recites the distortions caused by the necessity for dealing with a large population of poor citizens. The present result is one set of inadequate services given specifically to the poor in lieu of giving them money, and another set of general services which cannot be raised to the standards of the other urban publics because taxes must be kept down.

Welfare economists have suggested a number of tax, subsidy, and fiscal remedies to meet these difficulties. The quality of the metropolitan network and the historical record of federal attempts to supervise local government programs suggest that, whatever the set of remedies to be adopted, it should meet Jeffersonian standards — it should be clear, simple, obvious, and universal. The simplest and most effective program proposed so far is the guaranteed minimum personal income. Under this program every American citizen would file an income tax whose balance would show whether taxes were due from him, or whether he was entitled to income payments.

The proposal would correct many disorders in federal and municipal policy. With money in the hands of the poor, many of the existing and inadequate special poverty services could be abolished. The poor could choose, like other Americans, what they wanted from the society and the economy. As fee-paying citizens, they would become a powerful force for the improvement of many of the public services which their present impoverishment degrades. They would also have the means to move about the city and the metropolitan network seeking the jobs and residences most suitable to their needs. Since the poor are not one monolithic mass of single habits, talents, and aspirations, their new mobility and affluence would make possible the breaking up of the massive forms of residential segregation, unemployment, and maleducation whose very concentration now defeats remedial action. The former success of the very limited, but for its time equally radical, Social Security Act, suggests that such a policy would have an enormously favorable impact upon the entire metropolitan network and its constituent environments.

Municipal Government Reorganization

During the Progressive era, America's cities led the nation in experiment and adaptation to change because they were relatively rich and powerful governmental units. Until they become rich and powerful again, no matter how much they are subsidized and supervised, they cannot become sources of innovation. The present diffusion of metropolitan power and wealth is notorious, it has been a national scandal for at least a generation.

Since the beginning of the grants-in-aid program for highways in 1916 the federal government has imposed planning and administrative organization upon the cities and states of the nation. It is currently trying to impose land use, development, and transportation planning upon metropolitan regions. This planning and its planning agencies, however, cannot become effective until they are connected to strong political units. Only the conflicts and partial resolutions of the political process can produce effective plans.

Present conditions do not point clearly toward one kind of metropolitan reorganization. Mere consolidation of entire metropolitan regions will not necessarily produce effective local institutions. The recent performance of the massive New York City school, police, housing, and welfare departments does not argue for expanding their functions to embrace the entire metropolitan region. Similarly, it is hard to predict whether the education and welfare services of metropolitan St. Louis would improve if they were consolidated. Therefore, although it is clear that the long-run goal of federal policy must be to create strong local institutions, for the present this policy must be pursued in a flexible and experimental manner.

The current practice of the Urban Renewal Administration in administering its Community Renewal Program suggests the means for achieving the desired long-run federal disengagement. Under this program, cities make application for support for planning programs the cities themselves conceive. There are no fixed standards that are applied to these grants; rather, each city is encouraged to set norms it can meet and to work toward the goals it can fulfill. The common purpose of each grant is the nourishment of metropolitan planning and development capability in each city. Under the new Poverty Program, local initiative is also being encouraged in the formation of projects.

Now the routes to metropolitan reorganization are many. Some depend upon establishing sets of special-purpose districts, others on tax reorganization, others on state legislation for annexation and incorporation, still others on interstate compacts. If the federal government were to combine a policy of coercing these sorts of reorganization as a condition of its services with a flexible and experimental policy of allowing each metropolitan region to choose its own best path towards reorganization, the long-run goal of strong local institutions probably could be achieved. Until some policy like this is adopted, however, no substantial improvement in local planning or administration can be looked for.

Federal Urban Experimental Institutions

The lack of experimentation in metropolitan programs discourages the most sanguine observer. Waves of fashion establish new approaches, not the success or failure of tested projects. Fashions in architecture control much of the federal investment in urban renewal, while fashions in social science dictate changes in educational and social service. Clearly for a long time to come, the tired civil service of American cities and public schools cannot be relied upon as the source of innovation. By and large, private industry is not a source of relevant experiments. Universities may conceive experiments but cannot afford to carry them out in long-term pilot projects. Private foundations either lack the necessary funds or are so attached to fashion chasing with their "seed money" formulas as to be worse than useless for major metropolitan experiments. Neither can the professions be relied upon. The architectural profession, though committed to personal novelty, is antiexperimental and lacks even a good system for communicating its successes and failures to its membership. Looking back now, it seems sheer folly that a few high rise public housing towers were not built, managed, and tested over a period of years before such designs were allowed to fill the nation's cities with these expensive jungles.

The federal government did experiment with suburban housing in the 1930's by constructing a few green belt towns. These towns were an enormous improvement on contemporary commercial schemes and strongly influenced the fashions of postwar commercial builders. Can it be that the green belt plans represent the final and only solution to suburban planning and construction? A continuing series of federal planning and housing experiments would undoubtedly have a very favorable effect upon the quality of American urban planning and construction.

A federal program to create a permanent set of urban experimental institutions would meet more than just the need for testing out promising ideas at full scale. It would help to build a pool of talent which could later serve in state and local civil services. The present poverty program makes federal money available for temporary experiments, but no funds are offered to establish permanent experimental institutions. Under the current Education Act, regional experiment stations are to be set up under multiple university management with federal grants for a short term of years. Because of the ad hoc, impermanent nature of these arrangements, these regional centers will not be able to attract as high-quality staff as permanent, federally managed centers could.

Full-scale, long-lasting metropolitan experiments are almost nonexistent in health, education, and social service. Such experiments as do take place are temporary and subsidiary to the main functions of the hospitals, schools, universities, and agencies that carry them out. They cannot create cadres of imaginative, trained personnel who will carry their attitudes and successes throughout the United States. How few benefits accrue from giving a teacher, nurse, or social worker a year off to train at an institution that has never been able to experiment itself with the subjects it teaches? How much more would be gained by having a number of high-quality permanent federal demonstration and experimental institutions to which such personnel could be sent?

In conclusion, for the federal government to discharge its responsibility to a nation of metropolises it must substantially revise its historic patchwork of programs. It must disengage itself from detailed supervision of state and local civil service; it must institute strong national personal income, public works, and commercial regulatory policies; it must coerce local government into metropolitan reorganization; and it must establish a permanent set of urban experimental institutions.

The program outlined in this chapter is a minimum program. It will help, but it will not solve all the nation's employment problems. It will not cover the continent with beautiful cities or people it with citizens of stable ways. It should, however, make it possible for all American cities to do less damage to their citizens than they now do. It should make it possible for some parts of many cities to be beautiful, and should allow some excellent urban institutions to multiply and flourish. The net result could be a dynamic society that would encourage the country, its cities, and its citizens to keep pace with the possibilities of the modern world.

References

A responsible journalist's survey of the current performance of municipal government is Mitchell Gordon, *Sick Cities* (Baltimore, 1965); W. Brooke Graves has just completed the arduous task of historically ordering the many local, state, and federal programs in his *American Intergovernmental Relations* (New York, 1964); Theodore J. Lowi, *At the Pleasure of the Mayor, Patronage and Power in New York City, 1898–1958* (New York, 1964), takes a good plunge into the neglected history of municipal appointments. Coleman Woodbury, Ed., *The Future of Cities and Urban Redevelopment* (Chicago, 1953), espec. pp. 609–649, is fascinating as an account of how the urban world looked at the opening of the current federal urban renewal era. In this volume Woodbury gives a survey of twentieth century American urban experience. A good documentation of the collapse of the local civil service under the weight of federal programs is Searle F. Charles, *Minister of Relief; Harry Hopkins and the Depression* (Syracuse, 1963); while William E. Leuchtenburg's "Roosevelt, Norris and the Seven Little TVAs," *Journal of Politics*, XIV (1952), 418–441, is a fine demonstration of the great obstacles to interagency cooperation that prevented orderly federal regional planning in the past; a recent review of the federal-urban partnership is Roscoe C. Martin's *The Cities and the Federal System* (New York, 1965).

CHAPTER FOUR

FEDERAL RESOURCES AND URBAN NEEDS

Murray L. Weidenbaum

The future offers a wide range of choices among patterns of federal, state, and local taxation and expenditures. Cities need not be poor and the federal government rich. The choice of a fiscal policy for the nation of cities, however, requires a selection among goals: how much for the cities themselves, how much for business and employment stability, how much for redistribution of personal income, how much to sustain the structure of federalism?

Introduction

As a nation, we have a tremendous amount of discretion in making future allocations of our public resources. It is quite likely that substantial additional amounts can be devoted to meeting urban needs, but this shift of funds of cities will not come about automatically and certainly not easily. The three related purposes of this chapter are (1) to estimate the future volume of financial resources which could be available to meet

Murray L. Weidenbaum is an Associate Professor of Economics at Washington University. His former positions include serving as Executive Secretary of the President's Committee on the Economic Impact of Defense and Disarmament and Senior Economist at the Stanford Research Institute. He is author of *Federal Budgeting: The Choice of Government Programs* (1964).

the rising needs of nondefense public spending, (2) to examine the ways in which such resources might actually be released to state and local governments, and (3) to point out the inadequacy of our budgetary concepts and techniques for deciding among the public choices which lie ahead.

The most surprising finding of this chapter — in this period of continued deficit spending by the federal government — is the likelihood of federal revenue in the future outpacing the growth of current federal expenditure programs, and, hence, the vision presents itself of potential federal surpluses. These financial surpluses may also have a counterpart in human resources which will become available, and some attention will be devoted to both the problems and potentials of this surplus.

As Galbraith stated recently, "The great economic anachronism of our time is that economic growth gives the federal government the revenues while, along with population increase, it gives the states and especially the cities the problems. The one unit of government gets the money. The other gets the work." Despite the overstatement in Galbraith's testimony, the interactions of these two strikingly different fiscal conditions are likely to make available heartening potentiality for urban planners. However, we now have no satisfactory mechanism for reallocating large amounts of governmental funds among the various levels of government. Until we develop methods for rational allocation of such sums through the various levels of American government, expenditures will reflect more the wealth of tax-collecting agencies than the needs of our society.

Federal Budget Trends

A starting point for examining the future availability of federal resources for urban needs is an analysis of federal revenue and expenditure trends in the 1965–1975 time period. The purpose is not to make any recommendations as to the levels of governmental revenues and expenditures which are most desirable or even likely. Rather, the purpose is to estimate how much discretion there is likely to be in the federal budget. That is, will there be revenues above and beyond those required to finance programs and commitments that already are on the statute books? If so, the nation will have some significant choices between tax reduction, further expenditure increases, or some combination of the two.

Method of Making Projections

The various categories of federal revenues are here projected by extrapolating their past relationships to Gross National Product, and such related series as personal income and corporate profits, on the basis of assumed future levels of economic activity. In the language of economics, they are regarded as endogenous to the national economy.

Federal expenditures, in contrast, are considered to be exogenous — they influence the level of economic activity, but are not significantly affected by it. A combination of approaches is necessary in projecting the various functional categories of federal expenditure. For one category of programs, actuarial estimates are available of future expenditure requirements under existing legislation. The major examples of this nature are old-age and survivors' insurance and veterans' pensions.

Another category of expenditures consists of those for which relatively firm program estimates are available. The major example here is federal grants to states under the federal-aid highway legislation. For still another category of expenditures, statistical extrapolations can be utilized. Because, in the past, annual federal outlays for public assistance were closely associated with the number of persons in the United States over sixty-five years of age, these expenditures can be projected on the basis of the future age distribution of the nation's population.

However, about forty percent of government expenditure programs remains, those whose size is determined primarily through relatively subjective decision-making processes, or at least those which cannot be projected in an objective manner. These include national defense, agriculture, and housing outlays. Nevertheless, we can evaluate some of the factors that will influence program and budget decisions and also make reasonable estimates of expenditures in, say, 1975.

Perhaps the key program development affecting the estimates is the status of the defense program. It is clear that, after a short period of retrenchment, the military budget is heading upward again in response to the requirements of Vietnam. Rapid changes in the direction of the military budget has occurred in the past decade, as international incidents were interspersed with periods of thaw. The over-all trend, however, has been for defense spending to be a declining portion of both the federal budget and the Gross National Product; this long-term trend is likely to continue.

General Assumptions

It is also necessary to make numerous general assumptions in preparing budget estimates. The underlying assumption here is that the political, social, and economic institutions which set the pattern of life in the United States will continue to demonstrate a high degree of continuity.

The underlying tensions between the United States and the Communist nations are assumed to continue, although there may be periods when such tensions subside. Nevertheless, it is assumed that no major disarmament agreement will be achieved, and thus a continued high level of military preparedness will be likely. Limited conflicts may occur, but on a scale less than that of the Korean war.

The over-all level of economic activity in the United States, as measured by the Gross National Product, is assumed to increase at the average rate of three and three-quarters percent a year between 1965 and 1975, measured in terms of constant dollars. This growth pace is slightly higher than that achieved by the American economy during the 1955–1962 time period, but is required in order to prevent an increase in the over-all unemployment ratio. The rates of federal taxation are assumed to be those provided by current legislation.

The Expenditure Projections

Given these assumptions, a very striking shift will occur in the composition of federal expenditures during the 1965–1975 period, fundamentally a reallocation from the defense and space programs to the welfare and "Great Society" areas, such as education, social security, housing, and community development. During the coming decade, national security expenditures will decline in relative importance and for the first time in many years, the domestic civilian programs are likely to come to dominate the federal sector.

This shift in emphasis in the federal budget is far more than a financial one and will have important implications for changes in the distribution of income and wealth in the United States. The preponderance of civilian programs means a larger proportion of pensions and other "transfer" payments which alter the allocation of income among the various groups within American society. The proportional shift away from defense spending signifies a smaller proportion of federal purchases from private industry. These governmental procurements, which are mainly made for military activities, have been, since World War II, the major market for the major growth industries in the United States, notably electronics, aerospace, and scientific instruments. Moreover, it is precisely these industries that employ the lion's share of the scientists and engineers working in American industry.

The future budget situation envisioned here would not eliminate the large governmental market for our research and development talent. However, it would provide little long-term growth potential. Hence, normal increases in the supply of scientists and engineers would either move directly into nondefense fields or would replace ("bump") engineers or scientists now engaged in defense work, who would in turn be available for civilian pursuits.

The preliminary impacts of this reallocation of federal resources are already being felt. Numerous defense contractors are becoming interested in the potentialities of civilian work, particularly in the public sector of the economy, which responds to the unique type of market stimuli that they understand so well.

The emphasis on the public sector arises because past commercial diversification efforts of the major specialized defense producers have been unsuccessful. These companies generally are geared to the requirements of governmental rather than commercial markets. Hence, a major focus of current diversification efforts is on the application of the advanced engineering and technology—and especially the so-called large-scale systems management capability—to meeting nondefense government needs.

One of the most interesting developments is occurring in the state of California. The state government has undertaken a program of exploratory research to demonstrate how defense corporations can apply their sophisticated analytical techniques to important civilian areas. Awards have been made to several aerospace companies to do preliminary work in four fields:

1. A long-range plan for a state-wide transportation system.
2. An analysis of the State's mental institutions, to search out ways to improve efficiency.
3. A method of collecting, storing, and retrieving the masses of information used by the state government.
4. A system for handling the state's tremendous air, water, and soil pollution problems.

It certainly is conceivable that the type of talent which can be engaged in these projects may also find useful application in the similar problems that beset our major urban areas.

The Budget Totals

Some attention to the likely changes in the over-all fiscal picture should be helpful. Total federal revenues under current tax provisions could reach $185 billion by 1975. Federal revenues would become an increasing percentage of the Gross National Product because of the progressive character of the federal tax structure. (See Table 1.)

TABLE 1 Projections of the Gross National Product and the Federal Budget (Fiscal years; in billions of dollars)

Category	1965 *Estimated*	1975 *Projected*
Gross National Product	640.0	905.0
Federal Revenues	117.4	185.0
Revenues as Percent of GNP	18.3	20.4
Federal Expenditures	121.4	160.0
Expenditures as Percent of GNP	19.0	17.6

Federal expenditures under current programs and commitments will rise to $160 billion in 1975. Such an increase of thirty-two percent would be significantly lower than either the forty-one percent rise in GNP or the fifty-eight percent rise in revenues. This may be one of the fundamental findings of this study: under the current budget structure, federal revenues are likely to increase faster than the national economy and federal expenditures are likely to increase more slowly.

Hence, despite the current experience of a series of budgetary deficits, the future result of the current program and revenue structure of the Federal Government would reverse the situation. The budget results that will actually be obtained, of course, will be determined by the incremental decisions to be made during the coming decade.

To avoid any misunderstanding about the nature of these projections, it is important to emphasize that they are not the result of the exercise of judgment as to what are the most desirable or even likely future levels of total government spending. These estimates represent an evaluation of the future financial dimensions of current programs and commitments. There are numerous examples of possible new budgetary items which could involve large expenditures in subsequent years, some of which may very well be enacted. Typical examples of such new programs, which are not included in the estimates are the following:

1. Large-scale exploration of Mars and other planets.
2. Transforming the Department of Agriculture into a rural affairs agency.

3. An operational salt and brackish water desalinization program.
4. Federal financing of a civil supersonic transport development program.
5. Construction of a substitute for the Panama Canal.
6. Expanding the Social Security system in line with rising living costs and general improvements in the standard of living.
7. Expanding federal assistance to research and development, particularly to the "underresearched" industries catering to nondefense markets.
8. General pensions to all World War I veterans.

The projected gap between revenues computed on the basis of existing tax laws and expenditures estimated on the basis of continuation of current programs mainly signifies the amount of *discretion* that may be exercised by policymakers in the future. First of all, it is unlikely that an entire decade will go by without important changes in tax legislation and government programs.

Economic analysis has increasingly pointed out the adverse effects of a potential large surplus in the governmental budget. Such potential net inflow to the federal government is self-defeating, because it exercises a depressive influence on economic activity, thereby reducing governmental revenues from their potential, and preventing the actual realization of a large budget surplus.

Federal-State-Local Fiscal Relations

The prospective affluence of the federal government stands in sharp contrast against the narrow future means of state and local jurisdictions. There is hardly a potential budget surplus to worry about at the "lower" governmental levels. The reasons are rather simple.

The average state and local tax structure is relatively regressive, while that of the federal government is progressive. Under a progressive revenue structure, the tax bill rises faster than the taxpayer's income. The reverse is true under a regressive system, whereby the tax bite is a declining percentage of income as income rises.

The implications for federal-state-local relations are fundamental. As personal incomes of American taxpayers increase, the revenues under our progressive federal tax structure rise faster than income. Almost the reverse occurs at state and local levels. Many state and local taxes do not rise as rapidly as personal income. The average state and local tax structure is more inelastic than the federal, that is, less sensitive to changes in economic growth.

The story, of course, is quite different on the expenditure side. For example, the requirements for education, which dominate these budgets, continue to expand far more rapidly than either population or the economy as a whole. On the basis of rather conservative assumptions, the U.S. Office of Education has projected a fifty percent increase in public education expenditures in the next decade. The estimated increases are due, chiefly, to rising enrollment at all levels, especially in high schools and colleges.

Other pressures for rapid increase in state or local expenditures arise from the continued suburbanization of the nation, requiring expensive new governmental infrastructure for many new areas. Under normal incremental growth today eight out of every ten new private homes are being built in suburban communities. Continuation of such growth and movement would place increasing demands on the public services, utilities, and transportation facilities of the nation's metropolitan areas and their governments.

On balance, the outlook for state and local governments, on the basis of current tax structures and program requirements, is just the reverse of the federal situation — potentially large excesses of expenditure demands on states and localities over available revenues.

Thus far in the period since World War II, the rising requirements of state and local governments have been met in a variety of ways: by increasing tax rates, by imposing new taxes, by seeking grants-in-aid from the federal government, and by borrowing.

It is likely that each of these sources will continue to be

relied upon, but that some of them will be utilized with increasing reluctance. The debt of state and local governments has risen spectacularly in recent years; total debt of the states went up 339 percent from 1950 to 1964, while that of local governments rose by 236 percent during the same period. Constitutional debt limits and similar institutional restrictions tend to dampen further increases. New and heightened tax rates apparently are also running into increasing opposition and are in striking contrast to the two rounds of tax reduction at the federal level since the end of the Korean War.

For the future, only federal grants-in-aid programs are likely to expand easily since they are tied, in part, to the coming federal affluence. These grants, which are now running at about $10 billion a year, however, are hardly likely to increase by anything approaching the magnitude of the potential federal surplus of $25 billion estimated for 1975. They probably cannot keep pace with the potential surplus because they require state matching funds, and because one giant among them, the highway building program, will soon reach completion.

Ways of Aiding States and Localities

Despite the many political battles that will have to be fought in thousands of separate jurisdictions for revised state and local tax levies, there is no isolated solution to state and local finance. Local revenue problems can be rationally managed only in conjunction with a national policy for the potential federal surplus. Moreover, the sum of these many taxes is so large a proportion of the national economy that alternative tax proposals must always be considered for their effects on employment, personal income distribution, and the general level of business activity. Each of the major approaches for adjusting federal revenue to state and local taxation should be examined from a number of viewpoints: their tendency to expand or reduce the role of the federal government in the economy generally, and their tendency to expand or reduce the role of the federal government in state and local governmental affairs specifically; their effects on the progressivity of the over-all tax structure; their impact on the stabilizing effectiveness of the tax structure; their influence on the distribution of income among the fifty states (i.e., equalization between high and low income states); and their relationship to local government roles vis-à-vis the state legislatures.

Currently there are six major approaches:

1. Direct federal expenditures
2. Conditional grants-in-aid
3. Block or unconditional grants
4. Tax sharing
5. Tax credits
6. Income tax reduction

These alternatives are not mutually exclusive; some combination might be considered.

Direct Federal Expenditures. Increases in federal revenue could be devoted to activities conducted by the federal government itself in all fifty states. For example the federal government could institute new programs of an interstate character, such as the construction of air pollution control facilities. This approach would call for the largest amount of federal intervention, since no provision would be made for state or local government participation. There would be state and local benefits, however, since facilities could be provided which otherwise might have to be financed locally.

Abstaining from reductions in federal income taxation would maintain the progressivity of the over-all tax structure and the role of the built-in or automatic stabilizers against unemployment and depressed levels of business activity. This would not be the case even if reductions in federal income taxes were countered by increases in state and local revenues. Most state and local taxes cannot be easily manipulated for stabilization of the economy.

Conditional Grants. Another use of increased federal revenue is to expand "tied" or conditional grants to state and local governments for financing specific functions, such as medical research or airport construction. This approach would tend to give the federal government added influence over the allocation of funds in state and local budgets. It is sometimes claimed that a disproportionate share of state and local revenues already is devoted to providing matching funds for federal grants-in-aid ("We can't afford to lose the federal money.").

The great bulk of federal grants is made to state governments. In the case of a few important grant programs however, the national government bypasses the states and deals directly with localities. Examples include housing and urban renewal, federal aid to airports, and aid to mass transportation systems.

Unconditional Grants. Recently a great deal of attention has been given to the concept of block or unconditional grants distributed among the states on a per capita basis. The so-called Heller plan was such a proposal. This would, of course, reduce the role of the federal government both in the national economy and in relation to state and local government action. It would also exercise a moderately equalizing effect between high income and low income states.

The general idea of federal distribution of surplus funds has a long history. Thomas Jefferson, in his second inaugural address, suggested that surplus revenue be utilized for "a just repartition among the States . . . applied, in time of peace, to rivers, canals, roads, arts, manufactures, education, and other great objects within each state." For many years Congress debated such proposals.

This method of distribution — comparable to the Treasury distribution of 1837, discussed below — might be far from an unmixed blessing for urban areas because federal funds would be funneled entirely through the state governments. It could increase the problems that the typical metropolitan areas face in obtaining "fair" shares of state funds from their respective legislatures. Perhaps some imagination might be devoted to methods of including local as well as state governments as recipients of the federal funds. For example, block grants could be made available to those metropolitan areas that would consolidate the myriad of governmental units (fire protection districts, school districts, utility districts, local improvements districts, etc.). Although a possible spur to efficiency, this approach, of course, raises some fundamental questions concerning the role of urban areas in a federal form of government.

Tax Sharing. It also has been suggested that a designated portion of federal tax revenues be distributed to the states on the basis of source of collection. This would result in high income states, with high tax payments, receiving the larger shares. Like the block grants, this method would also diminish the federal role, because the state governments would be left free to determine the allocation of their funds. In general, it would also have similar effects on progressivity and stability aspects of the over-all tax structure. Although this proposal would create the same sharing problems for urban communities, it would tend to benefit the larger urban areas that frequently are located in states with above-average per capita incomes.

Tax Credits. This approach would provide federal income taxpayers a more liberal write-off of state and local taxes. This could help local, as well as state, governments by softening resistance to increases in state and local taxes.

Outright Reductions in Federal Income Taxes. This indirect approach to aiding state and local governments would permit them to increase their tax rates without increasing the total tax bill of the average citizen. It introduces major questions of interstate rivalry. The over-all national tax structure would become less progressive because the nation would be placing greater reliance on proportional and regressive state and local taxes and less on progressive federal taxes in financing the public sector.

The purpose in analyzing the impacts of the six proposals is to show that the choice is not easy. Given a society with plural objectives, no single fiscal approach would satisfactorily meet more than a few of them — and might adversely affect other goals. Direct federal expenditures might optimize income stabilization and income redistribution objectives, but bypass completely both state and local governments. Tax reduction decreases the size of the federal sector, but meets state and local public needs only indirectly, if at all. Tax sharing and block grants provide for the allocation of public funds among programs to be made individually by the states, who presumably are more familiar with the needs and desires of their residents than the national government; however, no provision is made for the burgeoning financial requirements of counties, school districts, and cities and towns.

A review of past periods in American history where federal budget surpluses were familiar yields results which may be useful for analytical as well as for anecdotal purposes. By the objective standards — at least of some — "the good old days" occurred during the years 1825–1836. These twelve fiscal years represent the longest period in American history in which the federal budget continuously registered a surplus. By and large, the revenue excesses were devoted to reducing the national debt. Apparently, the bureaucracy was not too resourceful in those days. Expenditures in 1832 were only a little higher than in 1825 ($17 million versus $16 million) and the potentialities for debt reduction were soon exhausted.

Numerous proposals were made for alternative methods of disposing of the excess federal revenue. The one adopted was to distribute to the states, according to population, the surplus above $5 million in the U.S. Treasury on January 1, 1837, which amounted to $37 million. Historians argue over the economic effects of this large budgetary surplus. In any event, the distribution to the states was halted when it was three-quarters completed; the Panic of 1837 had turned the surplus into a deficit, and this "unique and curious measure," to use the terms of one historian, was allowed to lapse.

The variety of uses to which the states devoted these windfall revenues is intriguing. Some used the funds to capitalize the state banks, others devoted the money to local debt repayment or public works. Some objected to the whole idea. The Georgia legislature stated that they would have refused the money had it not been for the provision that the share of any refusing state would be divided among the other states. Although, according to one scholarly observer, some of the funds were "lost" or "wasted on improvements," the major portion was utilized for education and other undefined "worthy purposes."

Improving the Allocation of Public Resources

Depending on which of the six approaches previously described are selected, or some other, there may be great danger of not obtaining anything close to an optimum allocation of public resources. The possibility certainly exists that we, as a nation, may use up potential increases in federal revenues for relatively low-priority programs, while state and local governments are forced either to defer relatively more worthwhile projects for lack of funds, or to increase taxes which have adverse effects on economic stability and growth or on distributional equity.

What may be required is the development of some methodology to allocate public resources on some more rational basis than at present. To date there has been no systematic attempt to appraise the desirability of the choices implicitly made in the allocation of government resources among the major alternative uses and among the various levels of government.

In practice, the actual allocation of funds among the major end purposes of government is the accidental result of a myriad of independent budget decisions rather than the outcome of conscious determination. What is needed is a mechanism to permit the following types of choices to be made: between greater welfare and economic growth, between agriculture and education, between air and surface transportation facilities, between direct federal operations and grants to state and local governments, and so forth. Table 2 shows some of the kinds of implicit choices which have been made in the allocation of public funds among the major levels of government. It is apparent that, as the emphasis in the public sector shifts to the nondefense functions, the responsibilities of state and local government expand.

Basically, the horizons of budget reviewers need to be broadened by enabling cross-comparisons not currently made, such

TABLE 2 Allocation of Public Funds Among Major Functions

Level of Government	*Major Governmental Functions*									
	National Defense	Education	Old Age Insurance	Health and Welfare	Natural Resources	Highways	Unemployment Compensation	Police	Housing	Air and Water Transportation
Federal	X[1,2]		X		X					X
State						X	X			
Local		X		X				X	X	

[1] The symbol X indicates level at which the largest portion of governmental funds is spent.
[2] Functions listed in descending order of dollar magnitudes, from left to right, based on Fiscal Year 1963 relationships.

as a trade-off between an extra billion dollars for federal natural resources development or for grants to states for education or more general purposes.

The current budgetary mechanisms do not answer or even raise such basic allocative questions. Yet, such types of decisions are no more novel than a family's choice to use the Christmas bonus for a new car or a vacation, or a company's desire to allocate an increase in earnings to raising the dividend rate or to embarking upon a new research program. The company or the family may use relatively crude analytical techniques in making such choices, but, at least for some of them, the alternatives are considered jointly. The recent development and extension of program budgeting and cost/benefit analyses for defense and water resources programs may have applicability to the broader questions involving the allocation of public resources. Without prejudging the question, such techniques might result in a more reasonable distribution of public resources to meet the needs of our urban areas.

Not only must professionals develop techniques for comparative programming and budgeting, but also a major task of political education lies ahead, as William Seward lamented concerning the uses of the potential federal surpluses of the 1830's. The following appears in a letter he wrote in 1836, when he was a land officer:

> The public feeling is scarcely enlisted yet in support of our noble and just measure of distributing the public revenue. People seem, so far as they fall within my observation, to be unconcerned, as if entirely ignorant on the subject.

References

General Economic Projections — Gerhard Colm, *Long-Range Projections for Economic Growth: The American Economy in 1970*. Washington, D.C., National Planning Association, 1959.

Government Budget Projections — Otto Eckstein, *Trends in Public Expenditures in the Next Decade*. New York, Committee for Economic Development, 1959; Murray L. Weidenbaum, *Federal Government Budget Trends, 1965–1975*. St. Louis, Washington University, Department of Economics, 1965.

Comparative Tax Structures — Richard A. Musgrave, "Incidence of the Tax Structure and Its Effect on Consumption," in Joint Committee on the Economic Report, *Federal Tax Policy for Economic Growth and Stability*. Washington, D.C., U.S. Government Printing Office, 1955.

Federal-State-Local Fiscal Relations — William B. Graves, *American Intergovernmental Relations*. New York, Scribner, 1964; Paul B. Trescott, "Federal-State Financial Relations, 1790–1860," *Journal of Economic History*, September 1955; Edward G. Bourne, *The History of the Surplus Revenue of 1837*. New York, G. P. Putnam's Sons, 1885.

Allocation of Government Resources — M. L. Weidenbaum, *Federal Budgeting: The Choice of Government Programs*, 1964 (reprinted in *Congress and the Budget*, Washington, D.C., American Enterprise Institute, 1965).

WORK AND THE QUALITY OF URBAN LIFE

CHAPTER FIVE

THE ROLE OF WORK IN A MOBILE SOCIETY

Marc A. Fried

Current research suggests that the American world of work is a hierarchy of sets of social and psychological requirements for performance. Evidence from studies of the urban working class shows that individuals and groups move through this hierarchy in a step-by-step fashion, often with great difficulty. Much of the pathology of urban life is thus the consequence, or companion, of work transitions. Professor Fried examines the implications of this view of the urban work environment, and proposes a reorientation of public policy to confront the needs of a population of experiencing continuous "crises of transitions" in work and in other social areas.

Our generation faces problems of work and occupation that are strikingly different from those faced by other generations. One of the startling and paradoxical features of this situation

Professor Marc A. Fried is Research Professor and Director of the Boston College Institute of Human Sciences and Research Director of the Center for Community Studies of the Massachusetts General Hospital. He is the author of numerous articles on the urban working class.

This report is part of a study entitled Relocation and Mental Health: Adaptation Under Stress, conducted by the Center for Community Studies (Department of Psychiatry of the Massachusetts General Hospital and the Harvard Medical School), Erich Lindemann, Principal Investigator and Marc Fried, Co-Principal Investigator. The research is supported by the National Institute of Mental Health, Grant No. 3M 9137-C3. I am indebted to Mrs. Ellen Fitzgerald for review of some of the materials on unemployment, for a perceptive reading of tables, and for many helpful discussions of these problems.

is that a high rate of unemployment is associated with economic expansion and widepread affluence. To focus the problem of unemployment and underemployment even more sharply, work has taken on increased importance for a growing proportion of the population in our society at the same time that a large labor force has diminished in technological importance. Many people who did not formerly enter the labor market or who would formerly have disappeared from the labor market now are vigorously seeking jobs: women with children, the aged, the infirm, the physically disabled. The unemployed have become once more a major concern of federal and local policies. This time, however, the unemployed are not viewed merely as economically disadvantaged but as people caught in the interaction of cultural deprivation and unpreparedness for jobs that might provide them with an adequate income.

From the point of view of public policy we face the necessity of increasing the availability of jobs that are appropriate to the economic, social, and cultural expectations we have imposed on low-status populations and, at the same time, increasing the opportunities for people to develop the occupational potentialities that will enable them to work effectively at higher status positions. There appears to be little concensus concerning the methods of achieving either of these objectives. Nonetheless, with full recognition that jobs must be available before people at any level of ability can fill them, we can turn to problems in the development of work potentialities and try to understand more adequately this side of the work equation.

In this essay I shall first consider some of the problems involved in the social and psychological preparation for industrial work as a basis for considering the stages of social development in work role orientations in a modern, technologically advanced society. I shall then review some of the available evidence concerning the relationships between orientations to work, social class position, and preparedness for urban, industrial life. In discussing this evidence, I shall lean on previously unpublished data on work orientations from a systematic sample of males who had lived in a working-class community.[1] These data then lead to an effort to understand the processes of occupational and social mobility and the effects of work and other social experiences on these phenomena. Finally, I shall try to point the implications of these findings and observations to contemporary policy issues, concerning population groups most affected by inadequate work opportunities and inadequate work preparedness.

Social Development in Orientations to Work

Newcomers to the urban, industrial environment and their children form a large proportion of the lowest status populations in cities. This is almost certainly as true today for migrants within the United States as it was prior to 1920 for foreign-born migrants. Extensive experience in the urban, industrial environment is, generally speaking, an essential prerequisite for upward social mobility in a modern society.[2] Thus, one of

[1] A more detailed report and presentation of the data on work orientations is in preparation: Marc Fried, "Orientations to Work in the Working Class." The data are based on postrelocation interviews with a systematic sample of 331 male heads of household who had lived in the West End of Boston prior to its demolition. The data were actually collected in 1961 and include a wide variety of information concerning general functioning as well as occupational experience and attitudes. The sample represented a wide range of occupation and of occupational levels but the large majority were blue-collar workers of varying degrees of skill and training. For a more detailed discussion of the sample as a whole, see Marc Fried, "Transitional Functions of Working-Class Communities: The Case of Forced Relocation," in Mildred Kantor (ed.), *Mobility and Mental Health* (Springfield: C. C Thomas, 1965).

[2] Many studies present evidence to support this view of the demographic composition of low-status worker populations and the relationship between urban–industrial familiarity and occupational mobility: Niles Carpenter, *Immigrants and Their Children, 1920* (Washington, D.C.: U.S. Government Printing Office, 1927); Oscar Handlin, *The Uprooted* (Boston: Little, Brown and Company, 1952); E. P. Hutchinson, *Immigrants and Their Children, 1850–1950* (New York: John Wiley & Sons, Inc., 1956); Stanley Lieberson, *Ethnic Patterns In American Cities* (New York: Free Press, 1963); Seymour Martin Lipset, "Social Mobility and Urbanization," *Rural Sociology, 20*, 1955, 220–228; Seymour Martin Lipset and Reinhard Bendix, *Social Mobility in Industrial Society* (Berkeley: University of Chicago Press, 1959); and Basil Zimmer, "Participation of Migrants in Urban Structures," *Amer. Sociol. Rev., 20*, 1955, 218–224.

the most critical questions concerning work and social mobility is the effect of such movement from rural to urban areas on occupational functioning and, more generally, on social adaptation.

The process of movement from a preindustrial, rural community to the technologically advanced and cosmopolitan society of a large city involves a major disruption and transition. It is a transition from a secure if unrewarding world to a threatening if open environment. The most basic and immediate shift in orientations required by migration from rural to urban areas is the development of those expectations, skills, and abilities associated with obtaining and maintaining a job in a competitive market. This is a marked change from rural conceptions of work as sporadic (although physically demanding) and as a part of daily life, integrally related to other experiences and relationships with family, friends, neighbors, and kin. But the shift in orientations is mandatory, and the migrant from a rural area must either accomplish it, return home, or develop a fairly total dependence upon public or private agencies that help to sustain him in the process of transition.

More often than not, the entire livelihood of a migrant to the city and the subsistence of his family are completely dependent upon his ability to obtain and keep a job. Even apart from problems of seniority and discrimination, the job situation for such rural migrants is precarious. Not only are they likely to occupy the lowest rungs of the job hierarchy, but given any sudden increase in unemployment, the more recent migrants to an area are those first affected.[3] In fact, the data from the Boston West End study of a working-class, mixed-ethnic community reveal large differences among relatively long-term urban residents. In the year 1961, of those who had lived in the same urban area during their childhood, 4.1 percent were unemployed; of those who had lived in other urban areas during

[3] Eva Mueller and Jay Schneidescamp, *Persistent Unemployment, 1957–1961*. (Kalamazoo, Mich.: W. E. Upjohn Institute for Employment Research, 1962).

childhood, 6.2 percent were unemployed; and of those from rural childhood backgrounds, 14.5 percent were unemployed. Thus, there is a realistic basis for a continuing sense of anxiety and insecurity about job stability long after the initial experience of finding a job in the city.

Before this anxiety can diminish sufficiently to allow the migrant a more expansive and exploratory attitude toward work, the basic skill of learning to obtain and hold a job must become generalized into a sense of security in this achievement. In general, people must have a moderately high degree of fulfillment of their essential needs and confidence in future fulfillment of these needs before they can have any freedom to move on to more complex and exciting forms of work expectation and of work orientation. If recent migrants find opportunities for work lacking or precarious, and if the stabilization of their work orientations at each level is uncertain, they may find the burden of moving on to new levels of work orientation virtually impossible. Given a moderate degree of security in work and a modest range of choices in work situations, most individuals can readily develop the kind of inner security necessary for moving on to new levels of orientation to work.

The process of learning to obtain and hold a job is the first level in a hierarchy of work orientations and might be characterized by the idea of *work as a job*. It is the basic requirement for any transition from a rural to an industrial situation. Neither the difficulty of the work nor the routinization of tasks, both of which may be familiar from farm labor or from other types of rural manual work, is as important as the differences in conception of a distinctive job, separate from other life activities. For the rural migrant a new set of values, a new conception of the meaning of restriction and freedom, a new basis for interaction and communication, especially among people of different occupational status, must be established for the effective achievement of this level of work orientation.

Jack Weller, writing in the *Saturday Review*, provides one example of the difference in conceptions of a job for the Appalachian mountaineer who migrates to the city for factory work. "A mountain worker may be absent from work for a week or two, and when he returns to face an exasperated inquiry he will report that he went 'home' for the funeral of a second cousin or some other relative not in his immediate family. Like many mountain men, he may be a first-rate worker and he may keep the job — but his boss will find it hard to believe that he has heard the truth."[4] The difficulty, one may suspect, is not merely in the difference in kinship values nor in the conception of responsibility, but in differing expectations of both workers and employers and in failures of appropriate communication. Yet, the establishment of an orientation to *work as a job* is not only essential but, as I have suggested, a sense of security in this accomplishment is a necessary precondition for the psychological freedom to consider subtler, more challenging, and more rewarding potentialities in industrial work.

A second level of work orientation in this hierarchy might be conceived of as *work as a task* and is the most likely stage of work development following from stability in maintaining a job. *Work as a task* implies an ability to shift from the most routinized performance of duties and obligations to a conception of discrete components of the work process as pleasurable, as an opportunity for the development of manual or cognitive skills, as a process that allows for a sense of mastery in the performance of tasks. The tasks involved may require primarily motor or intellectual abilities but the distinctive characteristic is the expectation of pleasure in mastery. This pleasure is evidently more difficult to achieve in completely routinized jobs than in those involving at least some modicum of choice and decision. From this point of view, the very nature of the occupational task defines some of the limits within which a conception of *work as a task* may develop. Walker and Guest (1952) and Blauner (1964), however, report instances of men disrupting their work on the assembly line to create greater

[4] Jack Weller, "Is There a Future for Yesterday's People," *Saturday Review*, 48 (October 16, 1965).

challenge in the midst of extreme routinization.[5] And the West End data reveal remarkable instances in which workers find pleasure in work situations beyond anything evident in the job itself.

With the development of a sense of mastery of manual or cognitive problems, workers have increased opportunity to integrate this achievement in a new level of work orientation, one we might call *work as an occupation.* This level of work implies the existence, even taking for granted, the pleasure of manipulative mastery in task performance. It goes beyond sheer pleasure in mastery, in that workers begin to develop responsibility for an entire work objective or the performance of an entire work role. They begin to evolve that form of work morality that we frequently associate with the Protestant ethic and the appreciation, on a more abstract level, of the utilitarian contribution of their own work activities to a larger social enterprise. In the orientation to *work as an occupation,* pleasure in the mastery of discrete tasks must be subordinated to the fulfillment of larger, if less immediately gratifying, work objectives. By the same token, the development of this work orientation facilitates a new sense of social participation through work and increased potential for mastery and achievement of a total work role.

Finally, with a sense of security in an occupational role, and a sense of meaning in contributing to a larger social objective, it is possible for urban workers to move on to a conception of *work as a career.* There is little doubt that, in our society, despite the enormous price it may exact, the orientation to *work as a career* provides immense intrinsic and extrinsic rewards. In this orientation, individuals must identify their own personal achievement with the occupational role they fill. Social participation and individual fulfillment become almost indistinguishable. Since this orientation belongs primarily to the professions and to people in high-status managerial and executive positions,

[5] Charles R. Walker and Robert H. Guest, *The Man on the Assembly Line* (Cambridge: Harvard University Press, 1952); Robert Blauner, *Alienation and Freedom: The Factory Worker and His Industry* (Chicago: University of Chicago Press, 1964).

I shall give it little attention in discussing working-class orientations to work.

Social Position and Differences in Work Orientations

There is enough evidence from a number of different studies using different models, different techniques, different samples, and different indicators to state that variations in work orientation or in the meaning of work are strongly associated with variations in social class position. Current research clearly demonstrates that *a hierarchical structure of work role orientations is strongly associated with social class position as a composite form of status and with each of the factors that contribute to social class position.*[6]

If we consider merely two sets of facts, the relationship between rural–urban background and occupational achievement and the relationship between occupational achievement and work role orientations, we have a substantial basis for the view that rural backgrounds provide minimal preparation either for the kinds of jobs or for the kinds of work orientations that are highly rewarded in the urban, industrial environment. Moreover, at any given occupational level, those workers who come from rural backgrounds show lower levels of work role orientation than do equivalent workers from urban backgrounds. However, it appears that parental occupational status establishes a base for direct occupational achievement and can, as it were,

[6] The differences in work role orientations, following the lines of this hierarchy, are extremely marked for such dimensions as educational achievement, occupational status, and urban–rural background. Combinations of these dimensions produce even more striking differentiations. Thus, 45 percent of the high-education–high-occupation group express the highest level of work role orientation (work as a career) but only 1 percent of the low-education–low-occupation group express this orientation. Similar material is presented in Nancy C. Morse and Robert S. Weiss, "The Function and Meaning of Work and the Job," *Amer. Sociol. Rev.*, 20, 1955, 191–198; Arthur Kornhauser, *Mental Health of the Industrial Worker* (New York: John Wiley & Sons, Inc., 1965); Eugene A. Friedmann, Robert J. Havighurst, et al., *The Meaning of Work and Retirement* (Chicago: University of Chicago Press, 1954).

overcome the barriers inherent in rural socialization experience. Taken together, the kinds of preparation for occupational achievement in an urban society represented by rural or urban childhood residence and by parental occupational achievement are very potent determinants of any individual's subsequent orientations to work and subsequent social class position.[7] These background factors set the stage for subsequent opportunities and achievements in industrial occupations. Later opportunities and achievements based on education and occupational skills are part of a long sequence initially affected by parental status and childhood experience.

To say that there is a hierarchy of work role orientations related to social class differences is not simply to postulate a ladder of satisfaction with work. These differences in work role orientations by social class are independent of job satisfaction.[8] Although the scales are weighted against meaningful work opportunities for low-status workers, an unskilled laborer may find important gratifications and comfort in his view of the job as a way of earning a living or of keeping occupied. Unfortunately, this gratification and comfort is largely due to

[7] Since the association of occupational status and work role orientations is maintained under all conditions, the implication of this statement is that if the occupational status of the parents is high, occupational achievement is likely to be fairly direct whether a higher level of work role orientations precedes or follows from actual accomplishment; and, on the other hand, if the individual comes from an urban background, in contrast to those from rural backgrounds, they are likely to show higher levels of work role orientation which represent a preparation for subsequent achievement. It is impossible to tease these factors apart in a direct, empirical analysis of the causal patterns but much of the internal evidence supports this interpretation.

[8] The weight of evidence is that job satisfaction is also related to occupational status (e.g., Arthur Kornhauser, *op. cit.*), a finding supported by the West End data using open-ended and indirect questions concerning job satisfaction. Some studies, however (e.g., Paul Lafitte, *Social Structure and Personality in the Factory*, New York: Macmillan, 1958) report no differences in job satisfaction by occupational status. When we use direct measures of satisfaction in the West End data, as does Lafitte, we corroborate this finding as well. Thus, the difference in results is likely to result from the kinds of measures employed. In either case, however, controlling by job satisfaction, the relationship between work role orientations and social class dimensions is maintained.

inadequate preparation for alternative conceptions of work and, thus, serves as a barrier to occupational mobility. Further experience in urban areas and wider familiarity with different occupational possibilities in industrial society introduce a note of conflict into these occupational expectations. In this way, it provides impetus for new work expectations and, in the presence of available job opportunities, a more widespread demand for more meaningful work.

The excessive narrowing of workers' skills and horizons has been an important consideration in several studies of the technology of industry.[9] Blauner's recent investigation of several different industries reveals wide differences in the sense of alienation from work encouraged by different sociotechnical arrangements. His major concern is the ways in which different occupations foster a sense of powerlessness, of meaninglessness, of social alienation, and of self-estrangement in work and, by contrast, the absence of these forms of alienation in other occupational structures. These variations cut across differences in occupational status although, within each type of industry, the status differences appear to follow familiar lines of least opportunity for the lowest status groups. Nonetheless, an important feature of his study lies in its clear revelation that work role opportunities inherent in the nature of the industrial process are potent factors in the development of higher levels of work rule orientations.

There is undoubtedly much that can be done to encourage the organization of industrial processes and of the jobs involved in these processes to provide wider opportunities for the exercise of abilities, skills, intelligence, and imagination ordinarily submerged in routinized blue-collar (and even white-collar) occupations. To some extent, changes are already taking place as a result of automation which eliminate many of the least demanding work tasks. Moreover, as Friedmann (1961) points out, there is a movement toward job enlargement independent of automation, brought about by management's realization that

[9] Walker and Guest, *op. cit.*, Blauner, *op. cit.*, Georges Friedmann, *The Anatomy of Work* (New York: Free Press, 1961).

the greatest efficiency and productivity are not necessarily achieved by the minute fragmentation of physical movements in a work process.[10]

In addition to the inevitably slow process of changing conceptions of organization and of work levels, we wish to increase fully the economic, social, and cultural opportunities inherent in higher status positions for the vast majority of the working population. But the process of preparing large populations for the demands and opportunities of higher status occupational positions, and the process of increasing access to jobs that allow for wide options and greater challenges, also inevitably moves slowly and gradually. It is essential, therefore, to recognize that planners' efforts to upgrade the occupational qualifications of the underprivileged involve, to a very considerable extent, facilitating a natural process of transition. *Changes in orientations to work from one level of social development to the next are ordinarily associated with the normal and gradual process of occupational and social mobility in an industrial society*. There is little likelihood that we can short-circuit the sequential nature of these processes or by-pass the important levels of experience in the urban environment, of educational background, and of the early development of work expectations and skills. At best, we can hope to encourage more effective transitions at each level of development through a deeper understanding of the total process and of the nature of social and psychological resources most vital to movement along the sequence of work role orientations.

The possibility of any form of upgrading, by whatever methods we may employ, is completely dependent upon the objective existence of many and varied occupational positions. Indeed, although it is reasonable to speak of upgrading the functional potentialities of underprivileged workers, it is also clear that we have not yet fully tapped existing markets of skills, abilities, and potentials. More often we find that an individual's work role orientation has gone beyond the evident opportunities provided by his actual job than that his work role orientation is inade-

[10] Georges Friedmann, *op. cit.*

quate to the demands of his job. The same conclusion is implied by the data on occupational aspirations. Objectively, 50 percent of the men in the West End sample were at the same occupational level as their fathers, 29 percent had moved up in occupation, and 21 percent had moved to lower occupations. The largest proportion of the occupational movements, both upward and downward, involved single steps rather than large changes in occupational status. However, many more men aspired to higher occupational positions than those they actually held. More than half (51 percent) aspired to occupations higher than their own, while 42 percent wanted occupations at the same work level as their current occupations. These figures take on even greater significance, when we realize that, at each level, those people who have not been mobile more frequently have mobility aspirations than those who have presumably realized their mobility aspirations through actual achievement.[11] Since those with mobility aspirations have relatively higher work role orientations than others in the same occupational status, we can further assume that their ambitions are not altogether unfounded. The critical point, however, is that there is a larger reservoir of both work aspirations and preparedness for higher levels of occupational functioning than can be realized within the limited job opportunities available.

Thus, to say that occupational and social mobility are normal processes does not negate the evident fact that there is considerable disequilibrium between desires, preparation, and achievement. When discrimination operates, this disequilibrium becomes more marked. Thus, given equivalent parental occupational background, urban experience, education, prior job experience, or similar work role orientations, Negroes will have a poorer chance of obtaining any job than whites and, particularly, will have a poorer chance of obtaining jobs at a moderately high level. However, all of these factors do affect the status of Negroes as well as white and are critical de-

[11] The index used for mobility, in this instance, is the discrepancy between educational and occupational achievement.

terminants of social mobility.[12] In order to understand the problem, or, for that matter, in order to change the situation, we must carefully distinguish the problem of discrimination from the other factors that impede or facilitate occupational mobility. Preparedness for effective functioning in an urban, industrial environment can be seen as an important problem in its own right, a problem that affects whites as well as Negroes, and one that may be understood and influenced apart from the manifest problem of discrimination.

Crises of Transition

The movement from a peasant village or a farm community to an urban, industrial area creates a total crisis of transition and, at the very least, we must ask how experiences in other areas of urban life affect the situation of work. The question is most appropriate for the earliest phases of adaptation to the city and to industrial work, since these migrant populations are least prepared to make rational decisions in their own interest.[13]

[12] The issues in Negro mobility are complex and different dimensions are easily confounded with one another to the disadvantage of effective action. On the one hand, at any level of accomplishment, Negroes are more poorly "rewarded" than whites of equivalent accomplishment. Even this is complicated by the fact that the same level of schooling does not necessarily mean the same educational preparation. On the other hand, the educational and occupational discrepancies between Negroes and whites have been diminishing over the past few decades. For an analysis of these changes, see Philip M. Hauser, "Demographic Factors in the Integration of the Negro," *Daedalus*, Fall 1965, 847–877. None of the extant studies takes account of the significance of rural to urban migration and its frequency among Negroes over the past few decades as a further deterrent to manifest changes in status at the present time. The assumption that discrimination is the primary or even the exclusive cause of these status differentials must be modified by an appreciation of the process of social mobility and the gradual nature of those acquisitions that make mobility possible. In ignoring these factors we impede rather than facilitate social mobility among Negroes.

[13] More specifically, those migrants to the city who are of higher status often come from other cities or large towns or have had experience in other urban environments; moreover, higher status migrants more frequently appear to move on the basis of prior arrangements either for jobs, educa-

Characteristically, the low-status migrant from a rural area, whether from a foreign land or from another part of the same country, moves into those low-rent areas that we designate as slums. This first move into the slum may occur for many reasons: the low rents; the slum's easy access to entry-points of the city and its jobs; cultural or ethnic similarity to familiar areas; the migrant's prior contacts and social relationships in the area, or the city's discriminatory exclusion of migrants from other neighborhoods. Yet, continued residence in the slum after cultural assimilation and economic achievement suggests an important psychological and social "transitional function" of the slum in the lives of many working-class people. For some, the transitional function of the slum becomes unimportant relatively early in their progress through the lowest status positions in the society; for others, it retains importance for a much longer period, even into the second and third generation after the initial movement of a family from the rural to the urban environment.

The critical feature of the transitional function of the slum is that it provides a set of institutionalized arrangements within a relatively homogeneous and geographically bounded area which are as small a departure from the closed community of rural life as it is possible to achieve in a city.[14] In view of the complex and diverse mechanisms of adaptation necessary for effective functioning in the city, any situation which makes few demands on the newcomer for rapid adaptation and change in family relationships, kin and friendship interaction, consumer styles, recreation and leisure involvements, or religious and community commitments is likely to facilitate his learning process. In the familiarity and stability of their patterns, he

tion, residence, or social relationships, than do lower status migrants. Similarly, at higher levels of social mobility beyond the unskilled and semiskilled job levels, there is enough prior contact with cities and with industrialized work situations to allow for selective decision-making.

[14] Fried, 1965, *op. cit.* Also, Marc Fried, "Social Problems and Psychopathology," in Leonard J. Duhl (ed.), *Urban America and the Planning of Mental Health Services* (New York: Group for the Advancement of Psychiatry, 1964).

can more readily focus attention on the altered demands and expectations of work situations. Otherwise the influx of unfamiliar and ambiguous social stimuli and demands would prove too massive and threatening to allow a meaningful adjustment to the critical expectations for occupational activity.

While the evidence is not conclusive, there is much to suggest that *the experience of stability, security, and a close-knit communal relationship in the working-class slum facilitates both the initial adaptations to occupational demands and subsequent movement toward higher levels of work orientation and of occupational achievement.* At the same time, it is also quite evident that most working-class people who have eventually achieved some of the most important forms of urban, occupational, and educational social experience are already in the early phases of the next transition. They may not be explicitly conscious of striving for status. They are more often striving for better occupational opportunities, for the possibility of further education for their children, less often for better housing and income. It is in these concrete spheres that their unfulfilled desires are manifest.

Apart from the explicit or implicit social ambitions of slum inhabitants, there is other evidence pointing to the slum as an environment for transition. Characteristically, patterns of community and peer relationships in the working class are linked to patterns of marital relationship. Friendship and kinship ties are predominantly local, and other people are readily accessible in a physical and social sense. If both husband and wife have friends readily available, the fact that they spend their leisure time apart from one another creates no special problems. The patterns of community and neighbor relationship and the patterns of marital relationship are linked cultural phenomena, each involving institutionalized and widely appreciated forms of gratification.

The forms of peer and marital relationship found in the slums are particularly crucial to transitions of status, because both of these patterns undergo changes with mobility. Thus, the families who are occupationally mobile, or who appear close to such mobility, may continue to maintain extremely close communal ties. At the same time, they are more likely to number among their closest friends people who live outside the immediate local community. This shift from a local to a more cosmopolitan attitude toward friendships accompanies a transitional phase of marital relationship. The earlier forms of companionship in working-class marriages shift toward joint family activities, such as increased participation by the husband in household decisions and tasks or in periodic family shopping expeditions. The important quality of this marital transition is heightened interaction in areas other than the most fundamental household, sexual, and parental functions.

In the West End data there is a striking correspondence of these shifting patterns of community and family relationship with a number of other aspects of personal history: longer urban experience, higher education, higher levels of work role orientation, or the achievement of skilled occupations.[15] The internal relationships in the data suggest that only with the emergence of a sense of mastery at work, minimally in the performance of discrete tasks, is the individual sufficiently free from immediate environmental constraints and realities so that he can consider the possibility of reaching beyond his local community for friendship relationships, of exploring the city, of a fuller family relationship, and of considering the possibility of larger vistas for his children.

If these observations and conclusions are correct, there follow several implications of practical and theoretical consequence. First, whatever the impediment to effective achievement in an urban, industrial society, the difficulties may be viewed as crises

[15] Bott observed the interrelationship of family and friendship ties but questioned the class basis for these patterns. Elizabeth Bott, *Family and Social Network: Norms, Roles, and External Relationships in Ordinary Urban Families* (London: Tavistock Publications, 1957). For further descriptive material see Herbert Gans, *The Urban Villagers* (New York: Free Press, 1962); John M. Mogey, *Family and Neighborhood: Two Studies in Oxford* (Oxford, Eng.: Oxford University Press, 1956); and Michael Young and Peter Willmott, *Family and Kinship in East London* (Glencoe, Ill.: The Free Press, 1949).

of transition in social adaptation.[16] Crises of this kind may occur at various levels of functioning, and they may even require assistance from resources beyond the individual's normal social relationships. But they are not necessarily pathological. When a child learns to walk, for example, he experiences a "crisis of transition" that results in effective mastery of an important part of his environment and a sense of increased control. Crises of transition in social adaptation are more problematic than this, particularly in the earlier phases of the process when a total life situation has changed. But the effective resolution of *crises of transition* is, in large part, a function of internal preparedness and external resources that can shift the balance toward success or failure.

This brings us face to face with the second implication of this view of major crises of transition in working-class populations. Special resources, like money, education, or social position can modify the situation and influence the chances of success. The scholar from Paris or the lawyer who moves to Chicago from Birmingham, no matter how uncomfortable he may be for a time, is more likely to adjust effectively to the change than those less privileged. The situation for the low-status migrant is quite evidently different and he is at a marked disadvantage in numerous ways. Most clearly for the Negro migrant, the situation is filled with impediments and potential sources of difficulty and threat. The absence of family and community resources to help in absorbing the shock of change can only accentuate the problem and the dangers of potential failure.

A third implication of crisis in transition is that failures of adaptation to the urban environment are manifested in a wide range of psychological, physical, and social problems. In some instances, it is quite clear that migration is a core issue in the emergence of overt problems. For example, rates of psychiatric hospitalization have shown quite consistent correlations with

[16] Erich Lindemann, "The Use of Psychoanalytic Constructs in Preventive Psychiatry," in *Psychoanalytic Study of the Child,* Vol. 7 (New York: International Universities Press, 1952).

various types of migratory movement and, in the most recent analyses, are particularly marked for those who have moved from one state to another. The concerted impact of several crises clearly produces severe disruption.[17]

Under extreme conditions, such as those of the Negro rural migrant, it is apparent that the successful development of the lowest level of work role orientation, the conception of *work as a job*, is both a difficult achievement and an essential requirement for adaptation to the urban, industrial environment. If we consider the wide array of changes necessary for facilitating this transition for the vast numbers of underprivileged, both Negro and white, the problem appears almost impossible to solve. The analysis of some of the component parts of these problems, particularly those that bear on work role orientations and occupational achievement, however, suggests a moral for social planning. All too often, as with urban renewal, we plan for more effective institutions and functions and refuse to confront the normal processes of change and the natural psychological, social, and physical resources available for facilitating change. Thus, we try to plan for impossible tasks when realistic goals are within our scope. Or, in our neglect of developmental processes, we fail to take account of the ways in which they may counteract our best efforts. Problems of work in our society and, most particularly, the occupational and social achievements of millions of underprivileged people are far too important to allow this habit of planning to negate its own objectives. A more direct consideration of the policy and service implications of both the processes and problems of social mobility in our society may be of help in directing our subsequent efforts.

Conclusions and Implications

Any attempt to deal broadly with the problems and potentialities of work in our society and its portents for the future

[17] Fried, 1964, *op. cit.*, Thomas S. Langner and Stanley T. Michael, *Life Stress and Mental Health: The Midtown Manhattan Study*, Vol. II (New York: Free Press, 1963).

quality of urban life emphasizes our extensive ignorance. We know amazingly little about work, especially about the psychology of work. In a society with an ideology of individuality and self-fulfillment, *work as a career* is an orientation most widely encouraged and represents a goal most widely sought, though there is scattered evidence to suggest that family life, community relations, peer interaction, and even cultural experience often suffer in the pursuit of career goals.

Whether or not this is the case, democratic idealogy and institutional forms require the proliferation of external choices for the vast majority of the population. In historical perspective, there can be little doubt that this is most nearly accomplished in highly developed urban, industrial societies. For the people involved, migration to urban, industrial centers is the first step in the emergence of a wider range of options and choices, a process that has gone very far in the United States. In this paper I have been concerned with the long process of transition between this first step, the movement from rural to urban areas, and the development of those occupational orientations that appear to be manifestations of modern, cosmopolitan conceptions of life and world view.

These transitions are only a small part of the massive burden of social change envisaged by the present goal of a "Great Society." Yet even a more limited concern with improving the situation of the underprivileged in our society suggests a great many tasks. There are, however, a number of discrete and distinguishable policy issues that can be effectively pursued with the hope of some slight success. And partial success along several of these fronts simultaneously would lead us far toward achieving these minimal goals. At least four separate policy issues can be distinguished and, although I will concentrate only on the last, the others must be mentioned to provide the necessary perspective.

1. The first policy issue that can be distinguished from all others concerns discrimination and its corollary, segregation. In its most extreme form, this means discrimination against

Negroes and segregation of Negroes in residential ghettos. Unfortunately, discriminatory attitudes run deep and are almost certainly produced, in part, by desires to maintain the security and superiority of one's own beliefs, institutions, and selfhood against all potential challenges. Nonetheless, efforts to understand and reduce discrimination must proceed as distinguishable policy matters, important in their own right and essential components of any larger progressive change.

2. Whether full employment serves to reduce discrimination or not, an aggressive policy of insuring more job opportunities is an essential requirement for diminishing the ravages of economic underprivilege. Full employment is not so much a solution to problems as it is a basic condition for their solution. Many existing problems would barely be touched by an increase in employment oportunities; the aged, the severely handicapped, the family in which the female head of household is the only potential breadwinner are not likely to benefit directly from greater availability of jobs. On the other hand, a very considerable source of economic deprivation lies precisely in periodic and chronic unemployment and underemployment, and it would be pointless, if not destructive, to upgrade skills and work potentialities without providing adequate employment opportunities. In fact, we have not yet explored the intrinsic "upgrading" potential of wider job opportunities themselves. If it is the case that each crisis and failure facilitates the development of further crises and failures, a drastic diminution in unemployment and underemployment might accomplish far more than merely economic improvement for the underprivileged. Moreover, it is more difficult to maintain discriminatory hiring practices when there are more jobs available than ready incumbents to fill these positions, and it is less functional for individuals to discriminate when they are not threatened by the economic competition of a "newcomer." Full employment oriented to the problems of underemployment as well as to those of unemployment is as critical a policy matter as any that exists today.

3. Beyond the reduction of discrimination and the develop-

ment of full employment, it seems essential to stimulate further a process of organizational change that is already occurring in our society. To the extent that we hope to provide meaningful opportunities, as well as the bare essentials for existence, we should reverse the process of job fragmentation which developed in the course of the industrial revolution. Automation appears to have accomplished this reversal to some extent by virtue of incorporating an entire series of discrete tasks into a mechanical process that a single individual can control. Job enlargement and the reorganization of industrial processing systems can go considerably further than at present to facilitate the development of more meaningful forms of occupational participation. The central importance of the social relationships and social interaction engendered (or impeded) by technical features of manufacturing and office work is an exceedingly complex subject; and we have much to learn about alternative methods and their consequences. The reorganization of sociotechnical systems in industry involves both managerial and union groups and covers a disputed area of jurisdiction and control. Nonetheless, as the largest single factor in upgrading occupational roles and occupational skills, it is a central area in which change must occur.

4. It may be that, were we to accomplish a major reduction in discrimination and segregation, and were we to achieve full employment and a reorganization of the sociotechnical systems that affect a large number of relatively low-status workers, we would have achieved the largest part of our goals. Even if this were the case, however, there would remain throughout the population a large number of people who, at any given moment, would need special attention. These people would be men and women undergoing various kinds of psychological, social, or economic crises. Without attempting to discuss current social welfare policies and procedures or to criticize them in any detail, I would like to recommend a very different conception of health and welfare services, one that stems logically from an analysis of mobility processes and work orientations. This approach, with its origins in the conception of mental health

services pioneered by Erich Lindemann, may be viewed as a *crisis-oriented* approach in contrast to the *population-oriented* approach that is now widespread.[18] If it is the case that the processes of social mobility in an industrial society represent a series of crises of transition and it is also the case that the normal process of adaptation to the higher demands and opportunities of urban life involves a sequence of changes in psychological and social functioning, it is possible to direct our attention to the stages of adaptation and, particularly, to the crises of transition themselves. In this view, effective adaptation that allows an individual to function within an increasing range of real, external options, is a result of the successive mastery of each of these crises of transition. That desires for such mastery are widespread, I have already tried to document. While we cannot deny the relevance of individual differences in ability to master these crises, differences that are often viewed as "personal effectiveness" or "social competence," the available evidence suggests that the major component of these differences lies in the preparedness attributes we have discussed and in the availability of stable social resources to help in meeting adaptive challenges.

From this point of view, the most effective forms of welfare services would consist in providing additional social support through each of the major and predictable crises of transition related to occupational mobility and also in supplementing family and community resources that are inadequate. If one cannot skip over stages in social adaptation but, at best, can master them with more certainty and greater rapidity, then every major crisis of transition must be met with increased availability of assistance. Tracing the problem to its source, it becomes apparent that one of the first and most important crises of transition that remains completely unattended surrounds the initial movement from a rural to an urban area. To what extent some of the subsequent phenomena of crisis are exacer-

[18] For further information on the crisis orientation see Chapter Sixteen in this volume, "The Reinstitutionalization of Social Welfare," by Ralph E. Pumphrey.

bated by our failure to assist this initial process, crises like family disruption, chronic unemployment, and psychiatric disorder, remains unknown, but one can reasonably suspect that these tragedies are significantly influenced by failures to cope meaningfully with the migration crisis.

It is important to observe that the conception of crisis shifts the entire emphasis of potential policies, programs, and services from "high risk" populations to "high risk" situations or predicaments. If we carry this conception of crisis through to its logical conclusion, it means the elimination of a financial "means test" that we now employ directly, and the social "means test" we employ implicitly. This conception would extend policies, programs, and services to the privileged who face crises of transition with inadequate resources for effective adaptation, so that anyone, regardless of his income, could receive help in times of crises.

Another important feature of a crisis-oriented approach to economic and social problems is the shift in conception from relatively stable forms of assistance (which may or may not be necessary) to the very rapid deployment of emergency resources. A person who loses his job, in this light, requires immediate assistance in the form of money or of subsidized work in order to maintain a basic sense of psychological and social security as well as economic stability. Our usual approach is based on the assumption that people in crises need to be motivated and, at times, degraded in order to pull themselves together to achieve their goals. The crisis approach assumes that people in transitions need only temporary assistance to stabilize their situations and that, in the large majority of cases, their own motivations and abilities can operate best under supportive, nonpunitive conditions. Certainly, some people live their lives in crisis and would require relatively long-term assistance. The crisis approach assumes that these people are in the minority.

This approach to major crises of transition in social adaptation holds many possibilities for altering the occupational positions of underprivileged populations in our society. In the long run, it is likely to accomplish most expeditiously some of the major goals of current programs for the poor. It can be equal to the task, however, only in conjunction with other policies and programs that deal with discrimination, unemployment, and routinized jobs. At the same time, the successful expansion of horizons, not only in jobs, but in psychological potentialities, in social orientations, and in cultural experiences is likely to increase the effectiveness of antidiscrimination and full-employment programs. The net effect should be a faster approach to true equality of opportunity.

The problems of underprivilege and inequality in opportunity are such fundamental issues that our failure to achieve their resolution must, of necessity, be a persisting source of agony in our society. To "solve" the problem, moreover, means no more than providing some basic common denominators for life in our society. This solution is far from the goal of a great society, far from the achievement of urban culture one might envisage. Yet the very difficulty in adequately formulating the problem, in adequately conceptualizing a reasonable solution, in moving rapidly toward achieving its clarification suggests that the development of resources to cope with these difficulties may require major changes in our society itself, changes that may contain the kernel of the long-range goals we seek. It is easy to ask others to change so that they are like us and achieve the rewards that, having sought and fought for, we cherish. It is far more difficult to ask how we might change and, in the process, to alter the very context and form in which the issue is posed.

CHAPTER SIX

WORK AND IDENTITY IN THE LOWER CLASS

Lee Rainwater

Many urban Americans do not live to be good providers and do not follow the paths of traditional success. They seek sanity, however, by struggling for a valid personal identity. This search is the vast human potential of the lower-class American. The conflict between this search for identity and the world of work is one of the major disorders of the American City.

Valid Identities

One pivotal need of any person, a need directly related to the performance of work roles in our society, is the need for a valid identity. That is, everyone needs to *be somebody*. The tremendous variation in the kind of person Americans can become suggests that *which* particular somebody one becomes is

Lee Rainwater is Professor of Sociology and Anthropology at Washington University. He is the author of *Family Design: Marital Sexuality, Family Size and Contraception* (1965), and *And The Poor Get Children* (1960), and a coauthor of *Workingman's Wife* (1959).

This paper is based in part on research aided by a grant from the National Institute of Mental Health, Grant No. MH-09189 "Social and Community Problems in Public Housing Areas." Many of the ideas presented stem from the discussion with the senior members of the Pruitt-Igoe Research Staff — Alvin W. Gouldner, David J. Pittman and Jules Henry — and with the research associates and research assistants on the project. I have made particular use of the ideas developed in discussions with William Yancey, Boone Hammond, Robert Simpson, and Marc J. Swartz. The ideas presented are also much influenced by discussions about the psychology of identity with Sidney J. Levy.

not nearly as important as that *that* somebody be recognized as a valid expression of the human condition.

Gregory Stone has observed that of the various investigators who have used the concept of identity almost all

> imply that identity establishes *what* and *where* the person is in social terms. When one has identity he is *situated* — that is, cast in the shape of a social object by the acknowledgement of his participation or membership in social relations. One's identity is established when others *place* him as a social object by assigning him the same words of identity that he appropriates for himself or *announces*. It is in the coincidence of placements and announcements that identity becomes a meaning of the self.[1]

It is exactly this coincidence of placements and announcements that I refer to by the term valid identity. For Erikson, the achievement of identity comes about when "the young adult gains an assured sense of inner continuity and social sameness which bridges what he *was* as a child and what he is *about to become* and also reconciles his *conception of himself* and his *community's recognition* of him." Erikson[2] sees identity as "a self-realization coupled with a mutual recognition."

Thus, just as society is a system that allocates roles to its members, it is also a system that allocates identities, each identity being a particular configuration of the role positions into which the individual has been recruited and which he has achieved, and the sense of uniqueness and connectedness that he has distilled from his experiences so far in life. The maintenance of a valid identity is a lifelong task, beginning in infancy and continuing until death. Internal or social pressures at any point in time can bring about a crisis of identity in which the individual is forced to call into question the validity of the person he had thought himself to be.

To maintain a sense of valid identity, then, the individual must find some degree of congruence between who he feels he

[1] Gregory Stone, "Appearance and The Self," in Arnold Rose, *Human Behavior and Social Process* (Boston: Houghton Mifflin Co., 1962).

[2] Eric H. Erikson, *Identity and the Life Cycle* (New York: International University Press, 1959), pp. 110–114.

is, who he announces himself to be, and where he feels his society places him. Individuals are led to announce a particular identity when they feel that it is in some way congruent with their needs. The society influences these needs in one very important way by its willingness to accept such announcements by a congruent placement. As individuals seek to hammer out identities that will be valid in terms of their own needs, they make use of the resources in the form of values, norms, and social techniques, which their culture makes available to them. Each individual tries on identities that seem attractive and possible out of the cultural material that is available to him and then tests these identities by making appropriate announcements. If these announcements meet with success the individual will tend to maintain the identity until such time as his announcement is no longer validated by others or until it seems no longer congruent with inner promptings. Others do not confirm the individual's announcements automatically; their placements are a function of their own motivations or strategies in the situation. Placements of announced identities are hard won in processes of interaction in which both announcer and placer have stakes in the outcome which affect the other's willingness to confirm an identity. One kind of power in interpersonal situations involves one individual's ability to affect significantly the identity process of another by choosing to confirm or deny the latter's announced identity.

Perhaps one of the deepest anxieties human beings can experience is that which comes from the loss of the sense of identity. Such a loss comes about either when there is a sharp disjunction between the self that is being announced and the needs pressing for gratification, or when the announced identity is not appropriately placed by others.[3] In either case, the identity

[3] The subjective experience of a disjunction between announced self and pressing needs is well known psychiatrically as "depersonalization," a state in which the individual says to himself, "I am no longer me," or, "My body does not seem to be part of me." In depersonalization the repressed needs seeking expression in behavior call into question the validity of the self-announced (conscious) identity.

becomes invalid for the individual once he recognizes the state of affairs. The anxiety which follows pushes him in the direction of seeking another kind of valid identity.

Lower-class, especially Negro lower-class, Americans live in a world which poses severe threats to the maintenance of a sense of valid identity. Ultimately this threat stems from the fact that their society does not equip them with the ability to satisfy the needs which the society itself generates. Deprived of the ability to achieve in socially legitimated ways, they are stimulated to seek out other means to satisfy their needs, means which the culture regards as illegitimate. Sociologists call such an environment *anomic*.

In anomic societies, the individual is not able to maintain a valid identity either because in his acting out of the roles in which he is placed by others he experiences such punishment in terms of frustrations of his needs that he cannot accept as valid the identity proffered him, or because his efforts to achieve a valid identity in terms of the cultural models the society recommends do not meet with placement on the part of the larger society. In either case, in the anomic situation the individual finds that efforts to achieve a valid identity along lines supported by the larger society are in vain. His identity is called into question either by intrapsychic pressures or by society. But, since a tenable life requires a sense of valid identity, the individual has no other choice than to try again. His efforts outside the range of what is deemed culturally appropriate mark him as a deviant. Nonconformity with cultural norms can be seen, then, as an organized effort on the part of persons to achieve a sense of valid identity in a situation in which they have not been able to achieve it within the confines of those norms.

In most cultures there will be one institutional framework within which the major validation of identity of adults is accomplished. In many nonindustrial societies kinship and such other institutions as age grades have this function; the most important things about a man are bound up in his kinship or age-grade statuses and roles, just as is the larger part of his sense of who he is and why he has a right to exist. In our kind of society the major validation of self for men is expected to stem from performance within the occupational order, and for women from performance of a complex of roles organized around the household.[4]

Sociological and psychological literature is replete with discussions of the identity problems inherent in the efforts of men and women to accomplish suitably on the job or at home. Robert Merton's analysis of the dynamics of anomie in American society takes off from a consideration of the importance of success as the major "culturally-induced, deep motivation" inculcated by American society. The limitless quality of the success goal qualifies it as an anomie-producing agent in terms of Durkheim's analysis. Merton outlines several adaptations to the American situation in which there is a dissociation between the culturally prescribed aspirations for success and the socially structured avenues for realizing these aspirations.

I will suggest, however, that we get further in understanding the behavior of the middle class, the working class, and the lower class by substituting a two-value model for Merton's one-value model of the road to a valid, socially endorsed identity. The first complex of values I will call *career success*. This is essentially what Merton is talking about in his discussion of success, although he gives success an unnecessarily restricted connotation by his insistence on money as the central goal. This does not fit the facts of American occupational or consumer behavior at any class level. It is more reasonable to argue that money is a handy symbol mediating the evaluation process individuals go through in deciding whether or not a person has become a *big* man. The central goal in striving for career success has to do with eliciting those responses from others that validate an identity as important, powerful, prestigeful, rich, significant. While it is true, as Merton argues, that the instutions of communication in our society (mass media, education, etc.) tend to

[4] "A man's work is one of the more important parts of his social identity, of his self; indeed, of his fate in the one life he has to live, for there is something almost irrevocable about choice of occupations as there is about choice of a mate." Everett C. Hughes, *Men and Their Work* (New York: Free Press, 1958).

reinforce heavily the success goal, evidence also exists to suggest that matched against these pressures are other pressures within the same institutions which serve to legitimate "lesser" goals at each status level along the way from total failure to whatever the pinnacle of success might be.

The second complex of culturally defined goals might be called the goals of *the good American life*. Whereas the career success goals point in the direction of becoming a big man, the goals of the good American life point instead in the direction of becoming *a good and happy man*. It is reasonable to view the goals of the good American life as having a considerable history, evolving in a clear line from what we think of as the central goals of peasant life.

Whereas the careerist seeks to be a big man, the adherent to this opposed goal complex seeks rather to be a good provider. The orientation is to consumption rather than production; to the security of ascription rather than the open-ended, onward and upward quality of career success.[5]

These two goal systems are in contention both in the minds of given individuals and between groups of adherents. It is likely that prosperity in the country generally tends to reduce the number of persons who concentrate sharply on the one-value success model. A poor middle class finds it difficult to see any solution to its need for a valid identity other than that of striving to somehow get to the top of the heap. A prosperous middle class or working class is better able to envision a valid identity achieved in consumption and "living well with the Joneses" rather than keeping up with or surpassing them.

These two contending goal complexes represent regions

[5] For a discussion of this life style, see Lee Rainwater, Richard Coleman, and Gerald Handel, *Workingman's Wife*, New York: Oceana Publications, 1959; Gerald Handel and Lee Rainwater, "Persistence and Change in Working Class Life Style," in Arthur Shostak and William Gomberg, *Blue-Collar World* (Englewood, N.J.: Prentice-Hall, Inc., 1964); S. M. Miller and Frank Riessman, "The Working Class Subculture: A New View," in Shostak and Gomberg, *op. cit.;* Herbert Gans, *The Urban Villagers* (New York: Free Press, 1962); and Edward J. Ryan, "Personal Identity in an Urban Slum," in Leonard J. Duhl, *The Urban Condition* (New York: Basic Books, 1963).

within the over-all continuum of level aspiration, and there is no doubt that in the ranking hierarchy of the culture the careerist outranks the man who simply wants himself and his family to live well. But it is important to be aware that defenses against any claim of blanket superiority for careerist goals are strong in both the middle class and the working class. While to most Americans democracy and equalitarianism mean that everyone should have a chance to achieve as high a status as he is willing to work for, it is equally clear that for most Americans democracy means also the right not to play that game and still keep a sense of valid identity.

There is no doubt that lower-class people are amply exposed to both of the cultural ideals just outlined. That is, they know that some people make it big by the jobs they have and the money they accumulate, and lower-class people also know that some people do not make it so big but do manage to live comfortably in homes which they own in safe, nonslum neighborhoods, surrounded by an increasing measure of material comforts. At one time or another most lower-class boys and young men certainly entertain aspirations in one or both of these directions. At some point in their lives, however, a very great many lower-class boys and men come to the conclusion that these two ways toward a valid identity are simply not within the realm of possibility for them. The experiences that lie behind this conclusion are varied, and we will consider some of them as we go along.

In any case, the lower-class person is left with the central identity problem of, "What now?" That is, if a valid identity for him does not lie in the direction of an occupational role (either directly or in the purely instrumental terms of allowing him to be a good provider) then he must seek in other ways to construct a self which provides some measure of gratification of needs and earns some measure of recognition of oneself as a social being. It is my central contention that the behaviors of lower-class persons which are considered deviant, either by the members of their own groups or by the larger society, can be regarded as efforts to attain some sense of valid identity, as efforts to gratify the prompting of needs from inside and to elicit a response of recognition as valid persons from those around them.

The Expressive Life Style

A comparison of the various kinds of behavior in which lower-class men engage suggests one over-all conception that captures significant similarities among seemingly different behavior patterns. This is the concept of an expressive life style as characteristic of lower-class people, particularly of lower-class men. This style involves the preoccupations that Herbert Gans has dubbed the action-seeking way of life and Harold Feinstein discusses as the cats-and-kicks syndrome. The literature on juvenile delinquency, particularly that which derives from participant-observation techniques, contains varied and rich examples of this orientation to action, but literature dealing with different kinds of deviant behavior, community studies of lower-class life, and in my case, field data from one particular lower-class community (the Pruitt-Igoe housing project, St. Louis), suggest that the various deviances add up to variations on one theme more than they do to really different themes.[6]

Let me present some of the essential elements of the expressive life style from the point of view of the individual who acts it out. I will use the metaphor of the development of the self-as-gift or self-as-currency and speak of the cultivation of a particular kind of *dramatic self* as both a goal for individuals living in a lower-class social system, and as functional for them in putting together a valid identity. In the expressive life style, instrumental orientations to living are fairly consistently down-

[6] See, in addition to Gans, *op. cit.* and Ryan, *op. cit.* Harold Feinstein, "The Cats-and-Kicks Syndrome," in Howard S. Becker, *The Other Side* (New York: Free Press, 1964); Richard Cloward and Lloyd Ohlin, *Delinquency and Opportunity* (New York: Free Press, 1960); Albert Cohen, *Delinquent Boys* (New York: Free Press, 1955); Walter Miller, "Lower Class Culture as a Generating Milieu of Gang Delinquency," *Journal of Social Issues*, XIV (1958); James Short and Fred Strodbeck, *Group Process and Gang Delinquency* (Chicago: University of Chicago Press, 1965).

graded and recognized mainly in terms of the bare necessity of keeping body and soul together from day to day; factors involving self-expressive behavior are emphasized, elaborated, and held out as of intrinsic merit. Since I am most familiar with the particular version of the expressive life style developed by lower-class Negroes, I will draw my portrait from data on these groups.

The Gift of Self: A Lower-Class Negro Adaptation

Several characteristics of lower-class Negro culture help individuals to create certain styles of the public self. The more dramatic examples of this style are

1. Negroes develop a particular language that accents a colorful use of words in a particular rhythm of speech.
2. This speech is used most particularly in verbal contests, storytelling, entertainment through lively conversation, philosophizing, and the like.
3. Historically, Negroes have developed highly interrelated styles of sacred and profane music and dancing.
4. In Negro peer groups there is a great deal of emphasis placed on the development of "rep" (a reputation) as a person of importance.
5. Negroes have been fond of nicknames that in some way pick up the essence of the person.
6. Negro religion has historically emphasized individual religious experience and the communication of this experience to others.
7. Negro religion has been extreme in its Protestantism in that emphasis on individual reading and appreciation of the Bible and its philosophy has been highly developed.
8. Negro religious institutions have developed a cast of public roles for their participants. These roles emphasize the expressiveness and attractiveness of individuals as objects for enjoyment — the preacher, the singer, the deacon, the testifier, and the possessed.
9. Negroes seem, at least in the urban setting, to be particularly interested in the cultivation, through physiological methods, of heightened states of nonrational self-awareness (as in the use of alcohol and drugs of various kinds, perhaps also in the

involvement with fighting and sexual experience). It is important to note that these individual experiences are all turned into social currency, that they are not simply enjoyed by the individual for his own benefit and pleasure.

All of these activities seem to be, in the main, nonutilitarian. That is, their primary purpose does not seem that of furthering the acquisition of goods and services, nor the satisfaction of purely biological needs. Acquisition and satisfaction can come to be secondary functions because the expressive style can be used as a way of gaining income, goods, or services, but these possible gains do not represent the main goal of that life style. Rather, all of these behavior patterns represent different versions of *one* common adaptation in lower-class Negro society that has as its primary goal the maintenance of reciprocity between members of the society on the basis of a symbolic exchange of selves, an entertainment of each by the other. As Jules Henry has noted, persons living in a hopeless world, a world in which it is difficult to defend against the fear of death, may develop as a survival technique mechanisms that focus energy on modes of action which continually tell one that he is alive. I would see the expressive style as a way of accomplishing this reassurance, of building and maintaining connectedness with others in the context of an over-all structure of relationships which provides few traditional, solidly supported, axes of affiliation, or of complimentary duties and expectations.

The given community to which Negroes must adapt is one in which there is low expectation of reward on the basis of ascribed status (familial, sex, etc.) and low expectation of payoff for achieved status. Instead you learn that you have to "go for yourself" at the same time that the "go for" inevitably implies reliance on the responses of others. One way of eliciting that response is through making oneself an interesting object, through the cultivation of an aura for yourself that elicits rewarding responses from others. If one is successful in creating a dramatic self, one has gained a kind of security since that self can neither be taken away nor spent up (at least in the short run). By establishing relationships of symbolic transaction and reciprocity with others similarly seeking to maximize a dramatic self, the self is constantly replenished. It is important to note that in all of these activities, there are two things going on at the same time. The individual is experiencing a heightened cathexis of himself as a total being, and he is accumulating status characteristics which can be fashioned into an attractive public identity.

This particular kind of self is currently symbolized very well in some rhythm-and-blues songs in which a central concept is that of "soul." The admirable person is one who has much soul (in one song, soul is equivalent to body since the singer indicates he has 170 pounds of soul). Among gangs, the word is "heart" but the two would seem to be interchangeable. We are accustomed in social psychology to thinking of the individual as having many selves, "a simultaneous multiplicity of selves," and of these selves as becoming activated differentially in different role relationships. However, psychologists are never able to get away from the idea that behind the various selves lies an individual's sense of a psychic division of labor. I am suggesting that in the Negro lower class there has been relatively little to encourage adaptations which multiply the selves in role-specific activities and instead a heavy emphasis on the development of the self as an all-purpose object, with a consequent placing of all eggs in the one basket of soul or heart.

Sapir observed that "the endless rediscovery of the self in a series of petty truancies from the official socialized self becomes a mild obsession of the normal individual in any society in which the individual has ceased to be a measure of the society itself." We are suggesting here that in lower-class Negro society there are instead wholesale truancies from a conventional self that cannot come into being, although in some circumstances it is necessary for lower-class Negroes to maintain that they do indeed possess such a conventional self.

Given the cultural goal of developing one or another kind of dramatic identity, much of Negro lower-class life turns about the problem of approximating that ideal and the variations in group and individual behavior conditioned by these strivings. Clearly some individuals realize the ideal more effectively than others. Some individuals are better storytellers, some are better singers, some are better drinkers, or better fighters, or better preachers, or better at experiencing a trance than are others. We would expect that the individual who does well at these things receives more fully the rewards that his subculture has to give him than does the individual who performs less well. The guy with heart or soul truly becomes a leader, whether it be in the church or the tavern, the street, the laundry room or the bedroom. People offer him recognition and he in turn provides them with opportunity for vicarious experience, for learning, and for a reaffirmation of the particular world view that lies behind this cultural ideal.

I do not wish to present an overly romantic view of this particular cultural pattern; we have much evidence that it is one that can wear itself out rather quickly. To say that something is an adaptation to a particular situation is not to imply that it is a perfect or even long-lasting adaptation. On the other hand, it is quite possible that the combination of rewards which the leaders or performers give to the others in the group, plus the ever-present hope that one will be able to make the performer role pay off for himself, serve to sustain the pattern even though it in fact pays off very seldom in the way those who serve this ideal would want.

The dramatic self in one or another of its forms, then, can be regarded as the valid identity achieved within the expressive style of life. It is a self markedly at variance with the conventional self legitimated by the dominant sections of American society. Only when the dramatic self is turned into an occupational role, as among Negro musicians and athletes, does it earn credit in the middle class. Otherwise the behavior that comes to be highly valued by the lower-class person seems to the middle class simply a detailing of the "shiftlessness," "irresponsibility," "lack of ambition," and "untrustworthiness" of a class of people who are of no account, that is, who do not have valid identities.

This expressive style is rather neatly fixed in Talcott Parsons' categories. The particular Parsonian pattern variable configuration that seems to characterize best the expressive life style involves the following categories: ascriptive, particularistic, self-oriented, diffused, and affective.

The ascriptive versus achievement orientation is of particular relevance in connection with work. The whole emphasis in the development of the dramatic self is on *qualities*, that is, on what a person *is* by virtue of his actions rather than on what a person *does* in action. The Negro language of the dramatic self is replete with terms for these desirable qualities — "rep," "heart," "soul," "being saved," "being happy." The institutional settings are most appropriately those of the street, the church, the household. The activities central to the cultivation of dramatic selves are those of *membership*.

In contrast, the job represents a place in the instrumental system: a system which involves the learning structures of the school and the performance structures of the work place. The aura of these institutional settings is heavy with emphasis on instrumental behavior and allows little play for the expressive. The activity central to the instrumental system is not that of membership, but of *individual production*, not that of exchanging selves but of making and doing something.

In the schools, the orientations tend to be those of affective neutrality, a seeming universalism, heavy emphasis on collectivity orientation, on achievements, and on specificity. Here the lower-class individual finds himself generally out of step on the first day and falling farther and farther behind as time goes on. The lower-class child learns early that there is a very low probability of achieving a sense of valid identity along these lines and turns instead toward the expressive orientations that promise some gratification now. At adolescence and later, in a company of like-minded peers and within striking distance of like-minded girls the lower class boy or young man sets out to *be* someone through the technique of developing the dramatic self, and exposing himself to experts at that technique.

By the time lower-class men move into the labor market, they find themselves possessing few of the skills that market desires and feel dubious about the possibility of gaining self-validation through performance of an occupational role. They feel estranged from the role model of job holder. Their estrangement leads them sometimes to exaggerate the ease with which they could do a given kind of work if given a chance and at other times to have very little confidence that the instrumentally oriented occupational world (addicted as it is to performance credentials) will give them a chance to have and hold a job.

In response to this estrangement then, many lower-class men assign a low priority to work stability in the way they actually live their lives.[7] They engage in behaviors, as Allison Davis noted twenty years ago, that inevitably lead to their being dismissed, or they quit their jobs because "no one's gonna give me a hard time, who do they think I am?" Similarly, they tend to stretch out the time between jobs by not being energetic in looking for a new job and fill in for money by falling back on kin or girl friends. In the meantime they have something important to do because they strive to sustain valid identities before an audience of their peers.

Davis sought to show that "just as the members of the higher skilled working class and of management act in response to their culture, to their system of social and economic rewards, so do the underprivileged workers act in accord with their culture." Davis demonstrated that social, rather than biological, determinism accounted for

> the habits of shiftlessness, irresponsibility, lack of ambition, absenteeism, and of quitting the job, which management usually regards as a result of the "innate" perversity of underprivileged white and Negro workers . . . [These] are in fact *normal responses* that the worker has learned from his physical and social environment. These habits constitute a system of behavior and attitudes which are realistic and rational *in that environment* in

[7] See Michael Schwartz and George Henderson, "The Culture of Unemployment: Some Notes on Negro Children," in Shostak and Gomberg, *op. cit.* For a discussion of psychological characteristics that interfere with lower-class workers' ability to perform skilled work, see Orville R. Gursslin and Jack L. Roach, "Some Issues in Training the Unemployed," *Social Problems, XII* (Summer 1964).

which the individual of the slums has lived and in which he has been trained.

While terms like normal, realistic and rational were perhaps overly sanguine, Davis' analysis of lower-class job behavior and motivation is a classic one that still carries the ring of validity. Our main concern in this paper has been with the contending possibilities of expressive and instrumental role systems in the lower class in line with Davis' observation that "the most powerful of all the forces that keep (the underprivileged worker) in his present way of life and work are the pleasures that he actually can attain by following his underprivileged culture." [8]

The Stability of the Expressive Style

A static analysis of the situation of lower-class men with reference to the instrumental versus the expressive spheres of their lives yields, then, a picture of relative disinterest in the kind of work that is available and that one is prepared for, and a strong preference (instead) for getting along in ways that do not require that one be a steady worker and good provider. I do not believe that this point of view is one that lower-class men or even boys hold without ambivalence, and I certainly do not suggest that this situation is in any sense prescribed by an on-going lower-class subculture. Rather, from the point of view of the lower class, these are expected, understandable, and even gratifying alternatives that one may legitimately choose in a situation in which it is not possible to be someone by working toward a conventional self as good provider or career man.

Up to now we have considered those forces in the world of lower-class individuals which tend to encourage the search after a valid identity in the direction of an expressive style of life, to the detriment of performance of the instrumental tasks of learning and earning an income. But we know that the situation

[8] Allison Davis, "The Motivations of the Underprivileged Worker," in W. F. Whyte, *Industry and Society* (New York: McGraw-Hill, 1946).

is not as simple as this. Lower-class individuals do sometimes seek to accomplish in instrumental areas, and any given person may from time to time seek to establish a validated image of himself by pursuing goals related to work and job stability. Even the individual who seems to be very much enmeshed in an expressive way of life may surprise us by "suddenly" devoting himself assiduously to a job, limiting his involvement in expressive activities in the interest of keeping that job, and directing the money he earns toward stable life style goals. How can this come about?

Presumably if an individual begins to shift the focus of his energies away from those bound up in the cultivation of a dramatic self, it must be because this activity is not gratifying some of his needs. One constant source of frustration to most lower-class individuals is their awareness that, despite the surface validity of the self they put forward, their behavior is not in line with some of the standards of the larger society which they have internalized, often in spite of themselves. And they are made aware of their deviance in this regard not only by ubiquitous middle-class representatives but by others in their own world who, for selfish or moral reasons, call the validity of their identity in question by suggesting that it is not in line with broad normative standards. Thus, there is always the attraction of seeking to become a valid person in a more conventional way even though experience seems to have taught one that the probability of success at such an endeavor is very low.

In addition, even those needs that are directly expressive of the values of the dramatic self do not always achieve gratification in the pursuit of the expressive style of life. Both because of shortages of the goods of this system and because of the aggressive competition for peer groups status, the individual's status as a successful practitioner of the cult of the dramatic self is constantly called into question and he experiences considerable anxiety because of this. While the general effect of such heightened anxiety is normally to intensify efforts to compete successfully within the system, under certain circumstances the individual may instead say to himself, "What the hell am I doing anyway, why don't I try to get a job and settle down?" The punishment the individual often takes from participation in the system (in the form of physical violence and deprivation, or of anxiety over exactly where he stands and how he is doing, and of shame or guilt connected with his activities) also can serve as a stimulus in the direction of performance of more conventional roles.[9]

So, for a variety of reasons, lower-class individuals are tempted from time to time to seek valid identities in occupational role performance. The individual either seeks and gets a job or begins to pay more than minimum attention to one that he has. His primary motivation for doing so may still be very much involved with expressive goals — for example, the wish to have more money so that he can have a fancier set of friends, or go out in the evening to more expensive bars and nightclubs, or buy an impressive car.

However, continued success in holding a job, or, even more, in doing well enough to merit an increased wage has the effect of increasing the individual's subjective probability estimate of achieving a valid identity in terms of the possibilities inherent in the occupational role. Probably very few lower-class individuals direct their aspirations toward career success, but the goals involved in the concept of "the good American life" are ones which they have internalized long ago and which appear increasingly feasible as the job seems more stable or income increases.

If at the same time a man becomes involved with having a family (with the entailed task of being a good provider, husband, and father), he will feel an even greater constraint in the direction of abandoning the goals of the dramatic self. Lower-class women tend to be more verbal and more energetic in their affirmation of the values of the "good American life" than do their men. There seem to be far fewer gains for women in the expressive direction, and they tend to be more preoccupied with the desirability of a decent and stable material standard.

[9] Cf. the discussion by David Matza, *Delinquency and Drift* (New York: John Wiley & Sons, 1964), pp. 50–59.

They are ready both to reward and punish the men in their households depending on how well they do as providers. Thus, for example, we have seen dramatic changes within the short span of a day or two in the authority which the unemployed versus employed father can have in his own household. When the father finds a job, his wife and children are willing to listen to him and do what he says. When the father loses his job, his wife becomes much stricter in her evaluation of his demeanor within the household. In one case, the woman had her husband ejected from her apartment because he scratched her furniture, was unemployed, and could not pay for its repair. Growing older encourages a more stable adaptation, too, since the available rewards of the expressive life style are greatest for the young and seem to decrease rapidly with age, thereby making a more stable life style more attractive by comparison.

The most important external factor in shifts from the expressive life style to a more stable life style is probably the willingness of employers to put up with behavior that they feel interferes with job performance. It takes time for the individual to shift his estimate of what represents the best bet for establishing a valid identity for himself. The elements of this shift involve not only his success at the job, but also some of the typical experiences he is likely to have in the pursuit of expressive goals. He needs to accumulate frustration in that area as well as gratification in the area of occupational role performance if he is to choose the latter route to a valid identity. It is interesting that in Davis' example of this process, the wartime situation was one which made employers more tolerant than they were likely to be otherwise, but at the same time the shortage of certain consumer goods tended to work against the young worker's finding success in his effort to become a stable husband and provider. These days we have the reverse situation, employers are not at all tolerant because there is no shortage of labor at the lower skill levels, but consumer goods are readily available and anyone can set up a household if he has the money to do so.

All of this suggests that the one major social structural variable which will affect the extent to which lower-class persons can move in the direction of a stable life style has to do with how tight the labor market is or can be made to be. Managers, given a chance to exercise their standards, are very intolerant of failure to measure up to norms of predictability in job performance. In such a situation the lower-class man who is making the transition from an identity centered on expressive behavior to one centered on instrumental behavior has very little time to do so, since the consequences of his expressive behavior are likely to get him fired. It seems likely that any modification of the labor market situation which makes it more costly to the employer to fire employees at this level will have the effect over time of allowing more of them to shift in the direction of stability. (Of course, such a market change must be arranged so that machines are not brought in to substitute for beginning workers.) Similarly, any manipulation of the market structurally in such a way that the wages of individuals at the very bottom level allow them to put together some semblance of the going material standards of the good American life will encourage stability. Stability will be encouraged because the paychecks the lower-class workers bring home are more likely to elicit reward, respect, and adherence to their authority in the family.

CHAPTER SEVEN

TOMORROW'S WORKERS: THE PROSPECTS FOR THE URBAN LABOR FORCE

Stanley Lebergott

The range of freedoms offered by cities, particularly the vastly greater number of potential employers, has long attracted workers from the countryside to the city. In recent years expanding urban welfare programs, plus the widening gap between the level of urban and rural discrimination, has intensified that flow, particularly of unskilled workers. These workers, because of the recency of their experience in urban environ ments and their lack of urban skills, tend to create high urban unemployment. On the other hand, the cities specialize in government and in certain service and factory trades whose growth potential is above average. The combination suggests above-national growth rates in urban output and urban unemployment in the decades immediately ahead.

The quality of life which the city offers its workers will decide the kind of labor force available for its industry. For the range of advantage the city presents determines which of its native sons will remain over the years, and which men of talent and enterprise will be attracted to it from other regions. The compelling advantages that draw workers to the city have changed little over the centuries. "Behold this concourse of men, for

Stanley Lebergott is professor of economics at Wesleyan University, Connecticut, and the author of *Manpower in Economic Growth: The American Record since 1800* (1964), and *Men Without Work* (1965).

whom the houses of huge Rome scarcely suffice" wrote an ancient observer.[1] "From their towns and colonies . . . have they flocked. Some have been brought by ambition, some by the desire for the higher studies (or) by the public spectacles . . . some have presented their beauty for sale, some their eloquence . . . every class has swarmed into the city that offers high prizes for both virtues and vices."

The freedom for worship offered by the city has long been well known. To be a Muggletonian, in the seventeenth century, or a Jehovah's Witness today, is easier under urban than rural conditions. The city proffers the unmarried a wide choice of mates; and, to the married, a wide range of schooling for their children. The reach of opportunity presented to the consumer is even more noteworthy. Instead of being bound to a rural monopolist — whether doctor, grocer or carpenter — he finds a host of services and tradesmen available.

Such advantages are compelling attractions to the worker — for he is believer, parent, and consumer as well as worker. But these attractions are extended many times over in the labor markets. Corporation president or janitor, the city worker benefits largely from his choice among potential employers. The Arabian slave in our day (as the Scots slave in Boswell's) must serve a single employer. And the mutinous, bloody history of labor in mining towns and on shipboard reflects how workers react when — though free — their margin of choice for quitting one job and taking another is restricted.

By contrast the city offers freedom after feudalism — chiefly because it offers so great a host of employers. By spending a quarter on gasoline or bus fare, the average Chicago worker, for example, can reach any of 100,000 employers.[2] Other Illinois

[1] Seneca, *Ad Helviam de Consolatione*.

[2] The number of employers covered by OASI is reported in *U.S. Bureau of Census, U.S. Bureau of Old Age and Survivors Insurance, County Business Patterns*, Part 1 ,U.S. Summary, First Quarter, 1959, pp. 22–23.

To this number we add the number of farms reporting regular hired workers, from *U.S. Census of Agriculture*, 1959, Part II, p. 249. (The number of opportunities for part-time work are undoubtedly greater in cities than on farms. Hence we understate the urban–rural contrast.)

We assume that the relevant area of Chicago is about 950 squares miles; that outside the city, 56,000 square miles.

workers, with the same quarter, may choose among only one fiftieth of that number.

For most occupations, of course, the worker finds no employer outside the urban centers. Hence, while the Chicago worker may have fifty times the choice of the "average" rural resident, workers in a multitude of occupations actually have a far greater choice. Such enticements have long brought migrants to the cities. "We are for the most part a congregation of strangers," said the mayor of St. Louis in 1823.[3] A century later the same bemused observation might have been made: half of St. Louis' population had moved to the area within the five previous years.[4] The rate of inflow was nearly eighty times the concurrent rate of immigration to the United States as a whole.[5] The nation has virtually banned immigration. But little has been done to limit the volume or character of migration to our states and cities. (It was surely a casual curiosity when in 1936 Colorado proclaimed martial law "to prevent and repel the further invasion" of migrants from sister states.[6])

One result of open migration can be briefly put. At a rough estimate, half the families living in American cities today have moved there since the end of World War II.[7] The qualitative

[3] Quoted in Richard C. Wade, *The Urban Frontier* (Cambridge, Mass.: Harvard University Press, 1959), p. 218.

[4] *U.S. Census:* 1960, *Mobility for Metropolitan Areas,* p. 200. To be exact, 55 percent.

[5] Immigration to the United States averaged about 250,000 a year; our 1960 population, 170 millions. Allowing for deaths among the immigrants would lead to a rate of about .06 percent.

[6] The quotation, from Governor Johnson of Colorado, appears in Carter Goodrich, et al., *Migration and Economic Opportunity* (Philadelphia: University of Pennsylvania Press, 1936), p. 670. The major limitations have been in the form of residence requirements for the receipt of relief.

[7] Annual surveys since 1949 by the Census Bureau report that an average of 6 percent of the residents in urban areas have moved in since a year previous. (*Current Population Reports,* Series P-20, No. 36, 39, and ff.) Had these moves been independent, then over the span 1955–1960 we should expect a 30 percent migration rate (5 years × 6 percent). However, the 1960 Census-PC (2) 2B *Mobility for States and State Economic Area,* p. 1, reports that only 17.5 percent of the urban population had lived in a different county in 1955.

We assume that this 40 percent reduction factor (30 to 17.5 percent) would, over the longer span from 1945, be 60 percent. (If we reckon in

impact of this migration is probably even more significant than the quantitative. Year by year, this migration increased the city's competence for unskilled work — and just as steadily diminished its attractions for skilled and professional workers. How has this come about?

1. The flowering of federal relief programs since 1933 (public and old-age assistance, aid to dependent children) enhanced the city's attractiveness to those who are weak and heavy laden — typically the unskilled.

2. The farm parity program zealously (if unintentionally) undermined the marginal farmer. The result? The least skilled farmers and farm laborers were pressed to seek their fortunes in the cities.

3. The Second World War began a massive overturn of that status in which American Negroes had lived for more than three centuries. This significant postwar reduction of discrimination in U.S. cities, plus rising aspirations among rural Negroes, created further forceful incentives for the unskilled to migrate to the city.

4. Concurrently, the cities were offering landlords increasingly urgent inducements to create slums — first, by the pattern of rent controls, and second, by the feeble enforcement of housing and zoning codes. These powerful incentives toward under-maintenance helped keep rents down below the level to which rising land and construction costs would otherwise have pushed them. The result was to expand the supply of slum accommodations — quarters that would otherwise have been unavailable to potential migrants.[8] All of these occasions conspired to make cities bigger bargains for unskilled workers — who flocked to them.

---

the heavy immediate postwar movement, the higher rates for the armed forces — not included — and assume some memory bias in the decennial report, the reduction ratio could hardly be greater than 60 percent.) There fore we reduce the 6 percent rate of 2.4 percent for each year October 1945–1964.

[8] No comment is intended here on the advisability of either policy — nor are we referring to the price trend for housing of a given quality. The low-income migrant is often in search of housing at the lowest possible money cost.

5. Meanwhile, federal aid to the depressed auto driver made it possible for skilled workers and business men to abandon the city as a residence, yet continue to make their skills available there. A great national building program smoothed the way out. Where building costs might have risen to impede the move, federal loan guarantees (FHA and VA) gave the new suburban housing a margin of advantage over existing urban structures that it would otherwise have lacked. The happy beneficiaries of these programs moved out of the city in droves. By 1960 a third of all the managerial and professional workers employed in our central cities lived outside them — or nearly twice the proportion for laborers and triple that for service workers.[9]

In sum, a set of federal programs helped tilt the urban world — spilling out the skilled and upper income workers, tipping in the less skilled.

From this complex of change, a new set of options for the future has appeared. To fix the future for the urban labor force in 1984, we must first decide what economic functions the city will then serve.[10] How can we do so? Merely to peer at the present will not be particularly useful. Nor will inspecting the past be much more rewarding. A look down the winding path from past to present may, however, afford us a tolerably realistic guide to the future.

Which economic functions has the city served? And which does it now have? We ask these questions since these functions help determine the nature of the city's labor force — just as the nature of that labor force (fixed in part by the incentives we have noted above) will help determine the functions of the city.[11]

[9] *U.S. Census:* 1960, Vol. 1, Part 1, *U.S. Summary*, p. 1–576.

[10] The year is chosen in part because prevision for more than twenty years is dubious, in part because it is a climactic Orwellian date.

[11] If this proposition is largely circular, it is meant to be so. For the relation is joint, simultaneous and powerful. Each causes the other, and to pretend that the determination goes only one way is to make the problem so readily soluble as to be uninteresting.

Urban Employment Specialization

To decide for what work the city possesses particular competence, we start from the census distribution of the labor force. That record reports the American city now employs well above average proportions of workers in finance, wholesale trade, transportation, public administration, and the services — but only the average for manufacturing, and below average for construction.[12]

To project the future from this present pattern would require extended analysis of the structure of the American economy, plus a set of guesses concerning the composition of future demand. Let us evade that enormous enterprise. Suppose that instead we review the 1900–1960 trends in U.S. employment (Table 1) to see how this mix came to be, and to get a first indication of how the 1960 urban pattern may shift in the future. We can then note some corroborative factors.

1. A look at the historic trend reveals that employment rose least in farming, factories, and construction. Trade and services more than tripled. Government rose fivefold; finance nearly sevenfold. The greatest increases, therefore, prove to be in just those industries in which the city now specializes. Suppose we refer only to the change since that 1953–1955 business cycle peak which preceded the recent decade of slow growth. Again the same ordering appears. Most segments of the economy decline, or increase feebly; but trade rises, service and finance rise still more, and government employment gains most of all. The sixty-year trend is not likely to come to an abrupt end.

[12] Of the total U.S. labor force in 1960, 58 percent was working in cities. By industry groupings, cities were the place of work for 76 percent of the nation's finance workers, 72 percent wholesale trade, 70 percent transportation, 68 percent business service, 65 percent personal service, 65 percent public administration, 63 percent retail trade, 62 percent professional service, 58 percent manufacturing, 58 percent entertainment, 54 percent construction. All data from the U.S. Census of Population: 1960, Vol. 1, Part 1, *U.S. Summary*, p. 1–576, except wholesale and retail trade percentages, which were estimated. These data report on place of work — hence differ from the usual figures, which refer to place of residence.

TABLE 1. *Employment Trends:* 1900–1960 (in thousands)

	1900	1960	Percentage gain
Manufacturing	5,468	16,796	207
Apparel	364	1,170	221
Printing	244	860	252
Toilet prep.	2.6	29	1,015
Drugs	9.4	96	1,021
Construction	1,147	2,885	152
Trade	2,502	11,391	355
Service	1,740	7,392	325
Government (civilian)	1,094	8,353	664
Federal	239	2,270	675
State and local	885	6,083	612
Finance	308	2,669	766

SOURCES:

Major Groups: Lebergott, S., *Manpower in Economic Growth*, Tables A-5, A-8 and *Economic Report of the President*, 1965, p. 220.

Manufacturing Detail: U.S. Census of Manufacturers, 1958, Vol. 2, Part 1, pp. 23-2, 27-2, 28C-4, 28D-5. For drugs the value of fine chemicals in 1900 was 5 percent of the value of all chemical products and that ratio was applied to chemical employment (wage earners plus salaried) to give 1,050 employees (*U.S. Census*, 1900, Vol. X, Part IV, pp. 612, 646, 648). To this total the number of employees in drug grinding and drug preparations in 1905 was added, a group not shown separately in 1900 (*U.S. Census of Manufactures*, 1905, p. 46).

Hence we may project continuing strength for precisely those industries in which the cities have come to specialize.

2. A second cheering consideration may be inferred from studies of consumer spending patterns. Uniformly these budget surveys tell us that increases in incomes bring about more than proportionate increases in expenditures for barratry, ballet, and bedpans. Hence the prospect is for rising urban service industry employment if U.S. income levels continue to advance.

3. Specialists have projected the trend in government employment differently with each change in foreign policy. For our purposes it may be sufficient to note that a rising level of employment financed by the government is most likely. Direct increases in government employment will occur if war prepara-

tions extend. But indirect increases will occur even if peace threatens man's accustomed way of life: the ingenuity with which Defense Department programs have been transformed from ones designed to shoot men into ones to shoot space capsules surely forecasts rising government employment. Moreover, state and local governments have been steadily adding to their massive payrolls.

4. The forceful past rate of growth in financial employment will presumably falter in the future. Computing equipment will be substituted for a wide range of financial record keeping and even for portfolio management. The slackening of employment would, however, only attenuate the rate of gain to a pace which would continue far above average.

Urban Manufacturing Employment

We must, however, look not merely at these major groups but within the massive total for manufacturing. Manufacturing is still our greatest single industry grouping. And it contrives so wide a range of products that aggregate figures yield only a pale reflection of reality.

Almost every factory product that we can imagine has been turned out in the city: the Gutenberg Bible, the hula hoop, the Rospigliosi cup, and the first steamship. Yet the city does not possess an equal and universal set of aptitudes. It enjoys a comparative advantage only for some products. In which ones have our cities specialized over the past fifty years or so?

The United States ushered the twentieth century in by electing William McKinley President — for the second time. In that year our major cities specialized, overwhelmingly, in producing articles for raiment and riot.[13] Fifty-five percent of the nation's factory workers were employed in these cities; and these cities claimed the higher proportions of workers in

[13] Data for 1900 from the *U.S. Census of Manufactures:* 1905, Part 1, pp. cclxx–cclxxii. These data relate to the 162 principal cities in 1900, and hence are not directly comparable with the all-urban total in Note 16.

Apparel	91%
Jewelry	75%
Tobacco	65%
Malt liquor	81%

They also employed slightly above their all-factory percentage in printing (60 percent) and foundry and machine shops (66 percent).

What changes had taken place in half a century, and what do these changes suggest for the future? (See Table 2).

TABLE 2 Factory Employment in 1958

	Total in Industry	Percent working in Standard Metropolitan Areas
All Factory Employees	100%	72%
Instruments	100	97
Miscellaneous	100	96
Apparel	100	93
Printing	100	92
Fabricated Metals	100	79
Rubber	100	78
Transportation Equipment	100	75
Electrical Machinery	100	75
Primary Metal	100	74
Furniture	100	64
Chemicals	100	64
Machinery	100	63
Food	100	58
Paper	100	57
Leather	100	54
Petroleum	100	54
Tobacco	100	50
Stone Clay and Glass	100	49
Textiles	100	34
Lumber	100	20

SOURCE:

Data for Table 2 are taken from the *U.S. Census of Manufactures*: 1958, Vol. III, *Area Statistics*, Table 5, for each individual state. They relate to standard metropolitan statistical areas with 40,000 or more manufacturing employees. Sixty-nine such reports are available. The totals summed from these reports were computed, by industry, as a proportion of total manufacturing, as reported in the same U.S. Census, Vol. I, pp. 1–4, 1–5.

A. Cities retained their special advantage in only two industries — apparel and jewelry.
B. They advanced markedly in printing[14] (today almost completely an urban industry), chemicals and instruments.[15]
C. For most industries they either lost ground (e.g., tobacco and malt liquors), or, having been about at the national average in 1900, continued there (e.g., leather, furniture, machinery). For manufacturing as a whole their share had declined slightly.[16] Persistent reallocation of resources has plucked away — with magnificent impartiality — most of the special advantages and and disadvantages which the city once offered American industry.

Future Trends

Can we predict the future any more closely? In the prior sections we have noted the strong national growth from 1900 to 1960, and from 1953–1955 onward, in precisely those major industry categories in which the cities have come to specialize — services, finance and government.[17] And we have seen that within manufacturing the cities retained or gained strength in

[14] For printing we use data from the *U.S. Census 1900: Occupations*, Table 42, summarizing data given for 161 individual cities for the number of printers, lithographers, and pressmen. These come to 60.2 percent of the U.S. total given in Table 2 of this reference.

[15] The evidence for instruments is speculative since no direct data are available. The bulk of the present-day instrument category includes instruments, clocks and watches and photographic apparatus. The 1905 data for these industries give no urban data, but do indicate that perhaps 40 percent of employment in these industries, taken together, was in the three states of Illinois, New York and Connecticut.

[16] Problems of comparability make it doubtful that the decline — from 50 percent for urban areas in 1899 to about 42 percent in 1954 — is significant. Estimates are those of Creamer and Woodbury, from Coleman Woodbury (ed.), *The Future of Cities and Urban Redevelopment* (Chicago: University of Chicago Press, 1958), pp. 253–255.

[17] Note 12 reminds us that the "tertiary industries" per se are not the magic key — for retail trade is not significantly more concentrated in cities than the nation. And while wholesale trade is so concentrated, that activity has been declining sharply in recent decades.

apparel, jewelry, printing, chemicals, and instruments. Now, in the nation, employment in apparel, and printing has not increased strongly over the past half century. Nor has chemical employment: only the (city-based) drug and toilet preparations component has boomed (Table 1). It is clear, therefore, that these mixed patterns of employment reflect more than merely fair shares in national growth. The city must have some special advantages to explain such particularly lively employment growth.[18] To predict the future we must pick out what forces lie behind this differential growth.

1. The first element of urban advantage relates to style, to variety, and seasonality. The city dominates U.S. apparel and jewelry production. But it does not do so because there is some elective affinity between them. New York City does account for half of U.S. employment in the manufacture of one major apparel line — women's suits and coats. Yet it accounts for only 2 percent of employment in another apparel line — work clothing.[19] A difference in markets or transport costs is hardly the key. For Detroit, Gary, and St. Louis together surely buy as great a share of U.S. work clothing (in which they do not specialize) as women's suits (in which they do). Nor is the dexterity and ingenuity of city workers an explanation. Surely, far more of each is needed to make missiles than matron's frocks. The special competence of the city is much more likely tied to the seasonality that characterizes the production of highly styled apparel, stickpins, etc. Short production runs for the couturier items, the improbable hem lines, afflict the apparel industry with an alteration between overtime employment and seasonal slack. Such other ventures characteristic of the city as ballet, the theatre, and jewelry production evidence similar seasonal variation.

[18] An adequate model of urban employment growth would, of course, have to explain the basis for expecting cities to share equally in national employment growth by industry — and not merely take it as par for the course. Here we concentrate on industries with above-national employment growth rates.

[19] *U.S. Census of Manufactures:* 1958, Vol. II, Part I, pp. 23A-8, 23A-13, 23B-7. The precise ratio for coats and suits is 46 percent.

Now the city dangles two special advantages before such seasonal firms. First is its network of private charities, social insurance, and public assistance. For without such subsidy the costs of carrying workers over the slack periods would bear directly on the city's apparel firms, ballet companies, etc. If passed on to the consumer in higher prices, such costs would reduce the sizable share of the U.S. market which these urban firms now possess. Secondly, the width of the job market in cities helps as well, making it possible for workers to find complementary seasonal work more readily than in rural areas. So long as cities continue to subsidize such industries through unemployment compensation, and so long as they offer complementary employment opportunities for seasonal workers, their special advantage for such seasonal industries is likely to persist.[20]

2. A common denominator links a second group of urban industries — finance and domestic service — namely a high proportion of women workers. We may also add chemical factories (not because the industry as a whole is of urban importance but because of its sectors that are disproportionately large in cities — drugs, cleaning materials, and toiletries). Nearly 85 percent of employees in urban drug manufacturing — and almost 100 percent for these other sectors — are women. We can make a similar statement for a second factory industry with a high urban proportion: instruments. Although women constituted only 18 percent of those employed by durable manufacturing in cities, they constituted almost twice as much — 33 percent — for the professional equipment and watch component of the instrument industry.[21]

Now it is well known that the money rates of wages for women tend to be below those for men. This differential may reflect some insufficiency as judged by employers. But it is more

[20] The bulk of subsidy is provided by consumers of goods and services produced in the state's less seasonal industries, since it is these who contribute disproportionately to the typical experience-rated Unemployment Insurance Fund.

[21] Data on the distribution of employees by sex and industry are from the *U.S. Census of Population: 1960, Industrial Characteristics,* Table 1, and Vol. I, Part I, p. 1–221.

likely testimony to the fact that many women workers seek only pin money — or should one say TV and new car money? Hence, they set lower reservation prices, provide "cheap labor" — i.e., cheaper than male labor of equal quality. The lively increase in the ratio of working women to men suggests that this latter factor is forcefully effective.

3. The city specializes in goods and services whose value the market is least competent to judge. How does the consumer assess the professional abilities of a teacher, a lawyer, a physician? Typically, he must adopt the opinion of others in the guild — other teachers, lawyers, physicians. Common criteria of the market, such as the consumer's own experience, or his neighbor's reactions, may be peculiarly irrelevant: the competence of the defendant to judge the capacity of his lawyer or the student's parent, his teacher, is in most instances low. Even quasi-objective measures may be delusive: the surgeon with the highest patient death rate may nevertheless be the best in town if all practitioners agree in sending him their toughest, most hopeless cases. A properly laid brick wall will show no faults for years. But what performance criterion can we have for a case of horizontal lines in a TV set, or of pneumonia in a human? Such a case may shortly be followed by another breakdown. Yet how competently can the consumer decide whether a relapse or professional incompetence was involved? Consumer market judgments are not restricted, but almost nonexistent, for a mass of other activities in which the city specializes: insurance, and government, including schools, hospitals, and other typically nonprofit enterprises.

Now automation typically represents employer response to increasing cost pressures. Its machines provide skills and services whose quality equals — sometimes exceeds — those supplied by humans and it does so at lower cost. But where the quality of service cannot competently be judged by the consumer, the producer can consider lowering the quality of service as a way to meet cost pressures. It is surely possible that the quality of services offered in schools, barber shops, and professional services has been lowered in recent years. To the extent that cities do specialize in such industries, then the trend of technological advance will have a lesser impact on their employment levels than otherwise: the deterioration in quality of service will protect against disemployment.

4. Urban industries may have had a relatively sluggish rate of productivity advance. If so, cities have been less likely to generate unemployment by technological displacement. Nationally, output per manufacturing employee rose by 66 percent from 1929 to 1957. But gains for industries in which cities specialize were far weaker: 33 percent for apparel, a mere 25 percent for printing and publishing.[22] The concentration of urban employment in such industries suggests that urban productivity advance may have lagged behind that for the nation as a whole. The heavy flow of unskilled labor into cities would be consistent with such a tendency. Any such future differential in automation, in particular, and productivity advance, in general, would mean relatively fewer men thrown out of work in cities than in the nation generally.

Thus, the trend of urban specialization would seem to forecast low unemployment rates, if not necessarily high wages, for the urban labor force. The city's concentration on seasonal industries, businesses that use a high proportion of female employees, on professions and services whose quality is difficult to evaluate, and on manufacturing processes least subject to technological substitution, all point to employment growth better than the national rate.

Rural Migration and Urban Employment

If our cities had walls and moats around them, this might be the end of the story. But they do not. All cities import both delight and disease from the ends of the earth. American cities import distress as well. Offering better work opportunities, better charitable assistance, fatter relief checks, they regularly

[22] Data from Table D-IV, John Kendrick, *Productivity Trends in the United States* (New York: National Bureau of Economic Research, 1956).

attract the unemployed from the countryside. They become so many Ellis Islands, practicing Emma Lazarus' exhortation, "Give me your tired, your poor, your huddled masses." So long as the city serves this function, it matters less how much unemployment of its own it generates than how great is the gap between city and rural advantage. Two factors are at work that will continue to keep that gap significant.

1. The differential birth rate. When immigration to the United States was a major factor, foreign nations supplied our cities with inhabitants—in 1880, a third of them. By 1960 that share had dwindled to less than 10 percent. But meanwhile the proportion of city dwellers born on farms had doubled, from about 14 to 27 percent.[23] From 1900 to 1950, the South provided close to 10 million migrants to the rest of the nation.[24] Assuming only limited change in attitudes toward birth control we can expect that for some decades millions of Americans will grow up in rural territory, then decide that life in the city is preferable to a marginal existence, even with birds and trees and running brooks.

2. A second massive force that is going to increase unemployment in our cities is the reduction in discrimination against Negroes. Recent discussions of discrimination have usually emphasized by how much unemployment rates for Negroes exceed those for whites. Yet the simple assumption that this difference testifies to discrimination in the hiring and firing of Negroes is not one to be accepted out of hand. Sure enough we find that nonwhite unemployment rates in Southern cities are almost precisely twice those for whites. But virtually the same ratio appears for the Northeast and West, where we do not expect

[23] Data for the fifty major cities in 1880 from 1880 U.S. Census of Population, *Population*, pp. 460, 472; data for 1960 relate to all central cities, and are from *U.S. Census of Population: 1960*, Vol. I, Part I, *Characteristics of the Population*, p. 1–316.

[24] Estimates of net migration by state appear in *Population Redistribution and Economic Growth, United States, 1870–1950*, Vol. III, *Demographic Analyses and Interrelations*, by Hope Eldridge and Dorothy Thomas (Philadelphia: American Philosophical Society, 1964) p. 243. We increase the data reported there to allow for migrants who died in the intracensal periods, the former relating only to survivors.

discrimination to be quite as intense. And for the North Central region, strikingly enough, the ratio is 2.44, or very significantly greater. Upon investigation, we find the same regional pattern in 1940, and in 1937 as well.[25] Is discrimination really greater in the North Central states? Or is another factor at work?

Simply put, these differentials seem to indicate that in their view Negroes are buying freedom. Higher unemployment rates represent one part of the purchase price. The 4 million Negroes who moved out of the South from 1900 to 1950 went, in disproportionately great numbers, to St. Louis, Chicago, Detroit, and to the North Central states. Lacking skill, experience, and education equal to that of the typical resident of these areas, they were in fact choosing more unemployment in the North, in preference to full employment as sharecroppers and laborers in the South. The move would not have been rational if only their short-term prospects in the labor market were involved. The makeweight in this equation was presumably the choice for a more open way of life.

Since economics follows morality in emphasizing the fundamental role of choice among alternatives, we may go one step further. If a relative freedom is in fact the guiding star for migrating Negroes, then every attempt to make our cities more habitable, to clean up the slums, to improve the training for the unemployed in the cities, to deal justice out with a more even hand — every such attempt will tend to increase urban unemployment, by attracting still more migrants from the rural regions.

Suppose our assumption is correct that the pattern of births and deaths in rural Southern areas will continue to provide a sizable pool of eligible migrants. Then it follows that every increase in the attractions of our cities will find sufficient responsiveness in these rural areas to repeat the experience of the 1940's and 1950's — and bring ever more rural residents to be unemployed in the North.

[25] These data are presented, and their derivation given, in my introduction to *Men Without Work* (Englewood Cliffs, N.J.: Prentice-Hall, Inc., 1965), pp. 13–14.

In sum, the prospects for the urban worker in the decades ahead will be to work in industries now fairly typical of the entire nation — but disproportionately in those industries in which cities have come to specialize in recent decades — government, finance, service, and certain factory industries. The trends toward convergence and identity are so great, however, that the urban worker's occupation will differ less and less from the national average. If cities were not open ports of entry to immigration, the urban workers' prospect would be for unemployment rates below the national average. But given the likely flow of rural residents, his prospect is for above-average unemployment rates in the decades ahead.

RESPONSIVE PHYSICAL PLANNING

CHAPTER EIGHT

SUBURBS, SUBCULTURES, AND THE URBAN FUTURE

Bennett M. Berger

The current myth of American suburban culture obscures a popular ambivalence toward cultural variety. As the range of urban planning expands, it will gain ever more power to encourage or harass the diverse modes of American life. If metropolitan planning and architectural programs are to be responsive to the qualities of urban life as it is lived in our cities, then planners and architects must learn to read this cultural variety and to design for it.

The Persistence of the Myth of Suburbia

I originally undertook the study reported in *Working-Class Suburb*[1] in order to observe the transformation of a group of automobile assembly line workers into the "suburbanites" who had become stock figures in American popular culture in the 1950's. It seemed to me that, having found a working-class population more than two years settled in a new suburb, I was provided with an almost natural experimental setting in which to document the processes through which "suburbia" exercised its profound and diffuse influence in transforming a group of

Bennett M. Berger is Chairman of the Department of Sociology at the University of California, Davis, and is the author of *Working-Class Suburb: A Study of Auto Workers in Suburbia* (1960).

[1] Bennett M. Berger, *Working-Class Suburb* (Berkeley and Los Angeles: University of California Press, 1960).

poorly educated factory workers into those model middle-class Americans obsessed with the problems of crabgrass and "conformity."

Well, it is now a matter of public record that my basic assumption was wrong. As the interview evidence piled up, it became clearer and clearer that the lives of the suburbanites I was studying had not been profoundly affected in any statistically identifiable or sociologically interesting way. They were still overwhelmingly Democrats; they attended church as infrequently as they ever did; like most working-class people, their informal contacts were limited largely to kin; they neither gave nor went to parties. On the whole they had no great hopes of getting ahead in their jobs, and instead of a transient psychology, most of them harbored a view of their new suburban homes as paradise permanently gained.

But I was cautious in the general inferences I drew from that study. It was, after all, based only on a small sample, of one suburb, of one metropolitan area, in one region, and it suffered from all of the methodological limitation inherent in small case studies. None of my findings gave me any reason to doubt the truth of what William H. Whyte, for example, had said of his organization men, but it also seemed to me that there was little reason *not* to believe that my findings in San Jose would be repeatedly confirmed in many of the less expensive suburbs around the country whose houses were priced well within the means of unionized workers in heavy industry, and lower-white-collar employees as well. I did, in short, question the right of others to generalize freely about suburbia on the basis of very few studies of selected suburbs which happened to be homogeneously middle- or upper-middle-class in character — especially when it seemed apparent that suburban housing was increasingly available to all but the lowest income levels and status groups.

The considerable bulk of research that has been done on suburbs in the years since I did my own work has given me no reason to alter the conclusions I drew then; quite the contrary, it has strengthened those conclusions. Today, in addition to my own study of a working-class suburb, and William F. Whyte's study of transient middle-class suburbs, and the study by Seeley et al. of *Crestwood Heights*, a stable, older, upper-middle-class suburb, we have Herbert Gans's study of predominantly lower-middle-class Levittown, New Jersey, S. D. Clark's survey of a variety of suburbs around Toronto, Scott Greer's study of a Negro suburb of St. Louis, Charles Tilly's suburban work around Wilmington, Delaware, and the studies of William Dobriner and John Liell of Levittown, New York — Liell's work being the first I know of to study a suburb over time, since he studied it in 1951, shortly after its founding, and again in 1960.[2] Now, with the cooperation of the National Opinion Research Center at the University of Chicago and the Survey Research Center at the University of Michigan, research is going beyond case studies to generalizations about suburbia based upon the study of national samples of population broken down in terms of place of residence.

None of this research can be expected to give much comfort to those who find it convenient to believe that living in suburbs exercises some mysterious power over its residents to transform them into replicas of Whyte's practitioners of "The Outgoing Life." There seems to be increasing consensus among students of suburbia that suburban development is simply the latest phase of a process of urban growth that has been going on for a long time; that the cultural character of suburbs varies widely in terms of the social makeup of their residents, and the personal and group dispositions that led them to move to suburbs in the first place; that the variety of physical and demographic differences between cities and suburbs (and there *are* some) bears little significance for the way of life of their inhabitants; and that some of these differences, although statistically accurate, are sociologically spurious, since the appropriate comparisons are not between residential suburbs and cities as wholes but between suburbs and urban residential neighborhoods. The

[2] The work of William H. Whyte, William M. Dobriner, and John R. Seeley and his colleagues is well known to students of suburbs. John T. Liell, Scott A. Greer, and Samuel D. Clark presented the results of some of their research at the meetings of the American Sociological Association in Los Angeles in 1963.

high degree of order that was asserted as characteristic of suburbia was a result of highly ordered suburbs having been selected for study, and in general the reported changes in the lives of suburbanites were not *caused* by the move to suburbia, but were reasons for moving there in the first place. In suburbs, as in city apartments, the degree of sociability is determined not primarily by ecological location but by the homogeneity of the population (although, as Whyte indicated, the particular flow patterns of sociability may be affected by the specific locations of domiciles). Social class, the age composition of residents, the age of the neighborhood are much more profound predictors of style of life than is residential location with respect to city limits. Transient attitudes (if they were there to begin with) apparently decline with the increasing age of the suburb, as the neighborhood settles into the style of life determined largely by its dominant social and demographic characteristics, a settling simplified by the economic homogeneity of specific suburban housing tracts. Analysis of national samples has provided confirmation neither of a trend to Republicanism in politics nor of a return to religion. Suburbs, in short, seem, as Reissman and Ktsanes characterized them, "new homes for old values." [3]

It seems, then, that there are no grounds for believing that suburbia has created a distinctive style of life or a new social character for Americans. Yet the myth of suburbia persists, as is evident from the fact that it is still eminently discussable over the whole range of our cultural media, from comic books to learned journals. One should not be surprised at this, for myths are seldom dispelled by research; they have going for them something considerably more powerful than mere evidence. And though nothing I say here can change this fact, it may give us some comfort to understand the sources of the myth, the function it performs for the groups by whom it is sustained, and the nature of its appeal to America's image of itself.

In my book, and then, again, later in an article, I undertook

[3] Leonard Reissman and Thomas Ktsanes, "New Homes for Old Values," *Social Problems*, 7 (Winter, 1959–1960), 187–195.

a functional explanation of the myth of suburbia. I pointed first to the fact that suburbs were rich with ready-made visible symbols: patios and barbecues, lawnmowers and tricycles, shopping centers, station wagons, and so on, and that such symbols were readily organizable into an image of a way of life that could be marketed to the nonsuburban public. I also pointed out that this marketing was facilitated by the odd fact that the myth of suburbia conveniently suited the ideological purposes of several influential groups who market social and political opinion, odd because these groups could usually be found disagreeing with each other not only about matters of opinion, but about matters of fact as well. Realtor–chamber of commerce interests and the range of opinion represented by the Luce magazines could use the myth of suburbia to affirm the American Way of Life; city planners, architects, urban design people, and so on could use the myth of suburbia to warn that those agglomerations of standardized, vulgarized, mass-produced cheerfulness which masqueraded as homes would be the urban slums of tomorrow. Liberal and left-wing culture critics could — and did — use the myth of suburbia to launch an attack on complacency, conformity, and mass culture, and found in the myth of suburbia an up-to-date polemical vocabulary with which to rebuke the whole slick tenor of American life: what used to be disdained as "bourgeois" was now simply designated as "suburban." In short, the *descriptive* accuracy of the myth of suburbia went largely unchallenged because it suited the *prescriptive* desires of such a wide variety of opinion, from the yea sayers of the right to the agonizers of the center to the nay sayers of the left.

But though I still think this analysis of the suburban myth makes good sense, I think too that there is something more, something, if I may be permitted to say so, deeper, profounder, and which I was only dimly aware of then. "Suburbia," I wrote, "is America in its drip-dry Sunday clothes, standing before the bar of history, fulfilled, waiting for its judgment." I suspect now that when I wrote this I was less interested in understanding the full significance of what I felt to be true than I was in simply turning a fancy phrase. But I think now that the notion that Suburbia *is* America is our society's most recent attempt to come to terms with the melting pot problem, a problem that goes straight to the heart of the American ambivalence about cultural pluralism.[4]

Cultural Pluralism and the Melting Pot

America has never really come to terms with the legend of the melting pot. That legend, if I may quote the windy text of its original source, saw America as the place where "Celt and Latin, Slav and Teuton, Greek and Syrian, Black and Yellow, Jew and Gentile, the palm and the pine, the pole and the equator, the crescent and the cross" would together build "the Republic of Man and the Kingdom of God."[5] Despite the hope that a unified American culture might emerge from the seething cauldron, it didn't happen; instead, the formation of ethnically homogeneous communities — ghettos — helped the immigrants preserve large segments of their cultures, and the tendency to endogamy, helped them preserve it beyond the first generation.[6] But in spite of the evident facts of our cultural pluralism (by which I mean the persisting correlation of significant differences in values and behavior with ethnic, regional, and social class differences), attempts are continually made to create an image of *the* typical, or representative, or genuine American and his community, attempts that have usually succeeded only in creating stereotypes — most familiarly, perhaps, a caricature of one or another variety of Our Town: white, Anglo-Saxon, Protestant, and middle-class. *Saturday Evening Post* covers, white picket fences, colonial houses, maple hutches, and such have historically played an important role in such attempts. The myth of suburbia is the latest attempt to render

[4] In *The Organization Man* (New York: Simon and Schuster, 1956) William H. Whyte asserted that suburbia was a "second melting pot."

[5] Israel Zangwill, *The Melting Pot* (New York: The Macmillan Co., 1909).

[6] Nathan Glazer and Daniel P. Moynihan, *Beyond the Melting Pot* (Cambridge: The M.I.T. Press, 1963).

America in this homogeneous manner, to see in the highly visible and proliferating suburban developments a new melting pot that would receive the diverse elements of a new generation from a society fragmented by class, region, religion, and ethnicity, and from them create *the* American style of life. Suburbia as America is no falser a picture, probably, than Babbitt or Our Town as America but it fails as a melting pot for the same reason that the original melting pot idea failed: like many other urban neighborhoods, specific suburbs developed a tendency to homogeneity, almost always in terms of social class and very often in terms of ethnicity.

The myth of American cultural homogeneity and the facts of heterogeneity reflect a persistent ambivalence in American society regarding cultural unity and diversity, between the melting pot idea and the pluralist idea. During and after the period of rapid immigration into the "teeming cities," for example, free public education expressed the need for some minimum "Americanization," whereas the ghetto expressed the impulse to cultural self-preservation (both by the natives who excluded and the immigrants who segregated themselves). In the rest of the country, Fourth of July style patriotic rhetoric expressed the gropings toward an elementary national identity, whereas provincial arrogance, and hostility to "the government" and to centers of cosmopolitan influence, expressed the affirmation of narrow local autonomies. The ambivalence was really a double ambivalence. Each polar position was itself unstable: to be truly tenable, a pluralist ideology must accord intrinsic honor and value to a diversity of life styles, and this it has never completely done; the salient features of minority subcultural styles have more often than not been regarded as stigmata by dominant groups, tolerable so long as they were temporary, that is, *transitional* to something approaching the dominant cultural style. On the other hand, the attempts of provincial, nativist, ("WASP") groups to secure their own style as *the* American style stopped short of supporting the emergence of broadly inclusive *national* institutions which would have facilitated that transition. The most enthusiastic celebrators of "Americanism" were precisely the groups who were most wary of integrating the varieties of the national life into a unified culture.

Indeed, a unified national culture has until quite recently been a most improbable prospect, since the United States has traditionally been a society without very powerful national institutions to promote that unity and pass it down the generations. Without an established church or a powerful federal government, without national political parties or a standardized educational system, enormous distances and poor communications enabled local economies to breed a highly differentiated system of *native* subcultures — in addition to those created by the immigrants. Even today, there are probably dozens of distinctive American types, to some extent stereotypes, perhaps, but which nevertheless call attention to the wide variety of *native* styles: Vermont farmers and Boston Brahmins, Southern Bourbons and Tennessee hillbillies, Beatniks and organization men, Plainvillers, Middletowners, and cosmopolitan intellectuals, to say nothing of teenagers, the jet set, and many many more, all American, all different, and none probably very eager to be integrated into a conceptualization of "American" at a level of complexity suitable for a *Time* cover story or a patriotic war movie.

It is not surprising, then, that when one tries to abstract from American life a system of values which can be called distinctively or representatively American, the task is immensely difficult. The most systematic attempt by a sociologist, that of Robin Williams in his book *American Society*,[7] is foiled by the fact that important groups in American society do not share the fifteen or sixteen values which he offers as basically American. There is no question that values such as "achievement," "work," "efficiency," "equality," and the rest have played an important part in creating the quality of American life, but important parts of the lower and working classes (important because of their numbers) do not share them, and important parts of the upper class (important because of their influence)

[7] Robin Williams, *American Society* (2nd ed.) (New York: Alfred A. Knopf, 1961).

do not share them. As Professor Rainwater's paper in this volume makes abundantly clear, the very poor are different from you and me, and (as Scott Fitzgerald is said to have remarked to Ernest Hemingway) so are the very rich.[8]

The Viability of Subcultures

The most durable subcultures in the United States have been the ones which combined class, ethnic, residential, and religious factors to create a symbolically enclosed community. This fact has been most evident with regard to the most recent waves of immigrants: an ethnic status, a lower-class job, a personal church, a local politics, a neighborhood composed of one's own "kind," provide most of the necessary conditions for the maintenance of a way of life. A successful subculture encloses the life of the person by providing a framework of institutions that removes or minimizes the necessity for him to go outside of

[8] There is nevertheless a persistent opinion, prevalent among civilized Europeans but by no means limited to them, that there must be some widely shared features of American culture which implant themselves in an American's face, in his posture, in the way he moves, and which, apparently regardless of class and ethnic differences, mark him clearly *as* an American, immediately recognizable among a crowd of Europeans. Several things need to be said about this conviction by Europeans that Americans are always culturally visible. First of all, the level of discourse is important. Americans in Europe may be recognizable by the cut of their clothes or by their hair styles or other identifying features *which are not really very culturally revealing*. Second, it is worth noting that Americans in Europe are still a highly selective and self-selected group; not just *any* American is likely to be found feeding the pigeons in the Piazza. The sharp feeling that one can recognize an American may simply be a response to a stereotype. It is remarkable how ubiquitous this feeling is and yet how rarely it is stated in language which can survive rational appraisal. (I know that I occasionally still feel that there is something culturally distinctive about "suburbia" despite the failure of research to turn up anything substantial. But reason insists that I regard this occasional feeling as evidence of my all too human tendency to be deluded by prejudice, rather than as an intuitive gift which transcends the rules of evidence.) Finally, when Americans think about Americans, their tendency is to think about what differentiates them; foreigners tend to think about what makes them alike. But in the analysis of culture, not seeing the forest for the trees is a less common (and less damaging) error than the tendency to think that "all ________ (in this case, Americans) look alike."

that framework to find what he regards as a "full life." For these institutions to be capable of functioning, that is, of facilitating the activities that affirm the values of the subculture and discouraging the activities that threaten them, the group's authorities must establish a kind of quasi-territoriality — some *place* over which they can effectively claim hegemony. Jews in the ghetto are the classic example of what I have in mind. The Amish represent perhaps even more thoroughly than ghetto Jews the extent to which a subculture can be maintained in a relatively hostile environment so long as the institutional and territorial conditions are met. An upper-class, aristocratic subculture can be maintained in a hostile democratic environment to the extent that it goes on in places (territories) others can't afford to enter and to the extent that it is *enclosed* by a system of exclusive and sequential institutions — from school and club to college and church, through special courting and kinship institutions which promote endogamy, to careers in strategic sectors of the economy. But these are all matters of degree. The important thing to remember is that a subculture is made viable *to the extent that* (the conditions are variables) the territorial and institutional enclosure provides sustenance and support to its norms, insulates the members of the group from outside pressures, and hence discourages, forestalls, or otherwise controls mobility.

But in an open society no subculture can be totally enclosed, and this is one important source of their instability. Although my emphasis on territorial and institutional enclosure suggests that physical and social *segregation* (for that is what it comes to) contribute to the maintenance of cultural pluralism, the fact is that most groups fall severely short of providing their members with an enclosed institutional environment, even those who want it most. If even so traditionally viable a group as the Amish can be periodically threatened by the demands of local authorities that their children remain in school beyond the eighth grade, the stability of the subcultures that exist without much institutional or territorial support is much more precarious. The failure of a group to provide a complete institutional environment means not simply that a bohemian may be compelled to shave his beard or a teenager to trim his beatle-cut; it means that the members of a group must go outside for the satisfaction of some needs, and hence to "pass," to regularly *seem* to be what he is not; he must pass through some parts of the institutional environment in a sociological disguise, and under such conditions is probably highly vulnerable to disaffection.

To speak, then, of the viability of subcultures is to speak of their vulnerability. But the vulnerability to institutional penetration from outside is just one source of instability. The other source is the subculture's own normative patterns. Cultural norms morally strengthen the ability of their adherents to cope with certain exigencies, to undertake certain activities, to move in certain directions, to create certain personal and collective styles; but they weaken the abilities of their adherents with respect to other exigencies, activities, directions, and styles. What is frequently forgotten is that norms which enable in some respects, disable in other respects — an insight made excellent use of by Thorstein Veblen, John Dewey, and Kenneth Burke, among others. "The poor *pedestrian* abilities of the fish are explainable in terms of his excellence as a swimmer." To conceive norms, then, with a kind of double vision, as enabling or adaptive for some contexts and eventualities and as disabling or abrasive for others, not only adds to a systematic vocabulary for analyzing subcultural dynamics, it also discourages the sentimentality characteristic of many "one-sided" ethnographies with a "romantic" point to make.

Thus, the bias inherent in a sentimental description of the warmth and solidarity of the Jewish family and in the psychological advantages it provides is corrected somewhat by Bruno Bettelheim's criticism of Anne Frank's family, in which a little less solidarity might have let them survive. Under conditions of Nazi persecution, the desire to remain together meant to be slain together, when, separated, they might have escaped.[9] Or,

[9] Bruno Bettelheim, *The Informed Heart* (Glencoe: The Free Press, 1960).

as William Foote Whyte made clear a long time ago, the cultivation of warm and loyal feelings to the persons and places of one's youth may nourish the spirit but it impedes social mobility — if social mobility requires, as it often does, geographical removal.[10] We need not even go back as far as Whyte. In this very volume, Marc Fried suggests that the homogeneous working-class neighborhood (or slum) is a way of providing a familiar and stable context for new recruits to the industrial work force which enables them to weather the several crises of adaptation to the industrial environment. Lee Rainwater's paper, on the other hand, emphasizes not the evolutionary or transitional functions of slum life but the distinctive culture that the lower class (particularly the lower-class Negro) develops, from the material of which "expensive identities" are cultivated, *may obstruct any further transition.* Rainwater's analysis of the *stabilizing* character of lower-class culture does more than balance the evolutionary character of Fried's treatment, since he illumines the way in which lower-class culture, by facilitating the achievement of certain benefits and satisfactions, obstructs the achievement of others. That Rainwater's Negro cats are poor climbers may be explainable in terms of their excellence as swingers.

Myths and Styles of Life

I have tried to suggest that the persistence of the myth of suburbia reveals a continuing tension in American society between the ideals of cultural unity and cultural diversity, and that the persistent attempts to find some transcendent principles or values which define the unity of American culture have been defeated by the persistence of important class and ethnic differences. Even under natural or "organic" conditions, then, "American" patterns of culture are enormously difficult to describe with salutary accuracy. This difficulty is exacerbated when a society becomes sophisticated enough to be self-conscious about

[10] William F. Whyte, *Street Corner Society* (Chicago: University of Chicago Press, 1943).

its culture and rich enough to do something about it. The maturity and the luxury of our civilization constrain its elites to define an "American" style, and the miracle of our technology arms us to manufacture it. Our society is wealthy enough to support a substantial class of intellectuals devoted to staying on top of contemporary events to "spot the trend," "see the pattern," "find the meaning," to "discover the style." And our media are such that these spottings and seeings are more or less instantaneously communicated to audiences of millions, whose demand upon the marketers of opinions and interpretations for sensible and coherent syntheses is greater than the available supply.

Under such conditions, we do not get serious historical interpretation of contemporary events; we do not even get responsible journalism; we get myths, which themselves become part of the forces shaping what is happening, and which hence function ideologically. The myth of suburbia fosters an image of a homogeneous and classless America without a trace of ethnicity but fully equipped for happiness by the marvelous productivity of American industry: the ranch house with the occupied two-car garage, the refrigerator and freezer, the washer and dryer, the garbage disposal and the built-in range and dishwasher, the color TV and the hi-fi stereo. Suburbia: its lawns trim, its driveways clean, its children happy on its curving streets and in its pastel schools. Suburbia, California style, is America.

Most American intellectuals have found this image repugnant, but the bases of their antipathy have never really been made clear. Somehow associated with these physical symbols of suburbia in the minds of most intellectuals are complacency, smugness, conformity, status anxiety, and all the rest of the by-now familiar and dreary catalogue of suburban culture. But the causal connection between the physical character and the alleged cultural style of suburbia has never been clearly established. It is almost as if American intellectuals felt, like some severe old Calvinist prophet, that physical comfort necessarily meant intellectual sloth. Perhaps we have been too well trained to believe that there is somehow a direct relationship between the physical structure or the esthetic shape of a residential environment and the sort of values and culture it can possibly engender — so that the esthetic monotony of suburbia could house nothing but a generation of dull, monotonous people, and its cheerful poverty of architectural design could breed nothing but a race of happy robots. The only trouble with this view is that there is little evidence and less logic to support it. Most of the adult suburbanites were *urban* bred, and hence presumably already shaped by the time they became suburbanites. And although it is still a little too early to tell what kind of culture will be produced by the generation bred in the manufactured environment of suburbia, we might remember that the generation bred in the endless and prisonlike New York tenements did not do badly.

But becoming aware of the myth of suburbia, and pointing to the disparities between it and what we actually know of suburbs we have closely studied, should not be confused with a *defense* of suburbia. Nor should anything I have said about the critics of suburbia be interpreted as a revelation of my personal bias in favor of suburbia. As I suggested earlier, myths are potent enough to survive evidence; they are not disarmed by understanding. Quite the contrary. Once myths gain currency, once they go, as we say, "into the cultural air," they *become* real, and function frequently as self-fulfilling prophecies. Life copies literature; fact is affected by fiction; history is constrained by myth. "If a situation is defined as real," said William I. Thomas, "it is real in its consequences," and I have no doubt (thought I have no data) that family decisions regarding whether to move to the suburbs have been affected (both pro and con) by the myth of suburbia. And despite everything reasonable I have said about suburbs, I *know* that the fact that I unreasonably dislike them has been conditioned, *beyond the possibility of redemption by mere research,* by the very myth of suburbia I have helped explode.

In the sense in which I have been speaking of them, myths are more or less noble fictions; fictions in the sense that they are *made*, their order imposed, and their appeal is to the emotions. They are more or less noble depending partly on the art with which they are made but mostly upon the extent to which one is in favor of the consequences they foster, and particularly of the forms of solidarity they promote. In the context of the debate over cultural pluralism, what is usually at stake is whose version of America shall become "American."

Pluralism and Planning

Whose shall? I want to suggest that the question is relevant to the way in which the future quality of urban life is planned. Like Emile Durkheim, who suggested that the punishment of crime was significant less as a deterrent or as simple revenge than as a collective reaffirmation of cultural values, I want to suggest that we look more closely at the images of solidarity which inform the proposals for dealing with social problems in general and urban problems in particular. For social problems, of course, have no objective existence—although the facts to which they refer may. It is objectively true that some people have always lived in dilapidated, unsafe, unheated, vermin-infested residences, but "slums" have not always been a social problem. Slums become a social problem when a large enough group of important enough people decide that poor people ought not to live in such places.

Americans have a propensity for finding social problems. By defining them as real and hence setting ameliorative forces into action, we affirm our humanitarian heritage. To find problems, to mobilize opinion about them, to shake our social structure by its metaphorical shoulders and force it to *pay attention* to these matters, all nourish our beliefs in progress and perfectibility. America is a country dedicated to the propositions that no evils are ineradicable, no problems insoluble, no recalcitrance beyond conciliation, that no ending need be unhappy; we are a most un-Greek democracy. Finding and dealing with problems, then, are necessary conditions for the verification of these propositions; the very existence of social problems to ameliorate reaffirms our principles more than any imaginable utopia could. But not just any problems at any time. Because at any given moment there is an indefinitely large number of social problems that are theoretically identifiable, public concern with some (to the exclusion of others) can be understood not only in terms of the salience of the difficulties of those who *have* the problems but also in terms of the relevance of proposed solutions to the dominant forms and rhetoric of solidarity.

When we set out to improve the quality of urban life, what we are most likely to be doing is altering the conditions under which weak and vulnerable sections of the population live. But the wealthy, who also have problems, are protected from the welfare impulses of others. The strong and the autonomous grant no one the right to alter the conditions of their lives — that is what strength and autonomy are about. Public concern over and desire to plan for "the problem of" the increasing proportions of aged persons in our society do not extend to Dwight Eisenhower, Harry Truman, or H. L. Hunt, all of whom qualify for the statistical category "aged," but not for our image of those who need help — although if consulted I might have several suggestions as to how they might spend their declining years more wholesomely. The people who have the problems that are defined as real are those who are vulnerable to public action, and thus to the implicit images of solidarity which underlie that action. I think it is essential that we be very clear about these images, for to plan for the *quality* of urban life is to be concerned with the *culture* of urban life, and hence with the forms of human solidarity which planning is likely both to foster and discourage.

I see three broad alternatives for those who are confronted with the problem of planning the quality of urban life. First of all, planners can simply abdicate from any concern for the cultural conquences of what they do, and instead interpret their mandate narrowly: for example, the improvement of the physical environment for the poorly housed. To the extent that they have been planned at all, most new, inexpensive suburbs have been developed in this way — with occasional exceptions, as in the gestures by the Levittowns toward the provision of some institutional facilities. More centrally located urban residential development for the poor and less than affluent has also been dominated by considerations such as square footage, hygiene, and domestic technology. Now to provide room, cleanliness, comfort, and convenience to people who have previously been without them is an important achievement, but it is not planning for the quality of urban life. Quite the contrary; the *quality* of urban life is precisely what is usually left out of consideration — perhaps as a luxury rendered expendable by the need to bring large numbers of people up to some minimum physical standard. Under these conditions of planning, images of human solidarity seem limited exclusively to households within which *family* solidarity may be symbolized by culinary and recreational technology (refrigerators, freezers, barbecues, TVs, etc.), whereas solidarities beyond that of the family seem irrelevant, alien, or distant. There is a sense in which this alternative is evasive because such planning *does* engender a quality in urban life, but it is the quality that most cultivated foreign observers complain about in most American cities.

Planning's second alternative, it seems to me, is to make a conscious effort to alter the environments of certain groups, with the overt intention of bringing their culture closer to some monolithic or homogeneous ideal. Presumably, this would be some more advanced version of the melting pot idea, in which either a bureaucratic or entrepreneurial version of a middle-class life style would be given as an ideal toward which the poor should be encouraged to reach. Here the aim would be to make the society more monolithically what it already dominantly is. This alternative founders on its utopianism, on its assumption that a cultural consensus can be engineered or induced in a society in which conflict is endemic and which will remain so as long as the interests of groups and classes remain opposed. In the absence of any ability by planners to wipe out class differences, we must expect, in any multiclass community, controversy not only over the appropriate means to reach agreed-upon goals but over the goals themselves and the priorities to be assigned to them. This is the stuff of politics and culture, and where interests and norms are rooted in a class-based style of life, the attempt by one group to elicit the commitment of the entire community to a specific goal will very likely threaten another group and elicit its opposition. Moreover, these political and cultural diversities have a right to exist and persist. We can be reasonably sure that the vulnerable and dependent groups most readily affected by planning would gladly be rid of their slums, their poverty, and the discrimination against them. Beyond this it is difficult to assume anything with great assurance except, perhaps, that groups develop an attachment to those aspects of their culture which have not been imposed by necessity, an attachment made evident by their tendency to take the culture with them when they move from one enviroment to another, and to preserve whatever of it that circumstances permit. On the other hand, utopian planning dominated by visions of profound cultural changes is always interesting, and such planners might well devote more energy to making these visionary ideals manifest and rhetorically vivid, if only in order to help others to know whether to be for or against the form of solidarity they envision.

Finally, there is the pluralist alternative, an alternative perhaps best expressed in the recent work of Herbert Gans, and, to a lesser extent, Jane Jacobs. Whatever reservations one may have about the work of either, each of them projects an unambiguous image of the kind of human solidarity they would like to see fostered by urban planning. This solidarity is loose and heterogeneous, composed of more or less autonomous groups and neighborhoods formed on the basis of ethnicity and social class; communities attached, perhaps, to the notion that good fences make good neighbors, but necessarily related to one another through political and economic accommodations long characteristic of urban life. If they are open to criticism as "romanticists" (although it is not clear to me why a preference for dense street life or an insistence that an ethnic working-class neighborhood is not necessarily a slum renders one vulnerable to such criticism), it should at least be said in their defense that they obviously care enough about the *quality* of urban life to evoke a strong and clear image of it —something their critics do not always do — strong enough in Mrs. Jacobs' case and clear enough in Professor Gans's case to make it easy for a reader to be for or against them.

I am mostly for them, since planning for pluralism seems to me not only the most sensible way of responding to the fact of persisting cultural diversities but the most honorable way as well. In making their assumptions, planners might first of all assume (since it is the most reasonable assumption) that most groups which are displaced by planning moves *will take their culture with them* if they can. Planners would do well to anticipate this, and to modify their plans accordingly, to facilitate the preservation of those parts of their culture that are not illegal and that the groups want preserved. This means that planning would have to be done for *specific types of people with distinctive cultural styles,* that is for a variety of specific, known tastes rather than for faceless densities with a given amount of disposable income for housing. A working-class group with a durable pattern of sexual segregation (husbands and wives living largely separate extrafamilial lives) requires for its sustenance residential and community facilities different from those required by a middle-class group with a culture pattern emphasizing companionable family togetherness.

Similarly, to the extent that the "dramatic selves" and the "expressive identities," which Professor Rainwater finds characteristic of lower-class Negro culture, play an important compensatory role for the severe deprivations suffered by this group, we might plan to provide facilities for the nourishment of this psychocultural pattern — even as we plan to eliminate enforced segregation. But even after *discrimination* on the basis of race disappears, we have no evidence to suggest that *segregation* will ever completely disappear. If the experience of other ethnic groups is any guide (and we have no better guide), many Negroes (like many members of other ethnic groups) will choose to live among their own "kind" even after they have virtually free choice of housing. However "kind" may be defined in the future, we can continue to expect ethnicity and social class to play an important role. Although we know very little, really, about which members of an ethnic group *prefer* to live in ghettos, or why, even after they can live wherever they please, the *fact* that many of them do is beyond question. We have no reason *not* to expect this to be true of Negroes also, and those who choose ghetto organization may just turn out to be those who have been influenced by the most militant Negro leaders, intent upon the preservation of whatever is distinctive in the Negro subculture.

I hope it is clear that these remarks are not the elaborate rationalizations of a conservative searching for an acceptable rhetoric to defend the status quo. Quite the contrary; they are the remarks of a sociologist who, being *for* the extension of the widest possible range of choice to all segments of the population, nevertheless knows that choices are hardly ever random, and that no man is so free that he is not constrained by the norms of the subcultures to which he belongs or would like to belong. To plan cogently for optimal diversity in tomorrow's urban world, we need the ethnographic sensitivity to describe the diversities of urban behavior and to discover the norms which constrain them. We need also the analytic skill to distinguish between those parts of a subculture which are inherently valuable to the people who bear than and those which, being merely instrumental adaptations to enforced conditions, will be readily given up when circumstances change. Finally, we need the practical skill at fitting physical environments to cultures so as to accommodate the latter without necessarily hypostatizing them.

CHAPTER NINE

THE RISING DEMAND FOR URBAN AMENITIES

Jean Gottmann

The recent growth patterns of the urban regions of the United States and Europe show that two types of areas are growing fastest — megalopolis clusters which offer the widest range of job opportunities and highest levels of cultural amenities; and the Riviera recreation areas which combine some social amenities with good physical settings. Both types of settlements are characterized by high levels of planned, man-made facilities. These trends, often persisting against government regulations, suggest the direction urban and regional planning must take if it is to be responsive to future demand.

A few weeks before the St. Louis Bicentennial conference met at Washington University on Planning for the Quality of Urban Life, the President of the United States sent a message to Congress on the problems and future of American cities, which, in its preamble, quoted the famous statement by Aristotle in his *Politics:* "Men come together in cities in order to live. They remain together in order to live the good life." [1]

Jean Gottmann is a professor of geography at the Ecole des Hautes Etudes, University of Paris, a visiting professor at Southern Illinois University, Carbondale, and the author of *Megalopolis, The Urbanized Northeastern Seaboard of the* U.S. (1961).

[1] "Message from the President of the United States relative to the problems and future of the central city and its suburbs," March 2, 1965, *89th Congress, 1st Session, House of Representatives, Document No.* 99; quotation from Aristotle, p. 2.

Urban life has always conveyed at one and the same time an idea of superior quality in the mode of living ("urbane," "urbanity") and also a hint at the difficulties and social problems in the process of organization and growth. This duality of contrasted characteristics of urban life has led philosophers, preachers, and politicans to express preferences for the small town or at least a not too large city. Such a middle-of-the-road solution appears less and less practicable today. There were, by 1800, only seven cities in the world grouping half a million people or more. There are more than two hundred of them today. Two million people agglomerated in one urban district appeared an extraordinary phenomenon a century ago; there are about seventy such urban concentrations today; and this number of very large cities is bound to grow fast. The President's recent message also forecast: "A half century from now 320 million of our 400 million Americans will live in such areas. And our *largest cities* will receive the greatest impact of growth" [our italics].

There is urgent need to examine the problem of planning for better urban life. There is rather wide consensus that present conditions are not good, that they are worsening, and that little has as yet been seriously attempted to arrest the decay and start improving the urban environment. Also, the solution adopted widely by the many who could afford it, that is, the flight to the suburbs, appears about to be reaching its limits in the larger metropolitan areas. The difficulties of transportation, especially for commuters, the worsening general conditions of scattered suburban life have spurred the search for new, different ways of improving urban life. Increasingly the opinion has been expressed that modern Western society in general, and the American nation especially, should be able to manage better the conditions and modes of their urban life; contemporary affluence, technology, and social consciousness ought to combine to solve the existing problems. It is also felt that improving housing, purity of the air and of the water, policing of the city, transportation, schools, and other services will not be enough, and cannot suffice, if treated piecemeal. A general plan for a "good life" is wished for.

The Conference at Washington University examined many of the specific trends affecting urban life; the debates demonstrated much dedicated soul-searching on the possibilities of achieving fuller employment, higher incomes, better integration, and so forth. Most of the search developed in the two areas at present in the limelight of the national political scene, that is, race relations and civil rights on the one hand, and the war on poverty on the other. These considerations are certainly basic to the quality of urban life in America, and in many other countries today. In a way, it could be observed that the conference debated "*urbi et orbi*," extending the perspectives of urban life to the "Great Society" as a whole. In a nation where 93 percent of the people draw their incomes from non-agricultural pursuits, such attitudes are understandable. One wonders nevertheless at the more special needs and means of the large cities and metropolitan areas; these, because of their size, of the density of population and of activities achieved there, have specific characteristics and problems. General affluence and civil good behavior do not solve specifically urban problems, although it ought to be easier to arrive at satisfactory solutions amid such economic and social advantages.

A better quality of urban life suggests abundant and widespread physical and cultural amenities made available to the city dwellers. The contemporary process of urbanization has not often provided for such amenities in the various cities and metropolitan areas. Although it has been accompanied by a rise in the standards of living and generalized affluence for a majority (the war on poverty has really focused on only one fifth of the American nation), urbanization has caused in recent years more pollution, not only of the air and water, but also of the landscape. Slums and junkyards are only two factors of "landscape pollution" among many; the decaying old business districts of many cities, old and blighted industrial or warehousing buildings, ugly and poorly maintained wharves, tracks, railway stations, etc., are all-important factors in the picture. What is called for is not simply preservation of the old cityscapes with which old memories have embroiled our emotions. In the fast-changing environment of these days, "the shape of a city changes faster, alas, than a mortal's heart," as Charles Baudelaire said, in the midst of the sweeping renewal of Paris by Haussmann in the 1850's. Our means for molding spaces and materials are greater now than ever; they call for a rapidly changing urban morphology, bringing more amenities, and an actually good life, into the cities.

The profession of planners in America has the reputation of attaching little importance to the physical amenities in urban design. Of Alberti's famous duality of the qualities required in the townscape, "*commoditas et voluptas*," only the former, meaning functionalism, efficiency, has apparently retained the attention of Americans. Many critics of the modern city in America have eloquently bemoaned this attitude of the planners. The constructive proposals offered by such critics have remained too often in the realm of conservation of monuments of yesterday and of the preservation of a status quo where it seemed still socially and esthetically satisfactory. This was the slowly evolving mood of the common mortal's heart, lacking realization of the dynamic momentum of this era. If in many respects man is a creature of habit, he is also and will remain a creature of progress and capricious fashion. Changes in urban and architectural design must follow the evolution of society's structure, of the common man's occupations and use of time, his aspirations and endeavors. In fact, where careful design has been applied, town planning in America has produced remarkable good results, thus the college campus, a major American contribution to modern urban design.

The style of the half century to come may be deduced to some extent from some of the obvious trends of present American society. We do not pretend to forecast the precise plastic characteristics of future fashions in the arts of living and building, but we may outline where the demand for styles of living and location is headed for. In fact, it has been on the way there for some little while.

Americans have always been mobile, and in recent years, owing to improved means of transportation, they have been very much on the move. Where have they been moving to? The statistics of migration within the United States are very telling. On one hand, most of the growing population has been gathering increasingly into the metropolitan areas. Although the total acreage of the latter has been expanding, a higher proportion of the population is now concentrating on a rather small percentage of the total land area. More square miles have their population thinned out than there are square miles on which the population is thickening. Despite the visual impressions created by the suburban sprawl, Americans are on the move to live in higher density formations than in the past. The regions being thinned out are not deserted; their lands and buildings remain quite productive; but small fractions of the land area are harboring increasingly a higher percentage of the total population.

Megalopolis, the huge urbanized area on the northeastern seaboard, in 1950 contained 21.2 percent of the nation on 1.8 percent of the land area of the conterminous United States;[2] in 1960 in this same area the population represented a slightly lower proportion of the nation, 20.5 percent, but its number had risen from 32 million in 1950 to 37 million in 1960, or by 5 million, meaning a serious increase in average density (from 596 to 688 inhabitants per square mile). If the nation as a whole had grown slightly faster (by 18.5 percent) in that decade and if the attraction of Megalopolis seemed to be weakening, other regions had considerably increased their share of the total population: California saw its population rise by 48.5

[2] See Jean Gottmann, *Megalopolis, the Urbanization of the Northeastern Seaboard of the United States* (New York: The Twentieth Century Fund, 1961).

percent and Florida by 78.7 percent. These two states aggregated 8.8 percent of the United States total population in 1950 and 11.4 percent in 1960. Most of these increases had thickened the population on less than half of the land area of these two states. Heavy densities were forming there, as in Megalopolis. At the three corners of the national territory small fractions of it held 32 percent of the nation[3] in 1960 on less than 5 percent of the area, as compared with 30 percent in 1950. This trend will probably be accelerated through the 1960's.

It is interesting to look at the figures of the net migration of whites (who have had freer choice of where to live) by States within the United States since 1940. A few regions, all distributed on the periphery of the country have attracted most of the net interstate migration of whites from 1940 to 1962:[4] the Southwest (mainly California and Arizona) and Megalopolis (i.e., the northeastern seaboard states, mainly from Connecticut to Virginia); two smaller but notable other corners of the country show a great and continuous power of attraction: Florida (fastest growing of all states) and the State of Washington. Finally, Texas and Ohio also attract migrants, though in thinner and less regular fashion.

With the exception of Ohio, the net migration obviously flows toward areas at the periphery of the national territory that are richly endowed with either cultural or physical amenities, or both, as is now the case of California, which has received the most massive inflow for the last thirty years. That the "geography of amenities" [5] plays an important part in the selection of location for people and a number of industries is increasingly recognized by students of statistics and by business managers. The lure of climate and landscape used to attract the wealthy, the people of leisure, the aged who could afford it. Thus the fortune began of the "Rivieras" in France and Italy, of the Californian and Floridian coasts in America.

[3] Statistics from the U.S. Bureau of the Census, *Statistical Abstract of the United States* 1964 (85th ed.; Washington, D.C., 1964).

[4] *Ibid.*, Tables 7 and 33.

[5] As it has been called by geographers, beginning with Edward Ullmann of the University of Washington, and James Parsons of Berkeley.

Now these areas are bustling with young, busy people, and with a variety of economic activities.

Such migrations of people and of job opportunities are not observed in the United States only. Similar trends are clearly at work in Britain (where a recent article is entitled "Shall we all go to live in the Southeast?"), in France (where the major growth areas are those of Greater Paris and the Mediterranean seashore from Monte Carlo to Marseille), in the Netherlands (where decentralization policies could not prevent the attraction to the *Randstadt Holland* encircling Amsterdam, The Hague and Rotterdam), in Switzerland (towards the Zurich-Basle and Geneva-Lausanne areas), and in most of the other fairly developed countries of Europe, Asia, and the Americas. The rapidly growing urban regions of the world may be, in most cases, grouped into the major categories which could be designated the "megalopolitan category" and the "Riviera category."

By "megalopolitan" is meant a category of urban regions formed around one or several large cities which arose as centers of commerce, industry, and perhaps government, and still are such centers. By "Rivieras" is meant another category, whose growth has been chiefly due to the advantages the area offered for recreational activities. One does not need to insist at great length today on the recreational advantages provided by the physical amenities found on the French and Italian Rivieras, in Southern California or on the "Gold Coast" of Florida; they have been advertised enough throughout the world in order to attract first, tourists, then residents, and finally industries. "Rivieras" grew by putting to work a set of attractive factors quite different from those of the "megalopolitan" areas. It is noteworthy, however, that in the past centuries, commercial, industrial, and governmental functions have always favored the formation and expansion of urban centers, but that recreation is a new function for large, growing urban areas; the Riviera type of urban ribbon is special to recent times and mainly to the twentieth century. As they expand, they also bring commercial and industrial business into the beautiful region, which had only physical amenities to start with. Cultural amenities follow. The Rivieras may extend also to encompass old centers of trade. Thus new large urban areas arise, which may ultimately acquire characteristics similar to those of urban regions of "megalopolitan" origin. "Rivieras," however, are likely to care more about the looks of their environment, as they know better from experience the economic value of attractive surroundings.

The massive economic success of regions richly endowed with physical amenities seems a logical development at a time of rising standards of living, lengthening of leisure time for the mass, greater mobility of people, and better education for all. These four trends concur in fostering the congregation of people in those areas where they will find a more pleasant life and broader opportunity. Megalopolitan regions usually offer the opportunity; they also have worked hard to provide at least some physical amenities. The original Megalopolis on the northeastern seaboard of the United States had the need and the means to provide recreational areas near its sprawling cities, to serve the leisure of its urban crowds. Coney Island was a start that became a popular image; but Atlantic City, the Catskills, Cape Cod with its neighboring islands, and many other parks and resorts were formed within Megalopolis itself or nearby. These local facilities are helpful but do not satisfy the swelling demand for more recreational amenities and of better taste.

The increasing concentration of population in a few urban areas, large in comparison with the old concept of a city but small as a fraction of the nation's whole territory, is an understandable trend. It began in fact with the industrial revolution and the flow of the labor force from the farms to the cities. But it takes on a sharper, more selective form, which threatens to decrease considerably the relative importance of the population in most of the national system with the exception of the faster growing areas. The parts of the country being thinned out do not like this prospect. In most well-developed countries legislation has been passed opposing the trends of concentration, aiming at a more equal distribution of the population over all the land, and in any case endeavoring to maintain the present distribution.

This legislation varies from country to country. It was started, in fact, early in this century with the purpose of limiting the exodus from the farms, and helping the small family farm to survive and prosper. Legislators often believed that the family farm was the staunchest pillar of democracy, of political stability. There was widespread distrust of the crowds of workers gathering in the cities. Thus, in the United States and in Western Europe, farmers were granted various advantages in terms of taxation, price supports for their products, and subsidies. Electoral districts were designed to favor the stable rural areas in the distribution of seats in legislative assemblies. The electoral weight of farming areas in the House of Commons has often been emphasized, though farmers account for less than 5 percent of the total population of Britain. The current debate on legislative reapportionment in the United States well illustrates how the designing of districts has favored for a long time the rural areas losing in proportion to the total population.

Such measures, which have been fairly generally adopted in the democracies on both sides of the North Atlantic, were aimed at advantaging the rural areas, in order to convince their populations to stay where they were. Greater political influence gave them the economic means of improving their opportunities at home, making these regions more attractive to their residents and even to in-migrants. At the same time, by restricting the growth of political influence of the rapidly expanding urban regions, these same measures seemed appropriate to discourage at least some of the process of concentration, reputed politically and socially evil. These calculations were correct, but they failed to achieve their main goal: the major concentrations and a few new ones continued growing at an accelerated rate, both in figures of population and in employment opportunity. Megalopolis, California and Florida in the United States, metropolitan Toronto, Montreal, and Vancouver in Canada, Greater London and the Southeast around it in Britain,

Greater Paris in France, the Randstadt Holland in the Netherlands, Greater Stockholm in Sweden, the Zurich-Basle-Berne triangle in Switzerland, the Milan-Turin area in Italy, etc. The countries at large complained that these metropolises were sucking up all their blood.

Then sterner legislative measures were proposed and in some cases approved. New regulations forbade new industrial establishments and even office buildings to come to the central cities or even regions of these areas whose growth seemed to be upsetting the existing political and economic balance of the country. Paris, Amsterdam, London have now lived for almost twenty years under rules, gradually tightening, aimed at strangling their growth. Some economic activities were thus induced to go elsewhere. The growth of these areas of "megalopolitan type" was probably slower as a result than if these rules had not been applied. Various activities in the cities and suburbs were inconvenienced by these rules. But it turned out to be impossible to enforce them fully. Growth went on. People continued to congregate in and around the condemned areas, creating more congestion there. Many plants or offices forced to look for another location found a site in another area of fast growth. Those that failed to obtain a permit in Greater Paris went to Amsterdam or The Hague, Geneva or Zurich, or to the Marseille-Riviera seaboard of southeast France. The central plateau and some of the southwest of France kept on losing population as previously. Similar examples could be cited in other countries.

The failure of political pressure and stern legislation to stop a trend of concentration in small areas, which elect only a minority of the various legislative bodies, forcefully demonstrates the power of the economic, social, and psychological forces at work in modern society and shaping contemporary urbanization. Basic to this process is the occupational evolution bringing about, gradually and quietly, a profound economic and social revolution, one of which most people are not yet aware.

The industrial revolution began long ago to reduce the labor force needed on the farms and gather more workers in teeming cities and towns to work in mines, manufacturing plants, warehouses, seaports, and on the railroads. As the work of mining and manufacturing became increasingly mechanized and automated, fewer people at work produced greater quantities of goods at lesser cost. In the United States the evolution of the labor force is more advanced in this respect than in any other large country, and this evolution has greatly accelerated in recent years.[6] From 1950 to 1964, the number of production workers employed in manufacturing has remained rather stable, oscillating around the figure of 12.5 million. Meanwhile, the total number of employees in nonagricultural establishments increased by about 13 million (from 45.2 to 58.5), that is, by as large a number of jobs as there were engaged in producing the huge manufacturing output of this country. But this rapid increase of 13 million employees was not found in mining (employment in which fell), or in transportation and public utilities (total employment in which oscillated during those 15 years around 4 million) or, once more, in manufacturing production. Although the quantities of goods produced and handled greatly increased in the same period (by about 68 percent), the number of people actually occupied in production and handling work did not increase; the productivity of their labor did. The new 13 million jobs were found in such fields as wholesale and retail trade (registering an increase of 3 million jobs), finance, insurance, and real estate (plus 1 million), miscellaneous services (plus 3 million), and government (plus 4 million, mainly on local and state governments). By 1963, these four growing sectors of the labor force totaled 32.6

[6] Professor Lebergott's chapter minimizes the trend by comparing 1910 and 1960 figures; moreover, some sharpness is lost by his keeping the production workers in the same category with other employees in manufacturing.

million employees, more than half of the total nonagricultural employment. At the same time, the figure of the nonproduction employment of the manufacturing industries (i.e., managerial, office, research workers, etc.) rose by 1.8 million (from 2.7 million in 1950 to 4.5 million in 1963). Obviously, the future of the labor force is in the nonproduction areas, in specialized and advanced services: Megalopolis on the northeastern seaboard has shown an advanced thrust in that direction, as we demonstrated in our study of this region.[7] Similar statistical trends are shaping up in most countries of Western Europe and in Japan.

We have now embarked on a new economic period which we may call the "white collar revolution." It heralds the passage of the bulk of the labor force into clean work requiring qualified skills, responsibility, continuing education. It means shorter work days and perhaps work weeks, more vacation time; therefore a much greater demand for *education* on one hand, *recreation* on the other (rather than actual leisure, for the white-collar worker often has to think about his work while away from it). For such a society, the modes of living will be substantially different from those determined by the industrial revolution of yesterday.

First of all, manufacturing and storage plants, which used to congregate in the cities and form the bases of urban growth, no longer need this concentration. As they employ fewer hands, they do not require large residential groupings in their immediate vicinity. Industrial and warehousing plants can now scatter along the railways and highways; they no longer congregate in cities or dense formations by necessity. Only a few categories of industrial establishments still need the proximity of one another or of a large market. The cities are losing their "black country" and busy manufacturing appearance of the industrial revolution period. In the white-collar era they can afford another, cleaner, more elegant look.

[7] See Jean Gottmann, *Megalopolis,* especially the chapters on "Commercial Organization" and "The White Collar Revolution." The figures in the preceding paragraph are from the *Statistical Abstract of the United States,* or calculated from it.

The second force now at play is the interdependence, still very strong, of those qualified services (we suggested calling them "quaternary activities" in our study of Megalopolis) which are growing fast and begin to form a sizable portion of the total labor force; that is, the administration of public and private affairs, the financial community, research and higher education, mass media and advertising, highly specialized professional services, style-setting recreational and artistic activities. These are all very tightly interwoven in their daily operation; to function well, business management needs government; they both need easy access to the best available information, research, specialized consultants' advice, higher education, and entertainment. The interconnections and complementarity of these economic, social, and cultural activities have always been important, and they made large metropolises grow in every lively civilized country. Now these activities are becoming major sectors of employment and, insofar as mechanization and automation will stay and grow with us, this trend does not seem reversible in the foreseeable future.

The managerial, recreational, and mass media functions are not only offering more jobs nowadays, but they have glamour and prestige; and they contribute an exciting element to the growing city of tomorrow. This special factor is important. It attracts a certain quality of manpower that could have the choice between several jobs in different locations. The story is now well known of the large corporation offices which considered moving out of Manhattan after World War II; they gave up this plan because of the difficulty of finding the quality of employees they wanted in the various scattered locations under consideration. The IBM Corporation built its largest European center at La Gaude, near Nice, in an extremely beautiful site of the French Riviera, largely to offer the young scientists and technicians they employ all the advantages of living and working amid the physical, cultural, and recreational amenities of this glamourous spot of Europe.

Many more examples of this trend, now general in the advanced countries, could be cited. There is little doubt that as the new generation enters the labor force in the coming years, better educated, aiming at employment in the growing and more fashionable sectors of the economy, there will be an increasing concentration around the urban regions that will develop the most pleasant mode of life, offer a wide and attractive gamut of amenities. Such local conditions are largely man-made; they require a great deal of enthusiastic planning, investment, and care.

The traditional definition of the geographical region called a "Riviera" was that it is a seaboard where the mountains come close to the shore and that it is generally oriented toward the southeast. That means the amenities of sea, mountain, and a sunny climate all together. In Italy, however, the necessity of the southeastern orientation was discarded in calling two regions, one "Riviera di Oriente," and the other, "Riviera di Ponente." In California the climate of the seaboard is adequate despite its orientation, and this is also true of the Crimean Riviera around Yalta and of the westward-looking Riviera around Sochi in the Caucasus. In Florida there are no mountains, but the Everglades provide another kind of amenity. Another Riviera may be shaping on the Gulf coast of Texas with San Antonio and even Houston. Airconditioning and other gimmicks may counterbalance some unpleasant climatic features. Along the foot of the Front Ranges, Colorado is developing something that may become an inland "Riviera," where some dams and bulldozing may provide water spaces.

The same technology that frees the worker from the hardships of toiling most of his life to produce the necessities of life is also making it possible to install amenities artificially, where nature itself has not provided well enough for them. If, as some economists believe, space becomes *fungible* almost like money and securities, and one location can easily be exchanged for another, this is also true to some extent for what makes a place beautiful, exciting, and fashionable, and therefore attractive to many.

One cannot expect to decentralize and scatter so easily the places of work of the major centers of present quaternary activities; but as the volume and congestion of the great centers of "megalopolitan" character increase, some delegation of authority and deconcentration will occur, chiefly toward some centers in rapidly growing areas. Those that achieve a "Riviera-type" status will usually stand a better chance to win awards in the national and international competition. And through such a process urban life will acquire a much better quality.

There is little doubt that modern advanced societies have the means to afford the needed planning and redevelopment. There is also evidence that the forces already at play on the economic and social scene will gain more momentum in the immediate future. The percentage of the aged population, retiring with sufficient means to select a pleasant place to live, is rapidly increasing in the total population. The number of young adults, who have completed their school years and do not yet have children, and are therefore particularly mobile, selective, and looking for excitement, will increase more rapidly than any other sector of the age pyramid in the next ten years, in the countries that experienced the baby boom after 1945. Cities in America and Western Europe should prepare themselves for the impact of these waves of demanding customers. The illusion that they may all be dispersed along great new highways with more television and other gadgets ought to be dispelled. Modern people are gregarious. When they leave on vacation, with a free choice of where to go, they do not scatter in solitude amid the vast open, quiet spaces that still abound even on well-developed continents. Most congregate in a few fashionable, well-advertised, very crowded spots. This ought to be kept in mind when planning for an urban life that people will look for.

References

CHURCHILL, HENRY S. *City is the People.* New York: Harcourt, Brace & World, Inc., 1945. (Paperback revised edition 1962).

GOTTMANN, JEAN. *Economics, Esthetics, and Ethics in Modern Urbanization.* New York: The Twentieth Century Fund, 1962.

GOTTMANN, JEAN. "Grandeur et Misères de l'Urbanisation

Moderne," in *Urbanisme* (Paris), No. 88 (June, 1965), 40–50.
GOTTMANN, JEAN. *Megalopolis*. Cambridge, Mass.: The M.I.T. Press, Paperback 8, 1962.
LAVEDAN, PIERRE. *Histoire de l'Urbanisme: Renaissance et Temps Modernes*. Paris: Henri Laurens, 1959.
ULLMANN, E. L. "Amenities as a Factor in Regional Growth," in *Geographical Review*, 44 (1954), 119–132.

CHAPTER TEN

A PLANNING INVENTORY FOR THE METROPOLIS

Joseph R. Passonneau

Systematic quantitative descriptions of the existing physical environments in American metropolises can tell what environments the many publics of the city now use and suggest what they will need and want in the future. A good inventorying system could thus prevent the gross errors of resource allocation and design which now produce unwanted and dangerous neighborhoods. Accurate inventorying could also separate with a clarity not now possible (1) *the architectural,* (2) *the social, and* (3) *the public services components of the urban environment, allowing more effective choice of planning strategies.*

Because I am an architect I am interested in the form of things, and particularly in the form of the physical environment, natural and man made.

To modern eyes the form of many preindustrial cities seems to have been very beautiful. Such cities and their buildings had a unity that grew naturally and largely unselfconsciously out of then current technologies and civic attitudes. It would hardly have occurred to a medieval mason that the window he was shaping could be formed in any other way, and the form of a medieval town was based on a technology so limited, on social forces so strong, and on values so profoundly shared that

Joseph R. Passonneau is Dean of the School of Architecture, Washington University, and author, with Richard Wurman, of *Metropolitan Atlas: 20 American Cities* (1966). He is former Chief of Architectural Design for the Tennessee Valley Authority.

the possibility of alternative organizations and alternative values did not arise.

In contrast with earlier cities, modern cities seem either dull, or ugly and inchoate. Today many more choices exist in the forming of window sills and in the forming of cities, and there is no consensus among values on which to base choices. Because we have not yet found effective, consciously guided processes to replace the unconscious, automatic processes that have historically shaped cities, the vitality of modern life seldom finds vivid and satisfying expression in modern city form. And while it is dangerous to make aesthetic judgments on anything as rapidly changing and, therefore, as continuously new to our sensibilities as the modern city, architect's judgments are echoed in objective evidence of another form of ugliness, the social pathology and individual and group misery in large parts of modern American cities.

A great deal of conscious planning, public and private, has been invested in American cities. Planning, or foresight, operates at many levels; it occurs whenever action is guided by controls that can be identified as other than habit or conditioned reflex. *City planning* is the welter of predictions, or decisions, by individuals (heads of households, dope pushers, Sunday gardeners, slum landlords, urban sociologists) and by private groups, (cartels, welfare organizations, the Mafia, real estate groups, Presbyterians) that shape cities.

Much of the activity of urban government at all levels can be described as city planning, institutionalized. While I believe this to be a useful definition, in this discussion I will deal with "city planning" in the narrower and more conventional sense: governmental manipulation of the physical organization of the city.

The fact that we intervene and that we propose to continue to intervene in the market is, of course, based on the conclusion that the free market (or rather our mixed economy) will not automatically produce the kind of cities that we desire. There are a number of reasons why this is so.

First, the "environmental market" is conditioned by a great

deal of public investment and public regulations. The construction of highways, urban renewal projects, the insurance of suburban loans, all condition the private market directly; the organization of our municipal governments and the arrangement of the federal tax structure have indirect but perhaps even larger effects on the nature and quality of our urban environment. We should, therefore, articulate the purposes of such public intervention, predict with whatever accuracy we can muster the probable effects of public action, and, after the deed, test to what extent our predictions were accurate.

Second, while there is a great deal of public investment that affects both the growth of cities and the public and private profits the growth produces, there is a gross mismatch between the public investment and the public return. Most of the benefits accrue to individuals in the form of windfalls, rather than to the public that incurs the cost. A highway, for instance, both creates and shifts values. The "sign value" added to the farmland along a throughway accrues from public action. It does not belong to the farmer — this "sign value" would disappear if the public took "its" road away. A recent ruling by a New York court upholds this proposition.

Zoning may create values, but it is even more clear than in the case of highways that the principal effect of zoning is to shift values from, for instance, owners whose property is zoned for residential use to owners whose land is zoned for commercial use. The fact that much of the "profit" from public investment and growth accrue to private owners rather than to the public that made the investment largely explains why we Americans build "cut-rate" cities and explains why expensive private investments are hung on an armature of inadequate public investment.

Third, the very long-term nature of most environmental investments makes inoperative those aspects of a market economy which are conditioned by short-term profits. Henry Cobb (who as an associate of I. M. Pei has designed many large-scale private developments) recently set out to prove that most of the finest urban residential developments had been created by private capital. He found that in the developments he admired, the original investor had, in most cases, gone broke. Yet over the long term each development was very profitable because of its intrinsic quality. And the pay-off on such nonreplaceable assets as architectural and historic monuments and certain natural amenities is sometimes a very long time in coming.

Fourth, both the scale of investment necessary and the nature of the private corporate investor make environmental innovation difficult. One of the neighborhoods (as defined in later paragraphs) studied by Ray Goldman, a graduate student working on neighborhood analysis, is the Chicago Lake Meadows project of the New York Life Insurance Company. Here the population mix began with a ratio of about 90 percent white residents and 10 percent colored residents. The mix is now 50 percent white and 50 percent colored. The creation of such a mixed population was an avowed goal of the project. The goal was accomplished because an entire section of the city was developed to exploit its intrinsic physical qualities (proximity to Lake Michigan and to downtown Chicago) and to create a new form of environment (apartments, schools, shops, in a parklike, protected setting) close to good public and private transportation. The existence of this project demonstrates how public and private investment can combine to implement public policy by creating new forms of environment; the rarity of such successful projects suggests how difficult they are to create.

Fifth, "downstream effects" from both private and public action exist both in space and time (and can be good as well as bad). One suburb pollutes "its stream" and gives its downstream neighbors typhoid, and on the positive side, old men plant apple trees under which they will never sit. John Dyckman points out that the Illinois-Indiana boundary does not stop Gary's sewage from flowing into the Illinois River, but it does prevent the people of Chicago from fighting to protect their water supply, or to preserve the Indiana Dunes, a major Chicago recreation area. Municipal boundaries within metropolitan areas also create downstream effects. The boundaries that separate Kinloch (an impoverished, Negro suburb of St. Louis) from Clayton (the suburban location of major shopping and office functions) are boundaries across which private money can flow from Kinloch to Clayton, but which impede the flow of public money from Clayton to Kinloch.

Finally, while we have begged the issue of standards of value[1] by which to measure environmental alternatives, it seems clear that many things that Americans value are not adequately available to them. There is an enormous demand for available public recreation, but many cities do not adequately provide such facilities; vivid natural surroundings are increasingly valued, but most cities mismanage their natural environmental resources; low-density suburban living seems to be preferred by families with children, but such environment is difficult for low-income families to find, and for Negroes it is almost impossible. Many people would clearly like safe, urbane, high-density neighborhoods close to the central city (Jean Gottmann argues that when Americans are free to choose—that is, before and after they have had families—they move toward the center of the city) but in few cities are such neighborhoods available. Pleasure driving is the major American recreation, but we largely ignore the visual qualities of roads. All of these highly valued environmental commodities require public action on a scale that is now difficult but possible.

Urban Programming

Since World War II conscious planning for large-scale residential urban construction has become a major activity involving large numbers of people and enormous sums of money. The resulting public housing, urban renewal, and private suburban developments controlled by public investment policy, seldom satisfy us either visually or socially, and many of these projects may rapidly lose even their present limited value.

[1] Questions of value are ancient, subtle, and "value" is difficult to measure; but without standards of value planning cannot exist. The residential "accounts" described here are a first step toward the articulation of environmental values.

A principal aim of this book is to suggest ways in which we can develop better conscious, rational processes to guide such public action. Will Thompson discusses how, by conscious manipulations of prices, we can achieve physical planning goals. Bennett Berger in his discussion of working-class and middle-class urban life shows that the city is a place of plural culture and that there are, therefore, conflicting demands on its limited supply of space. My own concern is with the development of "programs" for physical planning.

Before an architect begins an elementary school, for instance, he needs a program telling him how many students the school will house, now and in the future; how many classrooms, auditoriums, cafeterias, libraries, etc., will be required; and how much area is needed in each; performance standards for materials, proposed budgets, and the extent to which he must allow for expansion.

Programming even a modest building is a difficult and creative task. Besides establishing area requirements and performance standards it is, at best, a learning process involving both client and architect, during which they discover needs previously unrealized. The often told tale of the architect who designs buildings without an adequate understanding of his client's needs is really the story of an architect and a client who have not been successful in eliciting from each other the correct questions when they wrote their "program."

The architect working at the project scale of several city blocks and the planner making public policy decisions that affect the design of even larger sections of the city have an even more difficult programming task. They are working for a multiple client with a variety of aspirations and needs, a client who has few institutional processes by which he can articulate his needs even if he can identify them, a client whose identity may change a number of times during the useful lifetime of the environment being designed.

If we hope to shape the city's growth we need at least to know systematically the number and nature of the people who live in the city now and will live in the city in the predictable future, their present and future needs for homes, schools, social services, churches, shops, recreation. We also need a description of the city's other activities: factories, warehouses, central business functions, and their physical requirements. We must finally understand how all of them are connected and how these connections are likely to change.

Even given adequate knowledge of the city, there are few aspects of a complex urban project that the architect can program and design unilaterally. Many issues, such as the size of the space to be allotted to each person, the number of rooms per family, etc., will affect mental health, using the phrase in its broadest terms. Many decisions will directly affect the public investment involved. We should sort out those design criteria that are not purely architectural in the formal sense, as a first step in identifying the kind of programming help the architect needs.

The same process will identify the unique province of the architect as artist. At a modest level, the selection of color and texture of the brick is an activity that economists and aldermen should stay out of — whatever their skills at resource allocation. At a higher level, the evocative organization of forms and spaces that in the world's great cities both reveal our past and still delight us, is the professional province of the architect alone.

In the writing of programs for large-scale environmental projects, it should be a goal of public officials and architects that at least the following conditions obtain:

First, there should be no "redundant" building either in the private sector or the public sector. That is, we should not build in such a way that we simply move people about the metropolitan area without improving the aggregate quality of the city's dwellings.

Second, public policy and investment decision should make a variety of neighborhoods available to the "multiple publics." We should also have some systematic way of knowing what these multiple publics need and what they are likely to be looking for in the foreseeable future. This means that we must wrestle with the problem of assigning values to various environments, and, because land is so important a part of the physical environment we must be particularly concerned with understanding the nature of land values and the way land values change.

Third, public policy and investment decisions should make social innovation possible.

Fourth, we should program our environmental design in such a way that we can accomplish what Will Thompson has called in another context "double-entry bookkeeping in social accounting." For instance, we should try to understand the side effects that occur when we tear down a slum and build a civic center. We should try to understand more clearly the extent to which we create social capital when we invest in superior school systems. Each of us could add to this list.

Fifth, we should program our environmental developments in such a way that we can demonstrate the additional values created by public investment. This is the essential step in recapturing some of these development values in order to help pay for the original investment.

A Planning Inventory

It is apparent that programming the physical form for an industrial, individualistic, pluralistic, and changing society poses puzzling problems. But we can take a first step toward avoiding such past errors as redundancy in building and too-simplistic norms by setting up a physical inventory of the city as it exists. Such an inventory should be repeated periodically to test the efficiency of metropolitan programming and planning.

These accounts should be made up of the minimum number of neighborhood types that can both be usefully used to describe the city and that have significantly varying effects on public services and investment in environment. Stated in another way, we are looking for the minimum number of types of population and types of public service mixes that significantly affect aspects of the environment.

In these tabulations a neighborhood is defined as an area within which the variations in people and environment are not great enough to produce significant variations in the type and quality of public services or of public and private capital investments. Such neighborhoods have a special kind of homogeneity. By this definition a neighborhood might be an area combining very high buildings with many families in them and low buildings with few families. However, within the neighborhood the mix of high and low buildings and of family types would be uniform throughout the neighborhood, partly as the result of a uniform level of services and investments. Another neighborhood type could contain only young families of similar incomes, and another neighborhood might be made up of highly diverse population types. In each case the "mix" of population types and public services and investments in the neighborhood would be uniform across the neighborhood. (Figure 1.)

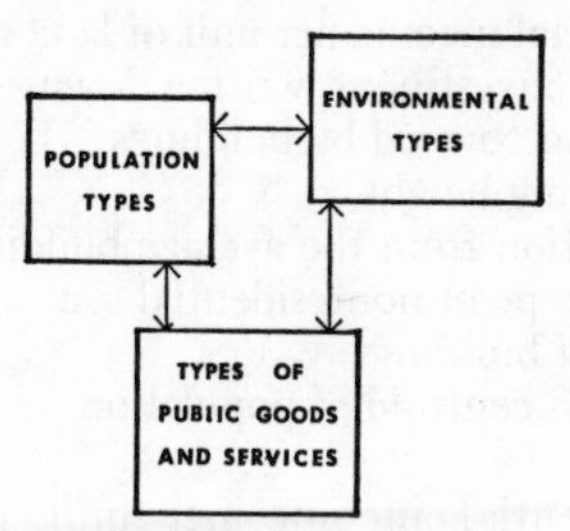

Figure 1 Categories of neighborhood characteristics.

The argument here is first that these three categories of "neighborhood characteristics" completely describe a neighborhood and second that the categories do not exist independently. For instance, upper-middle-class families will live in a variety of environmental categories, but not unless there is a high level of investment in education. Low-income rural in-migrants are found in a variety of "housing mixes," but such neighborhoods demand high levels of police surveillance and social and health services. And so on.

In St. Louis I have begun a model of a useful planning inventory. I have chosen first to analyze the residential environments of the city. The population characteristics included are

1. Average age
2. Variation from average age
3. Sex
4. Income per household
5. Education
6. Ethnicity
7. Percent of population in residence more than five years
8. Occupation mix
9. Total employed
10. School enrollment
11. Population density

The environmental characteristics are

1. Total residential income per unit of land area
2. Public capital investment, written down
3. Percent of land covered by buildings
4. Average building height
5. Average variation from the average building height
6. Amount and type of nonresidential use
7. Average age of buildings
8. Distance from centroid of population

The total residential income per unit of land area is a "proxy" for value of land and improvements. It has the merit that it can be calculated easily from census data and in some ways it may be a more useful indicator of land value than market conditions. Items 3, 4, and 5 describe quantitatively the organization of buildings on the site.

All of the neighborhoods (that is, all of the associated population and environmental types) make up a matrix of terms to which various values can be assigned (numbers of people, area in acres, value of land, etc.) depending on the characteristic of the city to be described and aggregated:

	A	B	C	D	E	F	G	H (Population types)
a	aA	aB	aC	aD	aE	aF	aG	aH
b	bA	bB	bC	bD	bE	bF	bG	bH
c	cA	cB	cC	cD	cE	cF	cG	cH
d	dA	dB	dC	dD	dE	dF	dG	dH
e	eA	eB	eC	eD	eE	eF	eG	eH
f	fA	fB	fC	fD	fE	fF	fG	fH

(Environmental types) (Neighborhood types)

Two of the three qualities of the total residential city are completely described within this matrix. These data can be mapped and presented in a publicly understandable and politically actionable way. (Figure 2 and 3.) We suspect that for

Figure 2 *Population distribution for St. Louis. (From* Metropolitan Atlas: 20 American Cities, *Joseph R. Passonneau and Richard Wurman. Cambridge, Mass.: The M.I.T. Press, 1966.)*

Figure 3 *Population distribution for New York.* (*From* Metropolitan Atlas: 20 American Cities, *Joseph R. Passonneau and Richard Wurman. Cambridge, Mass.: The M.I.T. Press, 1966.*)

each neighborhood (aA, aB, etc.) there is associated a typical level and mix of public goods and services,[2] although we do not have the resources to demonstrate this. For this sort of inventory to be useful there must be a systematic analysis of public investments and services. Indeed, this is where Federal research money should go if we are accurately to program future metropolitan growth.

[2] See *Towards an Integrated System of Regional Accounts: Stock, Flows and the Analysis of the Public Sector* by Harvey S. Perloff and Charles Leven, p. 197. These public goods and services would correspond to the "Regional Government Account" described in the Perloff-Leven monograph but broken down by neighborhoods as defined here.

These capital investment and operating costs of public services should be accounted for in the following categories:

1. Education and neighborhood cultural facilities
2. Local streets and public transportation
3. Social services and health services
4. Police and fire protection
5. Parks, playgrouds, and landscaping
6. Water, sewer, garbage collection

I also believe that, while we are aiming for a variety of residential choices, there is an order of quality of environments (aA, bA, cA, etc.) for a given population type. If this is the case, public policy should aim to shift the inventory of such neighborhoods in the direction of higher quality.

Further, the population types that will make up the future city will change in ways about which we can make rough predictions, at least if we respond to the ideas of Marc Fried and his colleagues. Public policy should anticipate the change in demand both in quality and kind of neighborhood.

Further, by shifting public services (such as the changes in education recommended by Professors Shaplin and Salisbury), we will create the need for new archetypal neighborhoods. Daniel Mandelker suggests other new (to the United States) residential archetypes and processes by which they can be created.

In summary, I have tried to describe one input necessary to create a better residential city and, therefore, to help shape Federal and local policy. Such policy should help avoid large public investment in inadequate environment, unwise allocation of resources between, say, education and low-cost housing and, at the highest level, provide a framework in which creative architects can help find new forms for our changing society.

References

LYNCH, KEVIN, *The Image of the City*. Cambridge, Mass.: The Technology Press, 1960. The M.I.T. Press Paperback 11.

MEYERSON, MARTIN with JACQUELINE TYRWHITT, BRIAN FALK and PATRICIA SEKLER, *Face of the Metropolis*. New York: Random House, 1963.

PASSONNEAU, JOSEPH R., "Emergence of City Form," *Urban Life and Form*, Werner Hirsch (ed.) New York: Holt, Rinehart and Winston, 1963.

PASSONNEAU, JOSEPH R. and RICHARD WURMAN, *Metropolitan Atlas: 20 American Cities*. Cambridge, Mass.: The M.I.T. Press, 1966.

PERLOFF, HARVEY S. and CHARLES L. LEVEN, "Toward an Integrated System of Regional Accounts: Stocks, Flows, and the Analysis of the Public Sector" reprinted from *Elements of Regional Accounts*, Werner Z. Hirsch (ed.). Baltimore, Md.: The Johns Hopkins Press 1964.

CHAPTER ELEVEN

REGIONAL PLANNING IN BRITAIN

John R. James

Although American urban problems are expressed in terms of dozens of large cities, our conventional planning and urban projects deal with only small fragments of the metropolitan network. In Britain, the scale of planning has evolved from small new towns to building clusters of large cities and molding enormous urban regions. Mr. James discusses present British methods and goals and indicates the future trend of linking national economic planning with urban regional planning.

The World Situation

These chapters have been written because we recognize the need to exercise some degree of control over the built environment. The subject is under discussion in every part of the world for we are witnessing an urban revolution of unprecedented scale.

How serious is the problem of urban growth throughout the world? It has been estimated that the peoples of the earth, now numbering 3¼ billions, will have doubled before the turn of the century. It is probable that the whole of this vast increase will take place in city regions — the twentieth-century product of a new mobility and technology, a new form in an age-old settlement pattern. Every national census shows the progressive decline of the rural population and the ever-growing population

Mr. John R. James is the director of planning in the Ministry of Housing and Local Government, London.

of the large cities. In England and Wales at the first census in 1801 less than one person in ten lived in a town or city of more than 100,000 people, but by 1960 six out of ten did so. In the United States less than one person in sixteen lived in such towns in 1850, but by 1960, again, six out of ten did so. In Russia and Japan half the population is urban; and in Argentina in spite of our popular conception of wide pampas and plentiful beef, maize and wheat, again six out of ten are urban dwellers.

Whereas lack of transport once set clearly defined limits to outward growth of our towns these limits are now being set in Britain by planning control, and in particular by the application to the large towns of green belt policies. The consequence of growth within defined limits during the nineteenth century was congestion; the consequence of the car during the twentieth is openness and spread. The old distinction between town and country has broken down; there is no longer a sharp, clean edge giving visual quality; and the pattern of administrative boundaries, created largely in the nineteenth century, is no longer satisfactory. From a planning point of view a central city cannot be looked at separately from the life of the region it dominates; it depends for the maintenance of its industry and commerce on workers who sleep elsewhere, for its recreation on the green belt and open country beyond, and for its future growth on planned overspill. This is true of all large cities: the only valid planning concept therefore is the city region that effects a marriage between the built-up core and the area that comes under its direct social and economic influence and is shaped and held together by its system of communication.

Our particular answer has come to us over the course of more than a century. It is not necessarily right for America with its different history and attitudes. British regional planning has its genesis in three separate strands of thought. First, there is the strongly held belief (Dr. Johnson and others) in the social values and economic strength of the compact and lively city. This is the part of our European tradition which makes most of us who visit the United States enjoy, temporarily at least, the vibrancy of New York, have an appreciation for Jane Jacobs, want to stay on in San Francisco and get out of Los Angeles. Second, there is the very powerful influence of our nineteenth-century social reformers — men like Owen, Rockingham, and Salt, who looked on the squalor, vice, and misery of the congested industrial cities and wanted to put an end to them. They led to Ebenezer Howard, the Town and Country Planning Association, and the new towns movement. Fifty years after the publication of *Garden Cities of To-Morrow* we got our New Towns Act. Third, we have a strong and passionate belief in the quality and values of the English countryside. We are countrymen and conservationists at heart. Wordsworth, Morris, and Ruskin stressed these values and were the precursors of such movements as the Friends of the Lakes, the Council for the Preservation of Rural England, leading to our National Parks and Access to the Countryside legislation and to our green belts. This trilogy of ideas has come together in our planning philosophy and acts of Parliament, and I should like to spend a little time on each of these three elements: the central city, the green belt, and the new towns as integral and interrelated parts in the physical planning of the city region.

The Central City

We have retained our belief in the value of the central city standing at the heart of the urban region — and especially in the old historic core wherever it has survived. In the terms of Professor Buchanan, this will usually form an environmental area from which all vehicular traffic, other than the essential minimum, will be rigorously excluded. This point of view was recently (February 1965) expressed by Lewis Mumford in evidence submitted to an Inquiry into the Oxford City Plan. He referred among other things to "the demonstrably fallacious notion that the way to reduce traffic congestion is to provide more facilities for private motor cars to enter the central area of the city, and sufficient off-street parking space to enable them to remain there." At the heart, too, will be the seat of those administrative, shopping, and cultural uses that are needed by the whole of the region, again forming distinctive environmental areas around which wheeled traffic will circulate rather than penetrate. We shall have to think increasingly of using more than ground level for the different uses to which we put this heartland; and also of moving out from the center those uses which are no longer relevant to the whole population. Circulation by tube trains at underground level, by car, and bus at ground level; by monorail, moving platform, and pedestrians at upper level are all quite feasible. The recent measures to prevent further office building in London are indicative of the recognition by the present Government of the need to reduce the intensity of nonessential central use. In all this we are trying to reject the destruction and depreciation of city centers. So far, out-of-town shopping centers are not for us — though in suburban form they will come. We are also beginning to reject the idea that there is no room for dwellings in the heart of our cities. The London Barbican project is an exciting, if small, beginning in the process of bringing people back to the city center from which high land values had forced them.

In the redevelopment of the slum and twilight areas that immediately surround all our city centers we face rebuilding on an unprecedented scale, though as yet we have not found the mechanism to do it effectively. In magnitude this task dwarfs the planning and architectural effort which is going to the building of our new towns. Land values are high, densities in Glasgow, Manchester, Liverpool, and London are often as much as 300 to 400 persons per acre, buildings and layout are obsolete, open space is negligible, and there is an indiscriminate mixture of row after row of by-law housing, primary schools, industry, warehouses, railway sidings, canals, and derelict land crying aloud for total renewal. Through these large areas new roads must be cut and more spacious surroundings created for future populations. It is our general experience that for every nine acres which are cleared of dwellings we can find only five on renewal for residential purposes. The remaining four are needed for incidental open spaces, better roads, car parks, playing fields, and improved schools. We are not aiming, anywhere, on redevelopment at net densities of more than 200 persons to the acre and often, as in Manchester, at not more than 90 persons. In consequence, we face a massive overspill of population from all our large cities.

This task, as in America, is clearly beyond the capacity and the will of private enterprise. The aggregation of small parcels of land in separate ownership into large units suitable for comprehensive development, the responsibility for re-housing the displaced families on slum clearance, and the financial loss of converting built land into open space, roads, or schools mean that the effort must be made by the public authority, supported by financial aid from central government. Some authorities, as for example London County Council, have done magnificent work; but in general progress is slow and somewhat unimaginative and is leading to a widening geographical separation of the social classes. Poorer families, on local authority housing lists, go back into the renewed areas; the richer seek the suburbs or market towns and country villages within commuter range. The two Englands are therefore not so much the North and the South but the inner and the outer areas of our large cities.

Green Belts

A green belt introduces by design an element of rigidity into the planning of a region, setting long-term limits to the expansion of the urban area it embraces. The Metropolitan green belt of Greater London was incorporated into development plans in the early 1950's, but it was not until 1955 that formal proposals were invited by the Minister for other areas. Eighteen green belts affecting more than half the population of England and Wales are still at varying stages in the process of formal definition and approval. Meanwhile, they serve as instruments of interim development control. As their boundaries will set limits to long-term urban growth, it is important that they should now be carefully measured against the future pattern of renewal and growth in the city regions as we see it.

Green belts are only part — an essential part — of a comprehensive strategy of containment and growth for each of the city regions. They cannot realistically be considered separately from questions of the best location for future development. These questions of where people are going to live and work need to be settled before the green belt boundaries are fixed. To do otherwise would be the reverse of sensible planning practice. The worst thing that could happen would be for the Minister to give them all final approval and shortly afterwards to have to modify his decision because no reasonable alternatives for housing and industrial growth lay before him. This would destroy public confidence (already well established) in their long-term character.

Any complaint of the restrictions that green belts impose on development needs to be weighed against their value for other purposes — maintaining the countryside, and sometimes a viable agricultural industry, between the large cities and towns, and protecting for public enjoyment the open wedges that sometimes penetrate the cities. And perhaps we have not hitherto stressed sufficiently the positive function of green belts, as distinct from their safeguarding and separating values. A green belt is an instrument of regional policy designed not only to resist urban expansion and sporadic development but to afford the opportunity for the creation of positive scenic and recreational values so that it lives up to its popular image, "the townsman's countryside."

To speak of "preserving" green belts in the light of the many claims upon it is to indulge in an illusion. What is needed is a policy of "creative conservation and imaginative landscape design," to use the late Professor Abercrombie's words, in order to secure by development control and landscaping that necessary changes do not spoil its finer qualities. Some green belt areas are not particularly attractive and here "creative conservation" is not enough. Imaginative landscape design is needed to make such areas both visually attractive and useful as parts of the green belt. Land near a conurbation is far too valuable to be allowed to remain derelict or unsightly.

New Towns

It was not until Howard took practical steps to deal with the disorders of London by suggesting that its surplus population should go into new towns that we were given the right tool for shaping the city region. Less than justice has been done to Howard's ideas. He was not concerned solely with garden cities. His mind was also seeking to resolve the problem of great urban regions by bringing into being for example, ten cities with a total population of three hundred thousand. He envisaged them as a single whole, integrated and bound together by a rapid public transport system. He called them a town cluster, a word which is reappearing with increasing frequency in British planning literature under the influence of the South East Study. He succeeded in founding Letchworth and Welwyn Garden City and by their success paving the way, in our pragmatic manner, for the New Towns Act of 1946.

Howard had thought of towns of 30,000 population. The Reith report, leading to the New Towns Act, proposed towns of 60,000, and with one or two exceptions this was the adopted size of our first brood. The real value of a fixed size is that nothing else can give quite the same economy in building and services, nor secure so readily the stability of community life and safeguard so easily that which is historically or aesthetically worthy of preservation. But I doubt whether there is much of intrinsic value in the common idea that the optimum size of a town should be 60,000 people. On the contrary, there is a lot to be gained from the variety and strength of an economy, administration, high-quality shops, cultural activities and amenities generated by the resources and purchasing power of a much larger population. In other words, there is an economy in scale that justifies new cities going well beyond this figure — but what this figure is for urban entities that look to the same center for most of their community requirements, I do not know. So much depends on the restraints people will willingly accept on the free use of their cars, and on the intensity and scale of traffic-generating land uses at the center. But by accepting Howard's concept of the town cluster, and by avoiding the form of present cities with radial roads leading into an embedded center, there appears no good reason why we should not successfully create new cities of a quarter or even half a million population. A whole variety of new urban forms might be worked out and their comparative costs and social merits estimated. Here is a very fruitful line for university research which I shall be happy to see studied for practical application in Britain.

For the sake of completeness I should like to add that by March 1964 the Government had advanced £359 million for the building of its new towns, that it is the Minister of Housing and Local Government (or the Secretary of State for Scotland) who designates the areas on which they are to be built, and it is the Minister who appoints the new town corporations, giving them all the powers necessary for the acquisition of land, construction of houses, factories, commercial buildings, and, where necessary, the provision of public services. When largely complete, ownership passes to the New Towns Commission, set up in 1961. Although the annual balance sheets take a great deal of interpretation, the first twelve towns in England and Wales taken together had reached the stage of profitability in about a dozen years.

Local Government Organization and the Role of Central Government

The facts point to the need for fewer and more composite urban planning units. The motor car and the spread of housing and commuting have everywhere blurred the clear distinction between town and country which first determined our local government system. The current proposals of the Local Government Commission, by increasing the size of county boroughs to give administrative expression to something like the whole built-up area, go some way toward creating local authorities fitted to tackle the traffic and redevelopment, if not the overspill, needs of the larger towns. So too did the proposals of the Royal Commission on Greater London which led to the creation of the Greater London Council, responsible as from 1st April 1965 for the administration of a single urban area, 600 square miles in size and containing just over 8 million people.

The concept of a continuous county in keeping with the physical and social entity of a city region and the evolution of our settlement pattern has its notable adherents, especially amongst professional planners. In such areas the planning matters of common interest to the million or so inhabitants which ought to be administered and decided on a regional basis are particularly those relating to roads and traffic, public transport, water supply, refuse disposal, clean air, shopping centers, hospitals, higher education, sports stadia, industrial location, new towns or major suburban development, and regional open space. Within such a county the personal and welfare services of local government would need to be administered, as now, by a lower tier of constituent authorities. But a radical change of this character in the structure of local government is far from being realized, and although it might bring great planning advantages there is also the danger that it might lessen individual freedom and local independence and equality.* The same point has been made in the report prepared by the Joint Center for Urban Studies (M.I.T. and Harvard) on "The Effectiveness of Metropolitan Planning" (June 1964).

The use to which we put our land and the scale of investment in the renewal or extension of our urban fabric are matters which concern several Ministers. Who then should exercise the initiative? In France, where the emphasis of four successive national plans has been on economic affairs, the Commissariat Général du Plan has a coordinating role among government

* In February 1966 the Prime Minister announced the setting up of two Royal Commissions for England and Scotland respectively, to examine the functions and administration of local government.

departments and serves the Prime Minister's Office. In Scotland it is the Secretary of State for Scotland and in Wales, the Minister for Welsh Affairs, but there the populations are small enough for a single ministry to be largely responsible for all the environmental services, for local government, physical and economic planning and land conservation. But this is quite impracticable for England, and you may have noticed that over the past two or three years we have been experimenting in a manner which you must have found confusing.

Nationally, the matters of deepest concern to the government have been not so much the planning of our city regions as the regional disequilibrium in economic growth rates, the relative decline of the coal, textile, shipbuilding, and heavy engineering regions compared with the Midlands and the South East, the high unemployment rates in the North and West and the outward migration of young people from Scotland, the North East and Wales. Social and political pressures from the less favored regions for a higher share of national investment, both public and private, led to the Toothill Report on the Scottish economy 1960–1961, to the Hailsham Report on the North East (1963), and to the report on rural depopulation by the Council for Mid-Wales (1964). All were concerned with programs for regional development and growth, and all took for their inquiries areas that were much larger than those of a city region.

This emphasis on economic planning places the responsibility with Mr. George Brown, deputy Prime Minister, and his Ministry of Economic Affairs. As with the French system it has a coordinating role among departments and is taking over the work of producing regional plans for the whole of Britain, including a re-examination of the basic premises in the South East Study (1964). Its senior officials will act as chairmen of Regional Boards of civil servants who will represent their departments in each of the provincial capitals.

Here, too, is the first real attempt in Britain to effect a marriage between economic and physical planning. European experience demonstrates that harmonious alliances of this character are far from easy to establish and that the exercise may perhaps be described as trying to put a half nelson on an octopus. The difficulty relates not only to the method and content of regional plans but also to the different regional boundaries that planners wish to adopt for different planning purposes. Their unanimity consists solely in rejecting the view that the administrative boundaries of the central city is satisfactory. They are constantly searching to put their studies into a wider context, hence the remark that regional plans refer to areas somewhat greater in size than the last one for which no solution was found or, according to Professor Haar, that an inquiry into the nature of a regional plan is something like the hunt for the smile of the Cheshire cat.

The South East Study

The most important essay to date in regional physical planning in Britain was published last year as The South East Study 1961–1981. It was written by officials of the Ministry of Housing and Local Government and was accompanied, on publication, by a government White Paper that accepted most of its conclusions and proposals.

The broad picture is that southeast of a line from the Wash to the coast of Dorset as shown on the accompanying map (see Figure 1, page 204), there are today over 18 million people or 35 percent of the population of Great Britain. In the last thirty years the population of the area has gone up by 3 million; and in the next twenty it is likely to increase by at least another 3½ million. It has a moderately high rate of natural increase, and it is the area of greatest attraction for immigrants from the Commonwealth and abroad, and for the young worker from other parts of Britain. About half of all the increase in employment in the country is to be found here, and, even more significant, it contains a highly disproportionate share of our growth industries. In London itself, with its 8 million people, the rate of employment growth (6.6 percent from 1955 to 1962) is actually below the rate for England and Wales (6.9

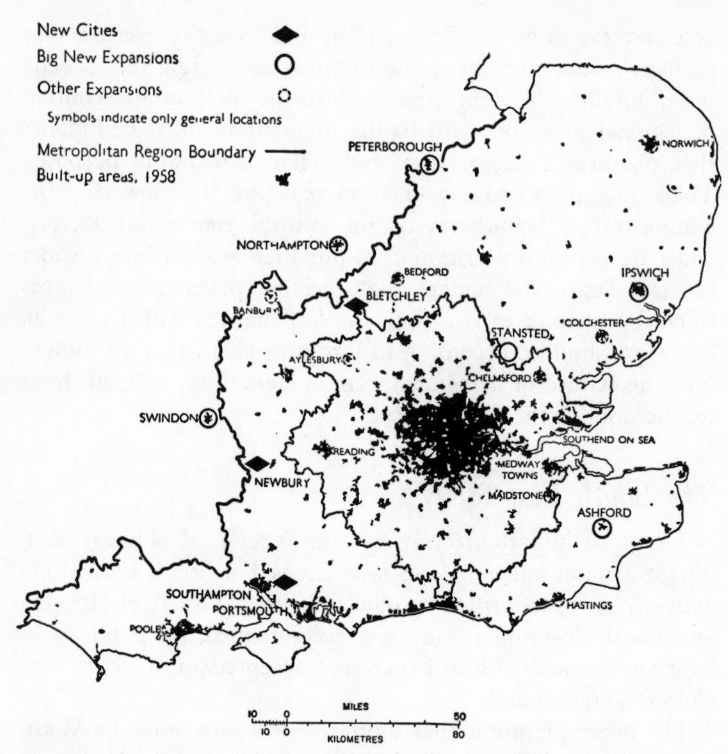

Figure 1 *Areas suggested for expansion in South East England. (From* The South East Study *by permission of Her Majesty's Stationery Office, Great Britain.)*

percent); but in the outer metropolitan region, extending outwards for some 40 miles from Charing Cross the rate of increase is over 20 percent. This is the region which contains the 2,000 square miles of green belt, the eight new towns, and a pattern of radial roads and suburban railways leading to the heart of London and welding this vast area into a single city region.

The particular and immediate concern of the Report is to draw attention to the magnitude and urgency of the housing problem for the whole of built-up London. Although its population is falling as a consequence of outward migration, the number of families requiring separate homes is constantly increasing. With greater prosperity, better housing, earlier marriages, and greater longevity, the average size of London's households has fallen from 3.02 persons to 2.85 in the last ten-year census period. Second, like all great cities London has its homeless, its over-crowded and its slums. The housing need to meet the requirements of present and future Londoners cannot be placed at less than half a million extra dwellings over a twenty-year period. But its available building land, even on reuse of railway land, the Arsenal at Woolwich, and more intensive use of Victorian and Edwardian property, is negligible. The plain fact is that provision must be made for about 350,000 London families outside London before the end of 1981. Without governmental intervention this is a task that is beyond any local authority, even one as powerful as the Greater London Council.

The question then is where these million people should live. The approved green belt (843 square miles) casts a tight girdle around the metropolis; it is one of the main achievements of postwar planning; it has a vital role to play, both positively for recreation and enjoyment and negatively for containment. It cannot, except marginally, be used as building land; and no Minister responsible for national planning would abandon it. The extended green belt (1,200 square miles) not yet approved by the Minister, is a different matter; but here too, great caution must be shown in changing its green fields into housing estates. Nor can much further relief be found in the eight new towns.

Over the course of the last ten years British planners have come to the conclusion that we must learn to build new communities on a very much larger scale than those attempted in the past. Nothing else will meet the needs of the population explosion which is upon us; and in an already highly urbanized society the addition of a further 20 million people by the turn of the century forces us to this point of view. In the South East Study we propose the building of three new cities, one of 250,000 in the area of Southampton-Portsmouth, the others of

150,000 each, near Newbury, and Bletchley. But in addition to these the Report proposes a further growth to Swindon, no more than twenty-odd miles from Newbury, of some 50 to 75,-000 people, and further additions to Northampton of 100,000 people and to Bedford of at least 30,000. Bletchley, Northampton, and Bedford constitute a triangle of towns that will be less than twenty miles apart. In other words, there will be new town clusters of well over one million people near Southampton, over half a million near Bletchley-Northampton, and approaching 400,000 in the Newbury-Swindon area.

All told, two-thirds of the prospective London overspill of a million people have already been agreed subject only to local inquiry. Teams of planning consultants have been appointed to prepare master plans. As yet there is no experience of attaching a new town to large existing communities. It is bound to prove administratively and technically more difficult and expensive than taking a green field site. The problem lies partly in the progressive conversion of the central area of the old town to cope with an increase in traffic flows, in securing the viability of both the new center and the old, in the incidence of local and central government payment for the new road network, and in the extent to which the new town corporation will need to exercise powers of compulsory purchase over private business and commercial interests. But the New Towns Act is a flexible and successful piece of machinery and much to be preferred to the Town Development Act of 1952.

Apart from lesser expansions, two further new towns are suggested in the Study, but both are dependent on other developments. The proposal for a Channel Tunnel to France makes a town of about 100,000 in the locality of Ashford in Kent an attractive possibility; while the need for a third international airport in the London area may be met near Stansted in Essex, and be accompanied by a similar-sized new town.

The South East Study has aroused much controversy. Most criticism comes from the fear that the large scale of government investment in new and expanded towns will further tip the scales against the economic regeneration of the less fortunate regions of Britain and further strengthen the magnetism of the South East. There is some justification for this fear. The answer, however, is not to hold back the relief of London's homeless and overcrowded and the economic life of the South East, but to speed the process of urban renewal and build more new towns in the Midlands and the North. Thus, although the regional studies for the West Midlands and North Western England are not yet ready for publication, the Government has already announced over the course of the past year or so more new towns — Dawley and Redditch in the West Midlands, Skelmersdale, Runcorn, Greater Warrington, and Leyland-Chorley in Lancashire, and Washington in County Durham, where incidentally the Old Hall was the home of the ancestors of your first President.

Further criticism has been voiced that any regional study should be preceded by a national plan, a viewpoint which was accepted by the Labour Party in their election manifesto last autumn. There is merit in this. A long-term look at Britain's future must aim at a national distribution of population and employment different from that which now exists and which was determined in the steam age of the nineteenth century. The Government is committed to an annual growth rate of four percent in the Gross National Product. Our expanding trade in recent years with the E.E.C. and E.F.T.A. countries of Europe, and with the East European bloc on the basis of bilateral trade agreements, must involve some reorientation of our trade and industry. It has already given a new importance to the eastern seaboard of Britain, a fact reflected for example in the growing activity of East Coast ports and the development in particular of the Tees and Humber estuarine areas. Our energy requirements are no longer so dependent on coal as in the past; the petro-chemical industry is developing rapidly; and deep-water estuaries in relatively unpeopled parts of the country are assuming significance as new growth points. Geological surveys of the North Sea basin for oil and natural gas may have a still more profound effect on our economy. A new and powerful axis of communication may be developed from the

Humber to the Severn, opening up new possibilities for urban growth well before the turn of the century. We may, therefore, be on the threshold of radical changes in the distribution patterns which have characterized the map of Britain from the time of the industrial revolution. It is right that regional planning should be seen in the perspective of national policies which aim at a smooth and ordered transition to new patterns reflecting new social and economic needs and new locational values.

References

Central Office of Information. *New Towns of Britain* (*C.O.I. Reference Pamphlet No.* 44). H.M.S.O., 1964.

Central Office of Information. *Town and Country Planning in Britain* (*C.O.I. Reference Pamphlet No.* 9). H.M.S.O., 1962.

CULLINGWORTH, J. B. *Town and Country Planning in England and Wales.* George Allen & Unwin Ltd., 1963.

HEAP, DESMOND. *An Outline of Planning Law.* (4th ed.). Sweet & Maxwell, 1963.

KEEBLE, LEWIS. *Principles and Practice of Town and Country Planning.* (*3rd ed.*). Estates Gazette, 1964.

Ministry of Housing & Local Government. *The Green Belts.* H.M.S.O., 1962.

Ministry of Housing & Local Government. *Planning Bulletins* (Nos. 1–7). H.M.S.O., 1962–1965.

Ministry of Housing & Local Government. *The South East Study, 1961–1981.* H.M.S.O., 1964.

Ministry of Transport. *Traffic in Towns* (Buchanan and Crowther Reports). H.M.S.O., 1963.

OSBORN, SIR FREDERICK J., and WHITTICK, ARNOLD. *The New Towns: The Answer to Megalopolis.* Leonard Hill, 1963.

CHAPTER TWELVE

A LEGAL STRATEGY FOR URBAN DEVELOPMENT

Daniel R. Mandelker

Current American planning law separates regulation from execution and distributes responsibility for implementation among numerous jurisdictions. The British "New Town" technique provides an alternative administrative and legal structure in which town planning and town building are more closely related. Professor Mandelker discusses three possible adaptations of British practice and the consequences of each for American community development.

Planning for improvement in the quality of urban life will require substantial changes in the character of our cities and urban regions. In this process, the legal system will play an increasingly critical role. Improvements in school facilities, in job opportunities and job access, in recreation, and in housing quality, all point to the need for legal machinery that can help make these objectives a reality. This chapter will examine deficiencies in the existing legal framework which impede the planning of our physical surroundings, will review and compare the English method for carrying out development policies, and will suggest changes in the American legal structure that can heighten its capacity for implementing planning goals. We will focus on the creation of entire new town communities as one

Daniel R. Mandelker is a Professor of Law at Washington University and the author of *Green Belts and Urban Growth* (1962) and of a case book on urban legal problems.

developmental technique for improving the quality of our urban environment.

Discussions about new legal forms and structures often lose sight of the objectives that new forms and structures are supposed to achieve, and an indication of these objectives will help clarify the aims of structural reform. We could begin our discussion with any of the several elements that are important to the quality of urban life, but housing quality certainly ranks high on any urban agenda. While throughout the nation an improvement in the quality of urban housing is taking place in the aggregate, de facto patterns of economic, racial, and ethnic segregation still force many to live in substandard surroundings. Concurrently, population displacement brought on by public programs of urban renewal and highway construction adds new burdens to those families whose incomes are below the level of adequacy. When low-income families displaced in these programs have improved their housing, the gain has been achieved through higher housing costs or dislocation from familiar neighborhoods and patterns of living. Forced displacement is inevitable in any program of environmental improvement, but we are not exploiting the possibilities that relocation offers for upgrading the housing of those who are affected.

Low-income housing needs are simply one of many social deficiencies that are present in urban society and that demand improved programs of public action. Among other problems, land is underutilized on the urban periphery, and the resulting inefficient commuting patterns may bear heavily on low-income groups. Housing conservation in older neighborhoods has also posed serious difficulties which have been hard to resolve.

Deficiencies in Existing Legal Machinery

Our governmental and legal machinery is not well geared to cope with these issues, and a catalog of existing difficulties may be helpful. Some of the major difficulties that block a more effective legal structure arise out of the federal character of American government. Policy-making in America is a mixture of decisions taken at national, state, and local levels, no one of which carries with it the mandate of compulsory implementation. The national government shapes policy through financial inducements, and state governments authorize their local units both to accept federal aid and to avail themselves of the substantive powers that are necessary to carry out selected programs. But the decision to act is local. This division of power among governmental levels combines with a division of responsibility among federal and local governmental agencies to fragment responsibility for the operation of critical programs, with the result that the lines of authority are unclear.

Tools for planning implementation are also scattered. Not only are they scattered among many municipal units within urban areas, but they are scattered among different enabling and authorizing statutes. The result is not only a lack of coordination, if all of the available powers are conferred on every municipality, but a lack of consistency, since not all the municipalities within the same area will usually possess the same powers. For example, municipalities may be authorized to conduct urban renewal programs, but counties may not.

The limitations arising out of the scattering of substantive power are reinforced by our system of local government; the system assumes a degree of local autonomy that impedes the attainment of regional objectives. These difficulties have arisen because municipalities are able to make parochial decisions without overriding restraint. In large part the problem is one of scale, as local communities may not be organized on a geographic basis sufficiently extensive or strategic to allow them to undertake the necessary planning and development decisions.

Substantive deficiencies in planning machinery should also be noted. One is that regulatory powers for the negative control of land use are separated from positive powers for the public development and redevelopment of land and community facilities, so that one cannot reinforce the other. For example, urban renewal agencies may plan the urban renewal project, but zoning power is left with the parent municipality. Conflicts of purpose may and do arise.

Private land development also falls under public control, but is not as well regulated as it might be because it is carried on in a context apart from the public regulatory decision. While publicly adopted regulations can encourage the desired development outcome through carefull allocation of land uses, they cannot compel development and must rely for their effectiveness on private entrepreneurs, who may not respond.

Timing is another problem in the execution of regulatory controls. A substantial period may elapse between the planning decision and the private development which replies to it. When development is ready to take place, it may be difficult, if not impossible, to execute because of an inflation in land prices. Inflation may have been brought on by landowners who hold out for the monopoly price conferred by a planning decision to allocate land to one use rather than another. In addition, changes in the pattern of community development can make the planning decision obsolete, and formal amendments to the regulations may not be easy to achieve. Feedback is all too absent in American planning, in which departures from regulations such as zoning ordinances must be handled as exceptional cases rather than as part of a continuing and self-corrective administrative process.

The New Town Idea

Improvements in the legal machinery for implementing policy goals will have to proceed in two directions simultaneously. At the same time that substantive improvements are made in legal powers, a more adequate framework will have to be provided for the exercise of those powers. New town communities present an opportunity for innovation which should be able to assist us toward both objectives.

An outline of some of the potential of new town development for improving the quality of the urban environment should indicate the usefulness of this device. New towns may be defined as entire communities which are planned and built as a unit, and which are self-contained in the sense that they include commercial and often industrial areas in addition to residential neighborhoods. This provision for a community of balanced land uses distinguishes the new town from the large-scale subdivision. Planning and developing an entire community from the beginning should present many opportunities for achieving more adequate urban surroundings. For example, the new town can become an important component in a regionally based program for improving housing quality and for handling problems of population displacement arising out of urban renewal and highway programs; development policies in a new town can be set to provide for the desired racial and economic balance in housing mix. If industrial, residential, and commercial areas can be planned together, diseconomies in land utilization can be eliminated and the proper relationships among land uses established from the start. Efficiency of scale is one of the most important by-products of new towns. Adequate recreational, social, and educational programs all require a minimum scale of urban development, so that a new town can be planned at a level that will permit it to perform effectively in all of these fields.

An evaluation of the potentialities for new town development in American metropolitan areas is made easier by the postwar English experiment in new town building, and this experience will briefly be reviewed here. The development of an English new town begins with the selection of a site by the national Ministry of Housing and Local Government, which is responsible for housing and planning policy. Often the site has been indicated in advance through a plan for the region in which the new town is to be located. After the new town site has been designated by the ministry following a public hearing, a nationally controlled development corporation is appointed to carry out the physical development of the site. While the new town legislation contemplated private as well as public development within the new town area, English new towns in practice have been built almost entirely by the development corporations. The ministry appoints the board of the corporation and maintains an informal audit of its effectiveness. All of the money for development by the corporation comes from public funds, and both the housing ministry and the national treasury department have the authority to review the feasibility of development proposals by the corporation before an advance of money is given.

National supervision of the development corporations provides the critical leverage through which new town policies are implemented, and the statutory foundation for this control is the ministry's order designating the new town site. Under English planning legislation the development of the new town would normally be subject to the supervision of the county, which is the statutory development control agency outside the independent cities. The designation of the new town site alters this relationship, as it confers both regulatory and development powers on the new town corporation within the area that is designated as the new town. However, designation does not automatically vest title to the designated land in the development corporation, and land within the designated area must be acquired as it is needed.

The building of a new town begins with the preparation of a master plan, a document that is required by the Ministry of Housing but not by the statute. While a public hearing is held on the master plan, and while it receives informal ministerial sanction, it remains an unofficial document that serves primarily as a flexible guide for the growth of the new town community. Nor does approval of the master plan authorize the new town corporation to carry out its building program without further review. Following the preparation of the plan, each development proposal must be separately submitted to the ministry for review and approval.

These development proposals, called Section 6 proposals for the statutory provision under which they are submitted, may themselves differ widely in areal scope and in character, as the statutory language that requires them is not stringent. In most instances the Section 6 proposal covers a neighborhood or a subneighborhood. While the ministry has the statutory authority to approve any proposal by the development corporation, and while its only statutory obligation to the county planning authority is to consult with it, the planning authority has come to play an increasingly important role in the planning approval process.

If we pause for a moment to see how far we have come, we can see that the creation of more satisfactory implementary tools for community development requires consideration of several variables. The important policies for the region must be identified and assigned their place on the urban agenda. Certainly the provision of an adequate housing supply ranks high on any list, and the difficulties arising out of the relocation of families in American programs of public improvement assigns housing a high priority. English new towns are a partial answer to the housing supply problem. Housing needs are regional, however. They cross governmental boundaries and require intergovernmental solutions, and the English system of national control is one way of resolving the intergovernmental issue. Finally, as a planning and development technique that could speed and improve the execution of our national and regional planning policies the English new town program has many advantages. These advantages can be listed:

Direction: Two complementary controls, the designation order and the Section 6 proposal, give the ministry a strategic authority over the direction of new town development. Perhaps the critical element in the English program is this extreme centralization of authority. Not only are sites effectively selected by the national ministry (no site has ever been withdrawn), but the ministry participates as partner in the development of the new town and retains a veto over objections by the local planning authority. Important development objectives can be implemented in the new town program, and through its review of individual development proposals the ministry can make its decisions selectively applicable to individual neighborhoods.

Timing: Under the new town system, the development decision is taken concurrently with the planning decision and the difficulties that arise out of the delays that occur under American planning controls are avoided. Ad hoc decision-making is prevented by over-all planning for the new town community.

Flexibility: The informal character of the new town master plan allows it to guide the development corporation's program without straitjacketing it too rigidly. As concrete proposals come up through the Section 6 process, they provide a corrective feedback, which permits the master plan to be amended de facto as development progress requires, or as changes occur in policy.

Scale: In the new town program, land can be assembled on a scale that is sufficiently extensive to achieve a unified and effective site treatment, and that allows the new town communities to be treated as part of a regional plan. American planning has been geared instead to a smaller scale, which often lies below the neighborhood level. Only American zoning for planned residential development approximates the English new town scale.

Initiative: Under the English system, the initiative for development within a new town rests first with the national ministry and then with the development corporation, as almost all of the building within the town is done by the corporation. This method avoids the weaknesses of planning implementation through the use of regulatory powers, which must depend for their effectiveness on the response of private developers.

Concentration of powers: The development corporation and the designation device become a significant method for concentrating both positive development and negative control powers in a single administrative process that is applicable throughout the new town area. What is important is not only the use of a single corporate agency that can undertake development and also do over-all planning, but the use of the Section 6 proposal to adjust the planning aims of the development corporation and the planning aims of the local planning authority. No such machinery is available in the American planning system.

Creating a New Town Program for America

Assuming that the English new town program can be exported as an effective development technique for implementing planning objectives in a metropolitan setting and for short-circuiting the obstacles of fragmented government, then the form which this program will take in an American context is critical. The federal nature of the American governmental system makes impossible the wholesale transfer of the English program with no changes, if only because the scale of the American continent prevents the close planning which has characterized the English new town effort. In this section, three "models" for the implementation of a new town program for America will be outlined, ranging from the high governmental commitment that characterizes the English program, to minimum governmental commitment accompanied by a maximum of private initiative. The impact of each program will be analyzed in turn.

Option I: Maximum Governmental Commitment

The English new town program probably incorporates the maximum amount of governmental direction acceptable in any society that avoids direct limitations on population movement. This first option describes an American new town program that would imitate the heavy governmental commitment of English practice, and by concentrating control in a public agency would make it easier to implement planning and developmental goals. However, our federal system complicates the task of working out an effective program under this option.

The federal government would no doubt be involved in a public new towns program, as federal loans and grants would probably be made available. But the availability of federal aid creates complications in federal, state, and local relationships because governmental responsibility for program direction must be fixed. Conditions implementing federal policy would be attached to federal aid, but, since federal legislation will have to accommodate a wide variety of state and local objectives, the impact of federal control will be blunted. For example, federal legislation could require as a condition to the receipt of aid that there be a "proper balance" of housing in new towns so that they would serve a broad range of income groups. But federal administrators would have difficulty in dictating the nature of that balance, a decision that can have important local repercussions. Furthermore, the impact of federal standards will be limited by the fact that they are enforceable as a condition to federal assistance. Federal control would be exercisable only through the withdrawal and withholding of funds in cases of noncompliance, a remedy that has not proved effective in other programs.

New town controls would be most directly imposed through state legislation and state administration, and the broader and more ambiguous the federal law, the more scope there will be for state control. Explicit standards controlling the nature of new town development would be unlikely in a state statute, however, for fear that the program would be straitjacketed. As a result, the degree to which program goals are attained will depend heavily on the nature of the development agency that is selected and on the effectiveness of state supervision if a state agency is not used.

Under this option, a governmental agency would do most of the development on the new town site. In urban renewal, the program most closely analogous, the public development agency is locally initiated and is closely aligned to the municipal entity that gives it life. It is subject to federal but not usually to state supervision. For new towns, the use of municipalities or counties to establish the new town development authority would create obstacles not present in urban renewal. One problem is that the selection of the appropriate governmental unit to creat the agency would be complicated by competition among local governments and by differences in their size, efficiency, and capacity.

Considerations such as these led the English to choose a

nationally controlled development corporation to implement their new town program, but new town building by a national agency would not be acceptable in the American governmental context. In America, apart from a locally initiated agency, the alternatives are an agency functioning as part of the state government or an agency functioning at the regional level. Problems of two-tier control will arise if a regional agency is used, and state supervision of that agency's development plans would be critical. Delays in implementation and a division of responsibilities might inhibit the effectiveness of the program. A state agency would eliminate the problems of dual control, but its acceptability is open to question. A state-chartered public corporation on the English model seems most satisfactory, but it would have to be under close state supervision.

Additional problems are raised by the methods to be used for the development of land within new towns. Urban renewal project land is usually sold to private redevelopers, and continuing control is a matter of covenants and local ordinances. This method might conceivably work in urban renewal projects that are limited in area, but it has obvious deficiencies in new town communities which are built on an extensive scale, which take time to complete, and which must be carefully coordinated in their development during the execution stage. Indeed, the division of responsibility between the redeveloper and the local authority has come under increasing criticism in the urban renewal program. Maximum governmental control of development within new towns dictates retention of title coupled with leasehold control of land allocated for development purposes. Except in public housing, such close government control of project execution is new to the American scene, and the statutory framework for such a program would have to be carefully designed. Project results in public housing dictate caution.

Option II: Minimum Governmental Commitment

Problems accompanying the close government control of development within new towns would be alleviated by a program in which the initiative for site selection and development rested entirely with private developers subject to minimum government supervision. Absence of governmental involvement would also reduce delays and speed development. As contemplated by legislation recently introduced in Congress, a privately directed program would rely on federally insured loans under the sponsorship of the federal housing agency to provide the capital for community improvements within new towns. On the new town site the development agency would be a private developer.

Nevertheless, the availability of federally assisted financing again raises the issue of public controls, and we must ask how much freedom we can tolerate in private initiative consistent with the objectives of federal urban policy. For example, if meeting the housing needs of low-income groups is high on the urban agenda, then the availability of federally insured financing with no guarantee that the new town will contain a proper housing mix is open to question.

As a minimum, private developers in any program that receives federal benefits will be subject to a racial open-occupancy policy, and even private new towns will have to be racially integrated under the President's Equal Opportunity Order. Enforcement of the order against racial restrictions in private housing presently rests with the Federal Housing Administration, the federal mortgage-insuring agency. Experience so far indicates that any system of enforcement that operates on a complaint basis will have limited success, and more effective sanctions are yet to be found. Furthermore, if the housing available in the new town is priced in the upper ranges, the economic barriers to purchase and rental will prevent meaningful integration. While public development is certainly no guarantee of a more favorable racial policy, a public agency is more amenable to control. The racial question is only one of many. To touch on public policy issues at any point unravels a series of problems that become difficult to resolve without substantially circumscribing the developer's freedom.

Another issue that cannot be evaded even in private development is the problem of relating the new town to its urban setting. Federal agencies show increasing interest in coordinating federally assisted programs with one another, and federal aid is usually made contingent on local adoption of a comprehensive plan. Even an FHA-administered program of federally insured loans would probably have a comprehensive planning requirement attached to it. Again, the implementation of a planning requirement will substantially circumscribe the developer's freedom and will bring other problems in its wake. The very act of designating sites for new towns will confer a monopoly value on property which will make landowners reluctant to sell to new town entrepreneurs. Public agencies would have powers of compulsory acquisition, and while these powers could also be made available to private corporations, the desirability of such a delegation is open to question. Conferring powers of land assembly on a public agency with authority to resell to private developers would help cure this problem, but would mark a substantial departure from a program in which public participation is held to a minimum.

Many of the problems that have been reviewed here could be eliminated if private developers stayed clear of any form of governmental assistance. However, apart from the financing and land assembly difficulties that would be presented in such an endeavor, the question arises whether we can continue to allow so important a component in the development of our urban areas to go unregulated. A federal requirement that the public regulation of privately sponsored new towns be a part of any comprehensive program for metropolitan planning is certainly not unthinkable. Apart from statutory requirements, private new towns on an extensive scale might be subject to the prohibition which the Fourteenth Amendment places on racial discrimination. But the real difficulty is that private new town development, if left unregulated, is likely to gravitate toward the upper-income market and leave the housing needs of urban areas unresolved.

Option III: Public-Private Partnership

While each of the options already discussed requires some participation by both governmental and private enterprise, an intermediate form for the development of new towns would consciously attempt to create a balanced system in which both government and private industry play major roles. This program incorporates a division of responsibility between the public and private sector which recognizes the role that each is accustomed to perform. Public community-building on a large scale is simply not in accord with tradition in this country. A mixed program would make the important tool of public land acquisition available at the land-assembly stage, and would leave to private enterprise its traditional role of residential development.

This option would borrow heavily from the federally assisted urban renewal program, in which the public agency performs the major task of land assembly, clearance, and preparation for redevelopment, while the private redeveloper executes the major share of the project. A similar program could be fashioned for new towns. A state or regional development agency could select the site, assemble the land, and prepare the development plant. Land could be leased or most probably sold to private redevelopers, each of whom would carry out part of the total plan. Some part of the project, probably the low-cost housing and some or all of the commercial and industrial centers, could be carried out by the public agency. For example, the public agency might build, rent, and manage the town's major commercial center.

Unfortunately, to shift the major responsibility for development of the town to private enterprise would leave too much initiative to private developers. If the public agency may only plan the new town, and must await a private decision to invest, there may be substantial delays in execution and the final product may be distorted by market pressures.

Urban renewal already provides an example of both such byproducts, and the problems of delay and coordination will simply be aggravated if the arena is shifted to the new town scale. Some of the major deficiencies of existing controls, such as gaps in timing and the inability to compel new development, would be present in a new town program of this type.

Other problems would arise from the attempt to combine both public and private enterprise in the building of the new town community. If some residential areas are to be built for rental purposes by the public agency, a mixed market in housing will be created which will present serious problems of product pricing. The value of land will tend to appreciate substantially as the town is built, so that values will be much higher on the completion of the town than they were at the beginning. A basic issue is whether land prices should be controlled at their original level, in effect giving a subsidy to purchasers of housing and other land on the new town site. Price control presents difficult problems, and in a mixed market the problems of maintaining prices at the same level in both the public and private sector are extremely complex. While initial sales by private redevelopers might be controlled, the public agency would need some method of reviewing subsequent sales in order to prevent landowners from cashing in on rising prices. Controls of this kind would not be tolerable in our society.

Other equally serious problems will be presented by the developer who buys land within the new town for speculation, or who in good faith buys with the expectation of carrying out development but for financial or other reasons is unable to complete his project. While the public agency could be given the power to recover any land that is clearly being held for speculative purposes, the delays and difficulties incident to exercising such a power might prove damaging to the development of the community. Take-over powers in the public agency would enable it to complete any part of the town which was left unfinished, but the agency may find itself more involved in the development of the town than it likes. Legislation would probably afford a priority to private developers who wanted to complete the project, and they might well exert pressure to alter the original plans. Whoever undertakes the job of completion, an unfinished project always presents problems that are difficult to solve.

Form and Function: The Aims of a New Town Program

This discussion should indicate that much of what can be accomplished in a new town program will depend on the legal structure under which it is carried out. If most of the initiative for new town development rests with private enterprise, for example, the extent to which we can accomplish stated social objectives will be limited by what private developers think is profitable. Accordingly, the choice of objectives to be implemented in a new town program will have a direct bearing on the formal structure which is organized to carry it out. At least three policy problems can be isolated:

1. *The urban level at which the programs will be executed.* We have to decide whether we are concerned with the developmental framework within which the new town policy is implemented. New towns potentially can have a substantial effect on the comprehensive development of a state or region, so that the size of the new towns and their location become critical. Sufficient governmental involvement to implement regional developmental strategies will be needed once we decide that a decision on these strategies is important. When an urban region is interstate the problems are even more difficult, although, hopefully, the structure for metropolitan transportation planning which is emerging under the federal aid highway act will develop into a more comprehensive process for planning in interstate regions.

2. *The character of new town communities.* We have already alluded to the developmental possibilities of new town communities. The literature on the purpose and function of new towns is vague, but at least three possible objectives emerge. One is that the new town should function as a force in the development and structuring of its urban region, and in ful-

filling this role one of its principal purposes is to assist in the improvement of the housing supply. A second possible role emphasizes the amenity values of planning and building a new community as an entirety. A third conceivable role, and one which has been little explored, would see the new town as an economic development agency, especially in regions where new industry is needed.

The character and level of public and private participation in a new town program will tend to vary, depending on which of these functions is emphasized. For example, internal amenities can be as adequately supplied by a private as by a public development agency, while insuring the desired mix in housing types would require more public involvement. The use of new towns for purposes of economic development might also require considerable public commitment, at least in the way of subsidy and other possible incentives.

3. *The scale of the new town effort.* What impact the new towns have on their regions will depend in large part on the scale of the new town effort. Communities of adequate size and in sufficient numbers are also necessary to provide scope for racial and economic integration. Suggested federal legislation which speaks of a program for planned neighborhoods, subdivisions, and communities reflects ambiguity both about the character of the new towns and the scale on which they will be built. Privately developed new towns can achieve a scale of effort at which they will begin to have an impact on their region, but without public direction the privately developed towns might either be underbuilt or overbuilt.

Conclusion

This chapter has assessed the legal capacity of machinery for planning and development in light of three objectives: the quest for improvement in the quality of urban life, the search for a remedy for existing weaknesses in presently available implementary techniques, and the need to balance the advantages and disadvantages of governmental and private participation in new town planning and development programs. One conclusion that emerges from this discussion is that the limitations of existing governmental machinery, coupled with the deadlock among governmental units at the local and metropolitan level, seriously impede any real attempt to implement our development goals more effectively. New machinery that can overcome these limitations is badly needed, and the new town program is one method of achieving a breakthrough. While it possesses some of the disadvantages of any ad hoc solution to social problems, and so aggravates the existing fragmentation of governmental programs in the urban field, the possibilities for review at upper governmental levels at least provides the opportunity for a more comprehensive setting.

Yet the problems of putting together an effective new town program are complex, and I have no ready answers to the questions of power and responsibility that have been raised by this chapter. What is clear is that our problems have outrun our programs, and that program revision to take account of the new challenge will not be easy. We need a synoptic view of the urban process, and we need to think free of the restraints of inherited categories. Thoughtful consideration of the new town community as a development strategy is one way to begin this reassessment.

References

For English policy, see SIR FREDERICK OSBORN and ARNOLD WHITTICK, *The New Towns: The Answer to Megalopolis* (London, England, 1963); DANIEL R. MANDELKER, *Green Belts and Urban Growth: English Town and Country Planning in Action* (Madison, Wis., University of Wisconsin Press, 1962). On new towns and land planning generally, see "Symposium: New Towns," *Washington University Law Quarterly* 1965 (February, 1965), 1–104; CHARLES M. HAAR (ed.) *Law and Land: Anglo-American Planning Practice* (Cambridge, Mass., Harvard University Press, 1964).

RESPONSIVE URBAN SERVICES

CHAPTER THIRTEEN

TOWARD A FRAMEWORK FOR URBAN PUBLIC MANAGEMENT

Wilbur R. Thompson

Metropolitan problems only in part reflect a lack of municipal financial resources. As much these problems reflect a steadfast denial of the need for entrepreneurial talent and expert management in municipal affairs. Using a price analysis of land-use planning and education problems, Professor Thompson shows how the urban public economy could be made to complement the private economy and to compete efficiently with it in the supply of public services.

Despite the headlines of the daily newspapers the economic problems of the large urban area are not responsive to Chamber of Commerce business chasing. Rather, economic progress in a metropolitan region will come from programs that enhance the productivity of the area. Small towns and cities living off one or two industries perhaps should struggle for new firms to achieve "balanced growth," but the industrial mix of a large American city is roughly as balanced and diversified as the U. S. economy itself.

Metropolitan areas with populations of a million or over tend to mix industries with very diverse growth rates, wage rates, and cycle patterns in roughly the national proportions. But the

Wilbur R. Thompson is a Professor of Economics at Wayne State University and former Director of the Committee on Urban Economics of Resources for the Future, Inc. He is the author of *A Preface to Urban Economics* (1965).

healing salve of moderate, stable growth cumulates in great size and creates new and intensely difficult problems in urban public management. If the challenge of the small urban area is how to grow, the challenge of the large urban area is how to handle the product of inexorable growth: great city size. This paper is offered as a modest contribution to the new profession of urban public management in very large metropolitan areas.

The fact that the diversified large urban area tends to grow stably and produces a roughly national-average income performance should not be interpreted to mean that affluence, equity and stability are no longer central goals, only that manipulating the local industrial-mix is not a realistic means to achieving them. The large urban area progresses not by outmaneuvering other urban areas for the most prized industries but rather by programs that enhance local productivity, much in the fashion of national economic policy. The rational management of our cities is, in fact, the essence of national growth policy.

The fact that we measure gross national product at the national level leads to the illusion that it is produced there. Output is produced and income is generated in very discrete factories, offices, and stores, located in distinct communities from which they draw workers who reflect the quality of local neighborhoods and schools, and from which they draw business services that reflect the general efficiency of the local economy. To the extent, then, that we build cities that are more conducive to good resource allocation, human development, capital formation, and enterprise, not only the local populace but the nation as well is enriched, especially to the degree that local innovations and practices can be copied elsewhere. In very real terms, as well as in a formal way, the gross national product is summed up from the parts to the whole. Our charge here is to look to the ways in which urban public management can create cities that are (*a*) more efficient workplaces, (*b*) more pleasant places to live, and (*c*) ever-better arenas for personal expression and development.

So large a subject matter cannot, of course, be squeezed into so short a paper. An attempt will be made to cast only the loosest net over some of the more powerful and promising reaches of urban public management. Specifically, the role of price, the importance of land-use planning, the provision of local public services, and finally the place of information, analyses, and innovation will be examined. While a policy orientation will be maintained throughout, staying largely to educational policy for brevity, the objective is to impart some feeling for the need to pursue a comprehensive approach, and certainly not to attain an operational status for any of the programs to be sketched here.

Rationalizing the Urban Price Structure

The city is such a dramatic land form that even close students of the city often fail to "see" the city as a highly complex network of relative prices. This is not surprising because many, even most, of the prices that push and pull at the form of the city are hidden or implicit prices. At the risk of simply exposing the economist's bias, the hypothesis is offered that this subterranean maze of rewards and penalties is the single most powerful force in shaping our urban life and is the root of many urban "problems." Moreover, not only have the "prices" of public services, utilities, land use, and movement about the urban area not been set, explicitly and rationally, by the public managers, but this group typically neither knows the structure nor appreciates the power of the instrument they unthinkingly manipulate.

The same "price" is usually charged for running water or sewers to a new householder regardless of whether he chooses to site his house near to or far from existing pumping stations. (Each household needs the equivalent of, say, ¾ inch of pipe cross section all the way back to the pumping station, regardless of whether it is aggregated with others into a trunk line for economies of scale over part of the trip.) Again, the motorist is subject to the same user charge for the extremely expensive system of streets, bridges, tunnels, and traffic controls he enjoys, regardless of whether he chooses to drive downtown at the rush hour and thereby pushes against peak capacity or at off-peak times when it costs little or nothing to serve him. To compound this distortion of prices, we set the price near zero (depending on how gasoline taxes are rationalized) and treat the scarcest urban factor of all — space — as if it were a free good.

None of this denies that pricing urban public services would be very difficult and in many cases impossible. Economists have, in fact, erected a very elegant rationalization of the public economy almost wholly on the base of the nonmarketability of public goods and services. The public economy is, for example, assigned the provision of those goods which are so indivisible that they must be collectively consumed (e.g., justice, public safety) and since individual benefits cannot be determined, nor can voluntary payment be relied on when exclusion from consumption is impracticable, compulsory payment (taxation) becomes mandatory and government responsibility is indicated. Again, because some goods are considered to be especially meritorious, we may elect to subsidize them to increase consumption of them (e.g., education, museums), and subsidies are often handled most easily through direct government provision of the service.

Where in the case of "merit goods" the majority induce ("coerce" through price) the minority to change their *personal* spending habits to a more *socially* beneficial (acceptable?) one, we can distinguish a separate rationale for public enterprise in the provision of those public services designed expressly for the poor. *Market prices* are clearly inappropriate for any public service that is designed to redistribute income in kind (e.g., social case work, unemployment counseling). In sum, the private market may not be able to process certain goods and services (pure "public goods"), or it may give the "wrong" prices ("merit goods"), or we simply do not want the consumer to pay (income-redistributive services).

But the virtual elimination of price from the public sector

is an extreme and highly simplistic response to the need to create a very sophisticated public price structure. Merit goods may be subsidized without going all of the way to a zero price. Few would argue for full-cost admission prices to museums, but a good case can be made for moderate prices that cover, say, their daily operating costs (e.g., salaries of guards and janitors, heat and light). This case is fortified by the fact that it is the middle- and upper-income classes who typically visit museums, so that free admission becomes, in effect, redistribution toward greater inequality, to the extent that the lower-income, nonusers pay local taxes (e.g., property taxes directly or indirectly through rent, local sales taxes). The low prices contemplated are not, moreover, likely to discourage attendance significantly, and the resolution of special cases (e.g., student passes) seem well within our competence.

"Free" public outdoor recreation facilities are probably even less defensible, especially when the user arrives by automobile, lugging several hundred dollars' worth of essential equipment (boats, tents, and portable TV sets) with which to complement the free public recreation facility. Full-cost prices may even be within the range of reason in such cases. The small, slum-neighborhood playground is clearly a very different matter.

Other pricing decisions that call for professional skill and ingenuity can be imagined. We may wish to subsidize a presumed merit good only for a limited period of time in the hope that by shifting spending patterns toward this good we may induce a learning experience which will shift basic tastes toward the good and permit eventual elimination of the subsidy. Below-cost prices for rapid mass transit could attract new riders, educate them to the advantages of a carefree journey to work, and perhaps increase the demand for public transportation. This is akin to "promotional pricing" as practiced in the private economy.

We may even find a place for user charges in public services rendered specifically to the poor. Social work agencies have often found that a nominal price for a virtually free service increases both the self-respect of the recipient and respect for the valuableness of the service. We might consider increasing our public assistance payments and charging *nominal* prices for public health services, family services, personal counseling, and for some surplus food.

Clearly, such an elaborate strategy of public price-making would call for professional competence not now available to city government — the new post of "city economist" seems indicated, a point to which we will return below. But the potential gains would seem to justify the effort. With local public expenditures pressing local tax sources unrelentingly, we need to save scarce tax money for those public purposes for which only tax revenue is appropriate, such as to finance new and more "public goods" and redistributive functions. To the degree that we could extract significant amounts of money here and there through select user charges, we would be able better to feed the "starved public sector" and to carry on various antipoverty programs.

Even granting that an imminent large federal government surplus may lead to a sharing of these revenues with states and localities, as brought out earlier by Weidenbaum, "a penny saved is a penny earned." Besides, we should not spend this impending bonanza prematurely. The secret to the great financial success of the federal government lies largely in the simple facts of a rising per capita money income, generated out of both real productivity gains and inflation, coupled to an income tax with a progressive rate structure, expressed in fixed, absolute dollar values. Thus as our incomes rise, whether due to real increases or merely to inflation, and even if our relative income position remains the same, we move into a wealthier tax bracket. It is more than a remote possibility that tax rates will be cut repeatedly over the coming decades. Even if the odds do favor significant redistribution of tax revenue from the federal to the state and local level, the great public needs of metropolitan area living dictate the exploitation of all promising revenue sources and user charges are one of the most promising.

Modifying the Urban Spatial Pattern

The land-use pattern of the city has attracted a modest amount of scholarly interest — city planners, geographers, social ecologists, and urban land economists. Most of the literature focuses on the location of industrial and commercial patterns and treats residential land use almost as a residual, gross aggregate; houses fill in the spaces between the key factory, office, and store sites. We have come recently, however, to appreciate the great social significance of the residential pattern, especially its form by socioeconomic class. The small city encompasses both rich and poor and, on this broad base of culture and tax-paying ability, builds good schools. But what was, at small scale, the relatively innocuous practice of clustering homes by size and value becomes, at great size, virtually complete socioeconomic segregation, as first grade-school and finally even high-school districts are exhausted by these ever-enlarging homogeneous enclaves. Not only does the slum child attend only slum schools (and the children of the affluent meet only "their kind"), but political fragmentation divorces tax base from public service needs and reinforces the cultural disparities within the metropolitan school system with great financial inequalities. The public school is, therefore, rapidly losing its traditional role of redressing the great inequalities in home and neighborhood life that obstruct attainment of the goal of equal opportunity. For perhaps one tenth of the population of our large metropolitan areas, equal opportunity is a myth and a mockery.

Perhaps no challenge confronting the urban public managers is as grave or as difficult as that of rearranging the residential form of the large metropolitan area to regain some reasonable momentum toward the goal of equal opportunity. The grand strategy is clear: we must attract some of the affluent back into the central city and move some of the poor to the suburbs. A promising set of tactics to achieve this is not nearly so clear. Surely though, some form of "urban renewal" is a logical element. Gross mistakes in timing the destruction of slum properties, too strong a bias toward downtown real estate values and urban aesthetics, and other sins of the past should not blind us to the potential that is inherent in fresh renewal strategies. We might, for example, experiment with renewing public facilities — social overhead — in our core areas. Better public schools, parks, and libraries — not just better than before but better than those existing in suburbia—might induce those families that place the least premium on cultural homogeneity and/or are least afraid of "strangers" to return. If we are to use taxpayers' money to subsidize core area renewal, a better case can be made for buying the pioneering of hardier souls by offering superior public services to all core area residents than for subsidizing luxury apartments (via the write-down of land values). Those who are most adverse to living near low-income families should be made aware of the need to provide some cross-cultural contacts and at least be willing to support extra rewards in the form of extra-high-quality public services to those less disinclined than they to take on the serious responsibility of serving as leaders and models.

Equally great potential for re-creating cross-cultural contact and responsible local public finance in large, politically fragmented metropolitan areas lies in the emergence of the large-scale residential construction company. We may well be at the beginning of an era of big builders creating indigenous variants of the British "New Town." The potential for creating new mixed-income communities in these satellites lies in the possibility that an integrated planning of house and community may produce a new living arrangement so attractive (or at least so fashionable) that socioeconomic heterogeneity is accepted as a price worth paying for a house and community in matched set. If, then, the state or its agent — a newly created metropolitan area housing authority, perhaps — were to approve large-tract new towns only if they embraced a very wide range of housing values, we might make considerable progress toward socioeconomic *re*integration within a few decades.

The tactics of establishing and maintaining "balanced" communities would need to be quite sophisticated. Since we have not learned how to build new houses priced within reach of the low-income family, do we resort to public housing or rent subsidies to house the poor? Or should we be content to begin with a slightly truncated range of high to low-middle-income housing and fill out the income spectrum in time, as the houses age, and filter down to lower-income families? Such a strategy would have the virtue of being more acceptable during the critical early stages and providing a more graceful transition to full cross-cultural contact. In such cases, the new towns would have to be built in stages so that new housing would be available at all times, to ensure the retention of the more affluent. In addition, continual construction and demolition — a widespread age distribution of housing — further ensures that the community will not be left with all old housing — massive blight — at some future time. In any event, the objective of creating socioeconomic heterogeneity at the high-school district level, at the least, is certainly not new and untried nor radical. If anything, such a program may be a bit romantic — a call to return to turn-of-the-century, small town America.

The Provision of Local Public Services

Another powerful lever in the hands of urban public management is control over the quantity and quality of local public services. The complementarity between the relative level of certain critical public services and the residential land-use pattern was suggested earlier: superior local public services might be used to lure middle- and upper-income families back into the central city. Better schools in the core area could, for example, become the means of creating a new population mix that could, in turn, be a significant step toward a better school system throughout the whole urban area.

Fiscal transfers from the outside would almost certainly be needed to finance superior education in the core area. In the context discussed above, the implication was that this would be federal money — a substitute for the federal subsidy in the write-down of land values in the current urban renewal program. Suppose we let this stand for now, and pursue instead the strategy most appropriate to regain for public education its traditional role as the great equalizer. How might a higher level of educational exenditures per pupil in the central city, however financed, be best managed to exert the greatest leverage toward equality of opportunity?

Certainly, the first reaction is likely to be a preference for reducing class sizes, recognizing thereby the value of greater personal attention for students who receive little or no education and guidance outside the classroom. But less obvious and certainly more controversial would be to apply the principles set forth earlier: price differentials to reverse current public service differentials. It is quite possible that higher salaries for teaching in slum schools would be an even better way to spend the higher school budgets. The better school teachers usually face the greater range of choice in post, and it would be surprising if they did not choose the pleasanter places to work much more often than not. Again, the more experienced teachers invariably graduate to the newer schools in the better neighborhoods after serving a brief apprenticeship in the older schools of the low-income areas.

Egalitarianism in the public school system has been overdone; even the army recognizes the role of price when it awards extra "jump pay" to paratroopers, only a slightly more hazardous occupation than teaching behind the lines. Besides, it is male teachers whom we need to attract to slum schools, both to serve as father figures where there are few males at home and to serve quite literally as disciplinarians. It is bad economics to insist on equal pay for teachers everywhere throughout the urban area when males have a higher productivity in some areas and when males have better employment opportunities outside of teaching — higher "opportunity costs" that raise their supply price. It is downright silly to argue that "equal pay for equal work" is achieved by paying the same money wage in the slums as in the suburbs. Even under the new Civil Rights law, which extends the prohibition against discrimination in employment from race to sex, no school system should hesitate to advertise *premium* salaries for teachers in slum schools under the "*Male Help Wanted*" column heading.

Further, price strategy may be supplemented with spatial strategy in the planning of better educational services. Even if it be granted that only by breaking up the great ghettos that are forming in our large metropolitan areas can equal educational opportunity be arranged, houses are a most durable good, so that even if hardened attitudes about socioeconomic mixing could be softened overnight, it would take years to attain integrated *neighborhood* schools. As a transitional device, the bussing of students to schools in neighborhoods culturally different from their own has been advocated, and some hesitant experimenting has begun. Too much should not be expected of this tactic, for our big city ghettos have grown so large that very long hauls would be necessary to go much beyond token mixing at the margins. Also, the low-income nonwhite school population in many central cities has already attained majority status, so that student exchanges between municipalities would be required to achieve significant mixing, a far more difficult objective. And our core area ghettos are still growing in size. Still, even if bussing is only a palliative in itself, it is a beginning, and a good experience in the few mixed schools that do evolve would serve to reduce unfounded fears of the unknown and soften resistance to the basic land reforms discussed above (e.g., income-balanced new towns).

Another spatial strategy designed to diversify student bodies is the creation of very large "educational parks" which serve this end simply by drawing students from school districts so large that no single socioeconomic group would be large enough to fill so extensive an area. Because we seek to promote not only more equal educational opportunity but also greater opportunity for all, a variation of this latter theme would be to establish specialized high schools that would draw from the whole metropolitan area, one emphasizing natural science, another social science, a third humanities, a fourth vocational education. Granting a tendency toward segregation in occupational orientation that reflects cultural background, as upper-class youths choose science, and lower-class ones choose vocational education more than proportionately, the prospect still remains that such cultural patterning would be less sharp than the residential patterning, on which base we now segregate. Moreover, the natural science high school could run the gamut from advanced physics to routine laboratory technique and achieve some cross-cultural contact in music and drama classes, physical education, and extracurricular activities at the very minimum. The inducement to suffer longer bus rides to school would be the simple but powerful fact that these schools would provide better preparation for college than do the comprehensive high schools with which they would compete. This is not trivial in a time of growing competition to gain entrance to college.

Information, Analysis and Entrepreneurship

The supply of information is critical to the organization and operation of the urban economy. Urban economics is distinctive in the emphasis that it places on the public sector, and decision-making in that arena is a very demanding business. We lack a satisfying theory of demand appropriate to the public sector or even good operational guides. Moreover, the information base necessary to implement an even moderately sophisticated set of decision rules is lacking. What urban public manager can specify even roughly the full private and social costs of a major public program or project? A decision for or against rapid mass transit has powerful effects on the form of the city, the budgets of the many political subdivisions, private property values, school districts and school populations, public investments in social overhead, location of business and industry, and employment and commuting patterns. What city administration has the in-house research capability needed to derive the relevant "prices" so that the electorate can make the proper "consumption" decision?

Again, have we explicitly elected to have a few very large

slums instead of many smaller ones from the base of (nearly) full knowledge of the long-run social as well as private costs and benefits associated with these two very different residential spatial patterns? We need to choose, in an explicit and informed way, the appropriate size of municipalities and other socioeconomic subdivisions of the metropolitan area.

The majority of the inhabitants of our very large metropolitan areas seem to prefer (*a*) very small local government, (*b*) financially independent local government, (*c*) residential patterns that cluster homes by income class, and (*d*) minimum standards in public service for all persons in the metropolitan area. All four preferences cannot be satisfied; the four conditions are not mutually consistent. Minimum public service levels can be financed throughout the metropolitan area only by consolidating small governments to mix different tax bases and public service needs (i.e., by giving up *a*) or by mixing the homes of the rich and poor at finer grain than we now practice to achieve a similar blending of fiscal needs and resources (*c*) or by arranging intergovernmental transfers, probably from above (*b*). We are a long way from assembling the data base, the research staff, and the public managers necessary to carry this message loud and clear to the electorate.

It has become quite fashionable to call for a local "data bank," and this is clearly a step in the right direction, but a mass of data is an intermediate product and no more, until it has been shaped by skilled analysts. The rationalization of the urban public economy will require much careful measurement, continual metering of change, construction of elaborate decision-making "accounts" that embrace social as well as private costs and benefits, formulation of sophisticated, machine-sensitive mathematical models that simulate the processes of the city, and decision models that trace out the likely ramifications of alternative policies and paths of development.

Assembling adequate in-house research capability in the public sector is no small matter. Consider, for example, the post of "city economist"; it is simply incredible that such a post almost literally does not exist. The author has been struck by the fact that the large automobile companies employ dozens of economists while the City of Detroit operates without benefit of a single, fully professional economist. This paradox borders on a travesty when one recalls that economics is a social science and the economist's skills are transferable to business only at significant discount. (This in no way denies the shrewd rationality of business in using the doctorate in economics as a proxy for intelligence, diligence, and above all persistence.) To turn the question around, if the automobile companies were required to operate within the salary structure of the City of Detroit, one wonders if they could make a car that would run. And the modern metropolis is a device infinitely more complicated than the automobile.

Certainly, one can explain this sorry state. Private business is exposed to at least some degree of competition (and/or product substitution) and must maintain a reasonable degree of efficiency to survive, while the local public economy is a near monopolist—and is a complete monopolist of the given piece of real estate on which it is sited. And since neither political party has threatened to apply expertise to local government, even political competition does not pose any threat to business as usual. The high salaries that would be needed to attract a first-class economist or other social scientist would, in fact, upset the orderly salary structure now in being and cause more than a little disruption and probably be a net political liability, at least at the outset.

Professional salaries competitive with private enterprise and enough above universities to attract very able "experts" would, of course, also touch off invidious comparisons among the electorate. The hope would have to be that "tax-economy leagues" could be sold on the proposition that, in the long run, a $20,000 professional would be cheaper than a $12,000 semiprofessional, and might often replace two of the latter. Pouring concrete in the wrong place is very expensive. If one could make just one key structural change in the city, a good case could be made for raising the salaries of just a handful of some old and some new posts in city government, even if this might mean overpaying the holders of those jobs for the first round. (There is, in fact, something to be said for encouraging mediocre legislators to raise their own salaries in the hope that they will thereby promote their own early retirement.)

But efficiency alone is not enough. As much as we would surely gain from a sharper quantification of the costs and benefits of alternative policies and/or paths of development, we probably stand to gain even more by breaking the existing technological and organizational parameters with scientific and social inventions and innovations. The business of managing our cities would seem to be the last holdout in this age of institutionalized research and development. Not only might the urban public economy do well to emulate private enterprise in forcing invention and product development with regularly budgeted sums for R&D, but it is almost mandatory that it do so to maintain technological and organizational complementarity and competitiveness with the private economy.

The Galbraithian paradox of private opulence amidst public squalor is probably as much a reflection of lackluster public enterprise as it is an underdeveloped sense of community. We have long accepted the notion that an affluent society with large holdings of discretionary income may independently *demand* many products and services. At the same time this society may be *sold* many other products and services for which demand has to be created. To date, the local public economy must be counted an unimaginative producer-designer and an unaggressive merchandizer, at least by Madison Avenue standards. Clearly, public mass transit is a weak contender for the crown of the private automobile industry and public housing has lost most of its early friends through debilitating form and dreary design.

If the public economy needs any element more desperately than it needs experts, it surely is entrepreneurs — social inventors, and promoters, in the best sense. Ideally, the urban public economy would have met the private economy's creation of the automobile with a complementary structure of relative prices (tolls, licenses, and parking fees) graduated by distance, time, direction, and mode of travel, and alternative mass transit vehicles of such high quality that the net advantages of this magnificent invention would have proved even greater than it has. Until we create a public economy that can effectively complement and vigorously compete with the private economy, we shall continue to have "urban problems" that are really little more than great disparities in talent between the private and public sectors of the urban economy.

The call for a more imaginative and aggressive group of urban public managers is not made from a base of innocence. Of course, mayors and councilmen shy away from being brave innovators; the electorate tends to vote against rather than for candidates and issues, and the prudent course of action is inaction. The scripts of the campaign speeches are documentation enough. Still, recognition of this fact of political life can only mean that we have to reach even higher in the ranks of talent to find public entrepreneurs that are as persuasive at selling new programs to the electorate as they are imaginative at designing novel ones. From this economist's point of view, the price most in need of change is the one we pay for urban public management — in order to enlist expertise and entrepreneurship to operate the most marvelous machinery ever created by man: the great city.

References

These thoughts are extensions of material drawn from a much larger and more comprehensive work by the author. See, Wilbur R. Thompson, A *Preface to Urban Economics* (Baltimore Md.: The Johns Hopkins Press, 1965).

The two most comprehensive works on urban economics are the nine volumes of the New York Metropolitan Region Study and the four volumes of the closely following Economic Study of the Pittsburgh Region. In both cases the results are summarized in the last volume of the series. See, Raymond Vernon, *Metropolis 1985* (Cambridge, Mass.: Harvard University Press, 1960, reprinted as a Doubleday Anchor Book, Garden City, New York, 1963); Pittsburgh Regional Planning Association, *Economic Study of the Pittsburgh Region* Vol. 3 (Pittsburgh, 1963).

A good collection of reprinted articles on selected subjects in urban economics has been recently published. See, Benjamin Chinitz (ed.), *City and Suburb: The Economics of Metropolitan Growth* (Englewood Cliffs, N.J.: Prentice-Hall, Inc., 1964, a Spectrum Book).

The precursor of the new field of urban economics is the much older and narrower field of urban land economics. A good statement of this rich tradition is to be found in Richard U. Ratcliff, *Urban Land Economics* (New York: McGraw-Hill Book Company, 1949).

CHAPTER FOURTEEN

URBAN EDUCATION IN LONG-TERM CRISIS

Judson T. Shaplin

Big-city school systems are already strained beyond their capacity to offer all their pupils a decent education. Problems of integration, lack of money, and undermanned teaching and administrative staffs have burdened these schools and will for years. Crash programs may obscure these enduring problems of urban education while the piling of nonacademic functions on the schools may further weaken their teaching function. Dr. Shaplin reviews the necessary conditions for improved city education and suggests a strategy of cooperation between school systems and supporting outside institutions.

The urban public schools, and particularly the schools of the inner city, are in deep trouble. Nowhere have the proposals for improvement been of a magnitude sufficient even to halt the decline of quality in the schools. Further, the schools are once again caught in crosscurrents of conflicting values and thus start anew the search for identity and clearly defined functions as society makes new demands.

Our urban schools face a complexity and difficulty of interrelated problems that defy solution. The urban population is changing and increasing rapidly, bringing into the schools greater proportions of the poor and of minority groups. It is

Judson T. Shaplin is Professor of Education and Director of the Graduate Institute of Education, Washington University, a senior education consultant in overseas work to the Ford Foundation, and a former city school committeeman. He is the author of *Team Teaching* (1964).

becoming increasingly difficult to obtain financing for the necessary expansion of the schools, to say nothing of the needed qualitative improvements. In addition, all of the related social service and social welfare agencies which support the children of the cities are in similar trouble, for the same reasons. New conditions of inequality of opportunity, in basic conditions of living and in education, are being created at a pace with which our current institutions cannot cope.

After three decades of special concern with the education of the gifted and "academically able" students, the attention of our schools is turning toward these massive problems of educational inequality. Since the late 1950's, and with ever-increasing intensity, now given impetus by the rising demands of the civil rights movement and the specter of increasing unemployment, we are becoming more and more aware of the extent and effects of poverty.

A new educational ideology or "fashion" is on the march, with a new terminology. We are now concerned about the "culturally deprived" or the "culturally disadvantaged." The ideology, based partly on research, states that we must reach the culturally disadvantaged youth, if not in the preschool years, then in the early school years, prior to alienation from school and from society. For older youth, counseling, training, and a variety of types of work experience are prescribed. We are turning to the school again as the one agency through which a majority of the children can be reached, and once again we are talking about special school programs with concerns for minority status, physical and mental health, family and social welfare, vocational training and employment, counseling and guidance.

Once again we are faced with the question of whether the public schools will be asked to handle these problems, or whether the schools can maintain a primary function of the development of intellectual skills and knowledge while society builds new and strong institutions, parallel and related to the schools but designed more specifically to meet the problems. This is the major question to be examined in this paper. The future quality of urban life depends greatly upon whether we can build new quality into our urban schools and whether we can create new and permanent institutions.

The Presidential and federal concept of a "War on Poverty" seems peculiarly inappropriate to the long-term social problems of the poor, though the sense of urgency and crisis conveyed is probably necessary to gain legislative approval. We are a nation of optimists and tend to hope that wars will be short in duration. The intent of recent federal legislation seems to be to initiate programs and then rapidly to shift responsibility to local and state levels. Political assurances are made that there will be immediately beneficial effects upon unemployment. Three lines of analysis suggest, however, that, if we are engaged in a war, we had better think of a Hundred Years' War.

1. Population Migration

With the long-term migration of the rural poor to the nation's metropolitan centers and an accompanying migration of the relatively prosperous and highly skilled to the suburbs, we may expect a further concentration in the inner city of the poor, the lower classes, and the unskilled. The inner-city schools must increasingly serve the economically and socially disadvantaged. All the attendant educational problems: poor language skills, poor motivation, punishment and alienation in the schools, early drop-out, and resultant unemployment are plaguing urban systems.

The situation is further complicated by the sharp residential lines which have been drawn for the Negro population and their consequent concentration into restricted and overcrowded areas. The continued in-migration of Negroes into the city and the out-migration of whites, coupled with the high birth rate of Negro families, provide an explosive quality to the overcrowded and growing Negro ghettos.

In the city of St. Louis, taken as an example of urban change, where more than 57 percent of the school population is already Negro, there is now a fairly steady annual gain in the system of 3,300 Negro pupils, with a loss of 1,100 white pupils, representing a net increase of 2,200 pupils annually. Population changes of this magnitude have catastrophic effects upon a school system, particularly when the residential lines are drawn sharply. In areas of greatest recent mobility, schools have turned from completely white to almost completely Negro within the span of a year or two, with a massive turnover of a large sector of the city in a five-year period. This has meant crowded schools, the bussing of large numbers of pupils to distant schools, the construction of supplementary buildings on the playgrounds of existing schools as well as large-scale new construction, and, of course, an exacerbation of educational problems with children.

A major effect of this population growth and migration has been retrogression with respect to residential and school integration. As Professor Wylie H. Davis states it, "On balance, de facto segregation in St. Louis public schools has patently worsened during the last seven years."[1] In the years immediately following the 1954 Supreme Court Decision, St. Louis was held up as a model for efforts in school integration. Since then, the forces of social change have wiped out all earlier gains and dwarfed present efforts, and there is no sign of relief. The same pattern of segregation is being repeated in all the nation's large cities.

2. *Financing the Public Schools in Urban Areas*

It is becoming increasingly difficult for the urban schools to obtain the money necessary to expand to meet the population growth and to provide the special facilities needed for the types of children now coming to them in large numbers. Help may be coming from federal sources under the new education legis-

[1] *Civil Rights U.S.A.—Public Schools North and West 1962*, Staff Reports Submitted to the United States Commission on Civil Rights, pp. 250–309.

lation, but it remains to be seen whether these funds can be applied to the central functions of the school or whether they will support supplemental and new functions.

The urban areas pay much more of the cost of public education locally and receive a smaller proportion of state and federal support than other school districts within their states. Further, most of the local revenue is derived from property taxes. Today 83.9 percent of the local school revenue in St. Louis comes from the property tax. The state programs of financial support do not recognize differences in costs for the various levels of educational programs and for special programs such as trade and technical education, classes for handicapped children, and evening and extension courses. Vocational and technical programs cost on the average 80 percent more per pupil than the elementary school program, and education for the handicapped is twice as expensive as that for the average elementary pupil. St. Louis in 1962–1963 served only 12 percent of the total public-school enrollment of Missouri but served 67.6 percent of those pupils in the state enrolled in vocational, trade, and technical schools. We can predict that needs for schools of these types will increase in the future in urban areas.

In many of the great urban areas, the taxable assessed valuation has actually decreased in recent times; and where there is an increase, it is less than in the rest of the state. St. Louis has shown a recent increase over a five-year period of 1.1 percent compared with a 15 percent increase in the rest of the state. The gain in school enrollment in a comparable period, however, was much greater; St. Louis has shown a loss of 10.6 percent over five years in per-pupil assessed valuation, whereas the rest of the state has shown a 3.1 percent increase.

In Missouri, as in other states, school districts find it extremely difficult to obtain tax rate increases, all of which must be approved by simple majority vote and some by two-thirds majority, and to pass bond issues, which must be approved by a two-thirds majority. There are many "submerged" issues in the elections. In St. Louis, for example, is a white majority population composed in large part of persons without school-age children or with children in the parochial schools likely to approve tax increases on bond issues when it is clear that the main benefits will go to a majority Negro population in the schools? Yet the loss of an election has drastic results. St. Louis lost four successive bond issue elections in 1960 and 1962, finally gaining approval in March 1962 with a greatly reduced and minimum bond issue request. In the meantime, the over-crowding of pupils required the rental of church facilities, the remodeling of existing minimum facilities, and large-scale bus-sing of pupils into schools in distant areas. Some of the suburbs, particularly those with working-class population, have similar problems. The repeated loss of bond issues and tax increases there has led to the abandonment of kindergartens, to double sessions in the schools, and to the charging of pupils for text-books.

Thirteen school districts in the suburban county spend more than the city per pupil, though only five have higher assessed valuation per pupil. The city effort thus is less compared with the county. Within the city itself, a determined effort has been made to provide equal treatment for all schools, so there are no gross distortions of expenditure between schools and districts; conversely, there is also no additional expenditure for schools with concentrated populations of culturally disadvan-taged youth, either at the elementary or secondary school level.

Summarizing the financial difficulties, we may say that both the cities and the states in which they are located have a capacity for greater effort, but a complex of political factors makes citizens unwilling to vote for increased support. Up to this point, the federal effort has been relatively small. The increased revenue available to the cities is not sufficient to keep pace with their growth and is totally insufficient to make significant inroads on the needs of the culturally disadvantaged in the war on poverty. All the financial evidence suggests long-term and increasing difficulties, which can only be met by increased support from local, state, and federal sources.

3. *Changing Policies of the Parochial Schools*

For many decades the urban public schools have had a partner in the education of city children, including the culturally disadvantaged in the inner city: the Roman Catholic school system. True, the parochial schools have been unequal partners, without access to public funds. In the 1950–1960 decade, nationally the Catholic school system grew at a 50 percent greater rate than the public schools, and this growth, of course, was concentrated in the large metropolitan areas. Now the situation is changing radically and the public schools are losing their partner, with the result that the public schools will be required to handle most of the future population growth, particularly among the culturally disadvantaged in the inner city, with the additional acute possibility that the public schools will also receive transfers from the Catholic schools of large numbers of elementary school children.

The Catholic school system faces an increasing financial and organizational crisis. Rising costs of construction have been a ban to expansion. Parochial school pupil-teacher ratios have been maintained at high levels during the expansion period, often forty-five to sixty pupils per teacher; now there is a growing desire for smaller classes and qualitative improvement. The Catholic school parent has been faced with both the rising costs of public education based on property taxes and the rising tuition costs of the Catholic schools. Particularly striking is the decline of the percentage of the religious serving as teachers in the Catholic schools in relation to the increased use of salaried lay teachers, for teachers' salaries are always the major item in a school budget. In the Boston area, where the percentage of the religious in teaching has been maintained at the highest level, the ratio of religious to lay teachers has dropped from twenty-five to one in the immediate post-war period to five to one at the present time. In the St. Louis–St. Louis County area, where approximately 29 percent of the children attend Catholic schools, the ratio of religious to lay teachers is less than two to one. The Catholic school system also faces the same critical problem of dislocation of school facilities that the public schools do, as white Catholic parents move to the suburbs, leaving behind empty classrooms in the urban parochial schools.

Partly as a result of these factors and partly because of changing views regarding the appropriateness of the public schools for Catholic children, basic changes have been taking place in Catholic school policies. In a number of areas, including St. Louis, bans have been placed upon the construction of new schools and the enlargement of existing schools. Any further expansion is being directed toward the development of selective, tuition-charging, academic high schools and institutions of higher education. As an extreme example, the Cincinnati diocese in 1964 dropped all first grades, shifting 10,000 pupils to the public schools. The Catholic school system in a major way is changing from a mass education system with emphasis upon elementary education to a system concentrating upon college-preparatory secondary schools and higher education.

The urban public schools can expect little additional help from the Catholic school system in times ahead, particularly in culturally disadvantaged areas where the majority of the Negro population is not affiliated with the Catholic Church. The full burden of handling the expanding urban school population at the elementary-school level and the costly vocational and trade elements at the secondary level will fall upon the public schools.

The main force of this line of reasoning so far has been to show that the urban school system is in an increasingly weakened position for fulfilling the tasks already assigned to it and is ill-equipped to take on any new tasks. As first steps in the long-term solution of the problems of disadvantaged youth in the cities one should argue, therefore, for the strengthening of the school in its present form, resisting the introduction of new tasks, and providing increased support for the tasks it has already undertaken and in regard to which there is a chance of improving present performance.

Strengthening the urban school today means concentrating

additional resources to schools in areas of disadvantage (often called compensatory education). It means action should be taken to: lower class size; increase facilities for remedial teaching, including individual diagnosis and treatment; concentrate administrative, teaching, counseling, health, and social welfare personnel in these schools in organized teams designed to provide both strengthened services for children and supporting organizations for school personnel; and institute a differential reward system for those personnel with the skill and willingness to undertake these tasks. All of these suggestions involve unequal allocation of resources and can be accomplished only if we can simultaneously gain broad city-wide improvements in all the schools — particularly competitive salary systems and reduced pupil-teacher ratios — so that the spread in allocation of resources does not become a factor furthering alienation of large sectors of the population.

To accomplish these objectives, we must intensify our efforts along familiar lines. On the financing side, it means the following: (*a*) increasing school revenue from local districts, including the development of new sources of revenue (sales, corporate, and personal income taxes) to take the pressure off the property tax; (*b*) changing state laws so that local tax increases and school bond issues are not so difficult to pass; increasing state contributions to public education, and particularly to change the state allocations so that the more expensive forms of education for which the cities carry greater responsibility receive allocations proportionate to cost; and (*c*) at the national levels to argue for federal contribution to public education for general support rather than for the special types of help which have characterized federal legislation so far in our history. On the policy side, boards of education and school administrators must be persuaded to develop programs providing unequal (increased) resources to unequal (disadvantaged) school populations. In this direction there should be substantial assistance from the new Education Bill just passed by the 89th Congress, and as quickly as possible we must seek the same kind of support from the states, so that continuation of the programs does not rest solely on the whim of the Congress.

In a number of large cities the public school system, because it is the largest and most powerful bureaucracy, has played the major role in federal antipoverty programs. Although this response of power attracting power is natural enough, it will hamper the long-run goal of providing a wide range of high-quality programs, serving our children both within the school system and auxiliary to it, if the schools take on all functions and other institutions are not permitted to develop.

In any plan for the sustained improvement of educational services we need to look carefully at the tasks and responsibilities of the school, to develop criteria for what the school will do and what it will not do in this concentrated effort. Ralph Tyler has stated the problem succinctly:

> Only by the fullest utilization of the potential educational efforts of home, church, school, recreational agencies, youth serving organizations, the library, press, movies, radio, T.V. . . . can this nation meet its educational needs. . . . Failure to encourage and to help other institutions to bear part of the responsibility inevitably weakens our total social structure and reduces the effectiveness of our total educational achievement. . . . Yet this is what we do when we in the schools assume responsibilities which can be discharged by others. . . . Few, if any, communities adequately utilize the educational potential outside the school. Instead, they waste precious resources of the school on jobs which others can do. . . . We need to organize a wide attack upon the total educational job, and we must clearly differentiate the educational responsibilities of the school from those of other agencies.[2]

In the same article, Tyler develops a few criteria which at least indicate directions for limiting the functions of schools. The school, rather than another agency, should teach basic skills such as reading and mathematics. It should provide learning when the essential factors are not obvious to one observing

[2] Ralph W. Tyler, "Educational Objectives of American Democracy," *The Nation's Children*, Eli Ginzberg (ed.), White House Conference Golden Anniversary, Vol. 2, 1960, pp. 70–92.

the phenomena, and when the principles, concepts, and meanings must be brought to the attention of the learner (as in many aspects of the sciences, for example). It is also the principal instructional agency in areas of learning in which the experiences required cannot be provided in the ordinary activities of daily life (geography and history). Similarly, school should provide for learning which requires more refined experience than is commonly available in life outside the school (art, music, literature). Tyler also advocates the teaching of human relations and ethical values, areas in which learning is going on in the community but often falls short of the ideal, this task to be shared by home, church, and youth organizations. He also argues for the teaching of the arts and sciences, particularly in the high school, to help students to form generalizations about the changing and developing world and to take an active, understanding role in this world. If such complicated matters can be stated succinctly, one might say that the central focus of the school should be upon the development of rationality and upon the learning of the symbolic systems and the communication skills essential to rationality.

A school organized systematically along these lines would look to other agencies in the community for a variety of activities: health information and nutrition; physical education, athletics, and recreation; expanding knowledge of the community and its cultural resources; training in skills required for modern living, such as driving a car; training in most aspects of work; treatment of emotional disorders; the training of children not capable of receiving academic instruction; and other activities now frequently included in the school program on a marginal basis. The question, of course, is whether we can guarantee that these functions can be performed in any other agency but the school, that we can in fact reach most of the children through other agencies. For any agency to have this capacity, it would have to have a strong local and state tax base in support of its programs, as do the schools. There would also have to be strong institutional bases for recruitment and training of personnel for the programs and clearly defined career patterns to attract personnel. We have a variety of agencies, both private and public, performing these functions, but few now have the financial support, organizational support, or personnel resources to provide such services to children on a scale parallel to that achieved by the schools. The present mood of American society and government, the concern for the culturally disadvantaged and the explosive pressure from the civil rights movement, provides an opportunity to identify those agencies which have such potential and to strengthen them, or to create new institutions capable of providing long-term service.

The task now is to identify some of the institutions that might be capable of sharing services to disadvantaged children and to indicate the ways in which they would be both different from and related to the public schools. As examples, programs serving three groups of children, at differing ages and circumstances, will be isolated for a preliminary analysis: (1) those serving the preschool child, (2) those serving the elementary-school child in process of alienation from school and society, and (3) those serving the school drop-out or potential drop-out with special problems of entry into the labor force.

1. The Culturally Disadvantaged Preschool Child

We are beginning to become aware nationally of the severe handicaps which the culturally disadvantaged child brings with him as he enters school. The family and community life of the young child under conditions of poverty is extremely limited and restrictive: limited access to material objects of all sorts; a restricted life space; limited contact and communication with adults; impoverished and dialectical language patterns; little opportunity for individual development of perceptual, manual, and conceptual skills. Stated in more psychological terms, there is severe stimulus deprivation.

In the past few years, as recognition of the problem has grown, there has been a ground-swell movement by social agencies and churches, supported largely by volunteers, to establish preschools in depressed areas. Many urban school systems have initiated pilot preschools, either alone or jointly with other agencies. As a follow-up to Project Head Start, subsequent programs are planned for year-long nursery schools and for support of nursery-school training programs. Directives of the Office of Economic Opportunity suggest that programs should be closely connected to health and social welfare agencies as well as to educational systems and under the direction and management of Community Action Programs rather than the public schools directly. Initially the federal support level is 90 percent, requiring a 10 percent local contribution.

The organization of the long-term institutionalization of preschools is an extremely complex problem. The potentialities of local Community Action Programs for attracting local and state tax support are not yet clear. These programs are usually given the form of nonprofit private corporations, capable of receiving donations and of entering into contracts with federal, state, and local government agencies (including schools) and with private nonprofit agencies (including church agencies and church schools). Whether the corporations are to serve merely as money-holding corporations, with other agencies as operating units, or whether the corporations are to serve directly as operating units is often unclear. At issue, of course, are delicate matters of state and local tax support to church-related and other private agencies.

Nursery schools have usually been supported by private groups of parents on a nonprofit corporation and tuition-paying basis in economically favored sectors of the society. Day-care centers have been supported by charity organizations, relying on the Community Fund and other private donations. Training programs for nursery-school teachers have had a difficult time in our colleges and universities, developing variously in schools of education, departments of home economics, or in child-development departments, infrequently in social work or medical settings, and often most strongly developed in state universities in rural areas away from the culturally disadvantaged population. The professional role of the nursery-school teacher has been a marginal one: part-time work, low salaries, almost complete dependency on private agencies, and marginal professional training and affiliation.

For the long term we should make every effort to develop preschool services to children within the context of local and state government agencies for child services, family and social welfare services, and public health and medical services — wherever seems most appropriate according to present local and state organization — but outside the context of the schools. This position is based on the argument that the younger the child is, the closer the relationship should be with the family and with the education of the family. Child-development centers should include preschools, health services, family counseling, and other social welfare services on as closely integrated a neighborhood basis as is possible. Capital construction programs will be required, since present agencies and the public schools in culturally disadvantaged areas are already fully occupied; these should fall within city capital-development programs, with state and federal assistance. Training programs will require a closer cooperation among schools of education, social work, nursing, and medicine than has been the case so far.

In the schools the kindergarten can provide the transition from community child-development centers to formal schools. We should make every effort in this period to institutionalize the public-school kindergarten as firmly as possible as a high-cost (low pupil–teacher ratio) facility. Wherever possible the kindergarten should be integrated with nongraded primary schools, so that children who need additional preparatory time in a less formal situation may be accommodated in flexible ways.

2. *The Alienated Elementary School Child*

Martin Deutsch has stated the problem succinctly:[3]

> Among children who come from lower-class socially impoverished circumstances, there is a high proportion of school failure,

[3] Martin Deutsch, "The Disadvantaged Child and the Learning Process," *Education in Depressed Areas*, A. Harry Passow (ed.) (New York Bureau of Publications, Teachers College, Columbia University, 1963), p. 163.

> school drop-outs, reading and learning disabilities, as well as life adjustment problems. . . . the effectiveness of the school as a major institution for socialization is diminished. . . .
>
> The thesis here is that the lower class child enters the school situation so poorly prepared to produce what the school demands that initial failures are almost inevitable, and the school experience becomes negatively rather than positively reinforced. Thus the child's experience in school does nothing to counteract the invidious influences to which he is exposed in his slum, and sometimes segregated, neighborhood.

It has already been suggested that the basic school approach to this problem should be a reduction of class size, the assignment of additional personnel in supporting teams, and the further development of individual and small-group remedial programs. The necessity now exists for the further development of two types of organization for alienated elementary-school children: one within the public-school system, the other external to it, but both serving all the school children of the community from both the public and the private sector. The weaker the effectiveness of the individual neighborhood schools, the more imperative will be the need for these types of centers.

First, within the public-school system, there is the need to establish separate schools or centers to receive the children for whom the regular schools have proved unsatisfactory. These centers should not be created in the image of the present elementary schools, but rather as radical departures from present practices. The need is for remedial learning schools or clinics with both diagnostic and treatment programs, on an individual and small-group basis. Few school systems are equipped now with facilities and personnel for this work or are able to apply the highly individualized and special techniques required to help the many kinds of educationally handicapped children, nor can the highly specialized personnel required be concentrated in regular school settings. The personnel of these clinic schools would, ideally, also serve as consultants to teachers in the regular schools. The staff of the clinics would include school psychologists, counselors, and social workers, as well as corps of special teachers, and would also provide direct links between the school and other social and welfare agencies working with the same individuals and families. These schools could serve as clinical facilities for university programs in special education, educational psychology, school psychology, school social work and counseling, all of which would need to be expanded to provide personnel for the new service.

Second, there is a need for medically and psychiatrically oriented child-guidance clinics, related to the medical facilities of the city rather than to the schools, to provide medical and psychiatric treatment for more seriously handicapped and emotionally disturbed children. With the exception of a few famous medical centers, child-guidance clinic services have not been well developed in our metropolitan areas, and both parents and schools have difficulty in finding proper medical treatment for emotionally disturbed children, who also frequently have severe learning disabilities. Child-guidance clinics are needed, organized under the auspices of city and county health departments. These clinics should be related to medical schools and teaching hospitals. If possible the clinics should be organized on the basis of the total metropolis because of the concentration of medical facilities in the central city.

Both types of centers are eligible for federal support under the Education Act of 1965, which authorizes grants for supplementary educational centers and services including the functions just outlined. The Act encourages service to all the children of the community, including the development of dual enrollment programs (a program in which a pupil is enrolled part-time in a private school and part-time in a public school for different parts of his school program).

3. The School Drop-Out or Potential Drop-Out: Age 16–21

The statistics concerning school drop-outs and their place in the employment market are frightening, particularly in view of increased numbers of young people entering the labor market in this decade and the decline in unskilled jobs available for those who do not complete school. In response to this problem, an extraordinary number and variety of special programs have been developed in cities across the nation, with stimulus from the Federal Manpower Development and Training Act, the Employment Opportunity Act, the Vocational Training Act, and the Economic Opportunity Act. The number and combinations of possible partners in projects for school drop-outs is greater than those available for projects covering the earlier years, involving: the schools; various city departments; state departments of labor and employment; private industry; private agencies; community action organizations; and multiple federal agencies.

The area of vocational, trade, and technical education has always been one of the most difficult for the public schools because of the rapid obsolescence of equipment and programs in the schools relative to the changing needs and technology of industry. The schools have also had the greatest difficulty in finding teachers who combine a suitable level of education and work experience at salaries which are not competitive with industry. In particular there is a shortage of top-level leadership in technical and vocational education, in both administrative and counseling positions. University training programs in both administration and counseling have been deficient with respect to technical education and the analysis of the world of work.

Many of the assumptions upon which the new programs are based remain to be fully tested. Of critical importance in all programs is the teaching of basic educational skills, often on a remedial basis, whether conducted under formal school conditions or under less formal situations in neighborhood centers or on the job. Another element contained in most programs is guidance and counseling, generally directed to job preparation and orientation toward work. Often counseling is the major element, but in many programs it is subsidiary to some form of work experience. Work experience may take one of two major directions: general preparation for work or preparation for specific jobs. Each type has its own difficulties. Those providing general preparation for work tend to overstress the virtues of work and the transfer of attitudes formed in any work situation, however unskilled or menial, to the specific requirements in a more skilled working situation. Those programs aimed at preparation for specific jobs face the task of assessing what jobs are likely to be open and usually end up preparing for a myriad of unskilled jobs.

Three types of programs seem to have a clear place in the schools as supportive of past efforts in the schools or of historic trends. These are: (1) part-time work programs aimed at providing the poor student with the financial resources to stay in school and complete his education to a higher level; (2) work-study programs in which the student alternates between school and work and in which special adaptations are made in the program; (3) counseling programs in the schools aimed at acquainting the students with the world of work and with the attitudes and personal characteristics required to hold a job and giving assistance in job placement, both in work-study programs and in part-time work programs. The greatest chances of long-term success will exist when local schools, in addition to being given federal assistance, join with city agencies and industry to provide jobs in the city agencies, the schools, and in a variety of industries. Jobs developed solely within the schools are much too limited and detached from the real world of work.

It is extremely important to provide training, counseling, and work opportunities for unemployed youth entirely outside the context of school for those youths who have been so alienated from school that it is impossible for them to return successfully to formal schooling. New York City seems to have a number of promising projects; a network of fifteen youth opportunity centers has been established under the New York Community Action Programs, including JOIN (Job Opportunities in Neighborhoods), Haryou Act, and Mobilization for Youth. A next step to guarantee long-term institutionalization of city programs will be the involvement of the states. Without direct state support and involvement, the prospects of long-term local-federal cooperation seem unstable.

The Job Corps of the Office of Economic Opportunity is operating on a different basis, entirely on federal subsidy, though with some participation of universities and industry under contract. Two types of centers are being established: (1) small rural centers providing general work training and work experience in conservation and similar areas; and (2) larger urban Job Corps Centers which will concentrate on training youths for urban work, combining job training with work experience. The operation of these latter urban centers is being contracted to universities and industries. We can only assume that the Job Corps is aimed at short-term "crisis" alleviation of unemployment, because neither the universities nor industry would seem to be likely to take over the expense of operating such a unit.

The lively interest in the youthful unemployed shown by existing government structures at the local and state level, particularly in employment divisions, which seem ready to cooperate and to seek appropriations, would appear to indicate strong possibilities for the development of long-term in-school and out-of-school institutions. There is, at present, one possible exception — the role of industry is not yet clear with regard to its service to youth at the point of entry into the labor market. Educational and training programs have increased enormously within our major industries, so that new employees find that taking a job is very much like continuing in school. The effort, however, is mostly directed toward high-level technical manpower development, with minimal contributions at the level of helping undereducated, unskilled, unemployed youths.

Conclusion

A superintendent of schools recently remarked that the federal programs represent an opportunity for the city schools to spend more of their own money. This is true also of the programs of the major foundations. The direction of new "crisis" grant programs does not always fit the long-term trends in the school system, and the federal and foundation funds are not available for the massive fundamental needs of the system—school building construction, reduction of pupil-teacher ratios, concentration of the teaching force in difficult districts, and raising sufficient funds to compete with the suburbs in attracting teaching and administrative talent. As has been seen, little free money exists for the city schools, and any matching endeavor with federal funds amounts to a diversion from other purposes. Further, the climate of crisis does not necessarily help to create a favorable environment for gaining tax increases for the city schools; indeed, the atmosphere of emergency and "rush" created by the fast-moving federal programs often creates conflicts for the long-term planning programs of the school system.

Innovation is taking place within our urban schools at an amazing rate, requiring major local direct expenditures as well as indirect expenditures in use of personnel and facilities. Further, these programs in certain instances tend to break the isolation of the school system, bringing schools into direct cooperative relationships with the universities, with private agencies, and with local and state departments of government. In a few programs, aided by Community Action agencies, there are possibilities of metropolitan area programs of cooperation. The "crisis" psychology of federal programs, however, has certain consequences which may defeat long-term planning and make more difficult the definition of suitable tasks for the various sectors of society in the education of youth, cooperation between the schools and other agencies, and metropolitan-area planning. First, the administrative capacities of the school system are limited and have now reached a flood crest. This overload on the administrative group leads to short-term decision-making rather than to long-term policy-making and inhibits the possibility of creating new institutions to perform supportive functions. Second, in spite of this administrative overload the public-school bureaucracy is by far the most highly organized and powerful institution in the city, capable of making unilateral decisions quickly. Therefore, decisions tend to be made rapidly by this bureaucracy, reducing the possibilities of long-term cooperation and the developing of extraschool institutions, which will require careful nurturing.

"Crisis" planning is also forced by the urgent demands created by population changes and by the extreme pressures exerted for integration. Pressures and counterpressures concerning integration have virtually paralyzed the city boards of education and administrative staffs. The magnitude of the problem is such that we can say with certainty that the schools can do nothing alone except attempt to hold a thin line of integrated schools on the margins of the sharply drawn residential lines and to take no directly negative, gerrymandering actions which will prevent the integration already achieved and that which is possible as neighborhoods change. There is room for the limited application of the concept of "educational complexes" advocated in New York City, in which the schools are reorganized into a 4–4–4 system (four grades primary, four grades middle school, and a four-year high school), allowing schools at each level to draw from a larger population area and thus crossing boundaries between Negro and white residential areas, always with the understanding that there is a "critical status ratio" below which a school cannot fall without alarming middle-class parents into removing their children. The deliberate planning of an integrated school may actually "tip" the neighborhood beyond recall.

A final comment must be added to this discussion of metropolitan planning and the creation of nonschool institutions for assisting in the education of our youth. The greatest help in all its problems could be given to urban education by breaking the residential barriers for Negroes, opening up new avenues for population expansion and for substantially integrated schools in the suburbs. Further breaking of the residential barriers within the central city alone will only extend and complicate school problems by fostering the growth of the restricted black ghetto. Simultaneously, there is a need for an opening of employment opportunities in both city and suburbs, so that Negroes can afford to move. We could also wish for a massive reintegration program in the city, bringing back white public-school families into the city, but this seems a utopian ideal. Fair housing and fair employment practices are the key to integration and must be closely related to cooperative school practices. The problems of the schools merely reflect the state of affairs in society at large.

New federal programs may well provide the stimulus toward greatly strengthening our total services to youth, disadvantaged and other, if we can keep our long-term targets in sight — educational planning for the entire metropolis, the strengthening of central school functions, the strengthening and creation of new youth service institutions with local and state tax support.

References

BLOOM, BENJAMIN, ALLISON DAVIS, and ROBERT HESS. *Compensatory Education for Cultural Deprivation.* New York: Holt, Rinehart, & Winston, Inc., 1965.

HUNNICUTT, C. W. (ed.). *Urban Education and Cultural Deprivation.* Syracuse, N.Y.: Syracuse University, 1964.

PASSOW, A. HARRY (ed.). *Education in Depressed Areas.* New York: Teachers College, Columbia University, 1963.

PETTIGREW, THOMAS F. *A Profile of the Negro American.* Princeton, N.J.: D. Van Nostrand Co., Inc., 1964.

RIESSMAN, FRANK. *The Culturally Deprived Child.* New York: Harper & Row, 1962.

SILBERMAN, CHARLES E. *Crisis in Black and White.* New York: Random House, Inc., 1964.

CHAPTER FIFTEEN

URBAN POLITICS AND EDUCATION

Robert H. Salisbury

The crucial problem facing the metropolis is how to achieve both stability and social integration in the face of prejudice, population mobility, and fragmented governmental structures. Professor Salisbury sees the school system as constituting an effective cutting edge for social and political change. He considers fiscal and organizational changes which might lead to a metropolitan school system and, at the same time, facilitate the growth of neighborhood-centered institutions incorporating the schools in broader, coordinated, programs of social action.

Big-city schools are having their troubles. Pickets, boycotts, and strikes have made the schools front page news as crisis after crisis has brought education into dramatic contact with the larger community. Reformers of many different social creeds have concentrated their critical fire on the schools and urged that they become more effective in behalf of one cause or another. Schools have been hailed as the mechanism by which the problems of urban life can be solved and blamed for the failures to erase social tensions.

Educators are thus beset by conflicting views of their proper function. Should they resist the enlarging of their role to encompass more diverse approaches to the training of children? Should they encourage other agencies to undertake retraining,

Professor Robert H. Salisbury is Chairman of the Department of Political Science at Washington University and recently coauthor of *State Politics and the Public Schools* (1964).

preschool and other programs to upgrade the poor and thereby minimize the role of the traditional school? Or should they welcome the far-reaching changes in the nature of their task which active participation in such activities might bring about? Are the schools to engage only in traditional, narrowly defined, educational tasks, or are they to become critical instruments of comprehensive social action in the urban environment? Essentially, these are all political questions, involving as they do conflicts of groups and ideas in the community which must ultimately be resolved by the actions or inactions of public agencies. They are questions, therefore, which a political scientist may properly consider.

Every facet of urban life involves the school system. We all know how vital the connection is between racial integration and the structure of public education. The relationship is equally close with regard to the problems of developing stable neighborhoods with decent housing, of improving employment and earning prospects for the city dweller, or even of increasing the portion of civility in the urban environment.

If the city is to be a tolerable place, I believe that educators must combine their resources and talents much more fully than they have done with other segments and programs of the community. I think the public schools are too "independent," too isolated from other agencies and groups with complementary jobs to do. The result is that none of the tasks is done as well as it should be; none of the agencies does the work that it could. In this paper I propose to assess the ways and means by which the schools have arrived at their present arm's-length relationship to the rest of the community, the costs of this relative isolation, and some strategies for and benefits of binding the schools more fully into the whole metropolitan political and social fabric.

The public school system of New York City has been described as "autonomous and inelastic." Nearly every other big-city system may be similarly described. What this means is that the schools are left largely to their own devices by other parts of the community political system. The ward bosses, the business interests, most of the unions and the other groups that fight it out for power in the city are largely absent from local school contests. They do not seek to dominate school decisions or to use the school system for their own purposes. Neither do they ordinarily provide support for the schools when some kind of public approval is needed. The struggles over school policy are confined primarily to rather specialized groups, most of them more or less professionally connected with education. School politics tends largely to be among the schoolmen. Autonomy is associated with inelasticity, however. That is, big-city school systems are largely unresponsive to external pressures for change or innovation. Let us examine the implications of these two aspects of urban politics and education.

In at least three fourths of the nation's big cities, the school boards are separately elected. Most city school budgets are beyond control by city officials. Even where the mayor appoints the school board, as in New York or Chicago, his ability or desire to intervene in its decisions appears to be very limited. Administrative appointments and promotions tend to be made from within the school system, very often according to seniority. This practice helps minimize internal conflict, a result that has its political uses. It also, of course, is associated with resistance to new ideas and programs that might upset existing relationships.

Isolated, too, are the two primary modes of interest group activity in the city schools. In some cities and in most of the smaller communities the predominant organization of schoolmen is the local affiliate of the National Education Association. Combining administrators and teachers, its major themes emphasize the unity of all educators to establish a professional climate, promote the schools, and to protect them against "outside pressures." The NEA rival is the American Federation of Teachers. The AFT pays little attention to the content of educational programs. It is concerned about the status and perquisites of classroom teachers, and its willingness to make relatively strong demands upon urban school administrators has won a large majority of big city teachers to its banner. By virtue of its program and membership the AFT is more divisive of the education establishment than is the NEA, which places the highest priority on consensus. Internal division among school people might permit the educational innovator to drive a wedge into the system. But AFT concerns have so little to do with program, and are so much designed along rather conventional union lines to protect the status of the "worker" and to equalize conditions for everyone in the same status that proposals for educational innovation meet little encouragement.

The drive toward consensus among schoolmen, whether encouraged by myths of professional unity fostered by the NEA, or by reliance on seniority, or by the notion that every teacher may someday be a superintendent, is very important for any discussion of present or prospective school policy. One important aspect of the myth of consensus is that it enhances the prestige of the schoolmen. Educators, like many other professional or semiprofessional groups, rest much of their claim to influence over educational policy on expertise. It is argued that they know more, by training and experience, than do laymen. As long as there is substantial agreement among educators, the claim to detached, professional expertise is plausible. If there is disagreement among "the experts," however, the board or the public must make its own choices among the alternatives. Hence domination of school policy is likely to fall to the schoolmen themselves to the extent that they can stick together. Lay or public control is enhanced by division among educators.

The consensus myth is closely linked to another aspect of educational ideology — the unitary nature of the community. "*The*" school serves "*The*" community. Everyone regardless of age, family status, income, or religion is assumed to benefit from public education. Although there may be some diversity within the school program to accommodate different interests and tastes, the predominant norm is unitary. Education is education, so to speak, for everyone equally. Curricular and administrative structures reflect this position, which is part a creed for present belief and part a goal for future achievement.

Moreover, the myth of the unitary community has reinforced

the commitment among schoolmen to resist "special interests." "Special interests" are those who, according to a rather primitive view of things which is still widely shared, make "selfish" demands upon public authority. By definition, "special interests" go counter to the "public interest" that a "nonpolitical" school board may be free to serve. Internal community division spawns "special interests"; a unitary community embodies the "public interest." In the latter case there remain no legitimate divisive questions, and the schools may function according to the recommendations of the experts, i.e., the schoolmen.

Out of these customs of schoolmen comes the overwhelming preference for nonpartisan administration of the public schools. Not only in law but almost universally in fact the urban party organizations have played an ever smaller role in school affairs. Rather, boards are chosen and lay support is provided with the active involvement of "parents" and "citizens" groups that, in their form and their style of action, stress their identity with the whole community.

The myth of the unitary community has served a number of useful functions in the growth of the public school system. It helped facilitate the growth of a profession that, whatever its shortcomings, provides an extraordinary range of educational services to an enormous population and in a manner utterly beyond the ken of the little red schoolhouse. Consensus among schoolmen has helped them throw off the pressures of superpatriots and has played a role in reducing the impact of political machines and partisan election contests.

Yet the unitary community is a myth and not a fact, and there is some reason to suppose that the myth is rapidly becoming disfunctional. The modern city is not homogeneous. Moreover, among its various major groupings there is substantial disagreement about public education. Negroes want a school system which will act as the cutting edge in an effort to restructure life chances so that they no longer will depend upon race. Negroes at every income level are also more willing to pay for school and other public services than, for example, are Irish, Polish, or Italian city dwellers. The latter may resist integration.

They may also resist public spending. They may be indifferent to public education, partly because they are large consumers of parochial school education. The result has been a community in which Negroes, combined with upper-middle-income whites, support school expenditures and "Blue Ribbon" school boards while lower-middle-income whites, many of whom are Catholic, are indifferent, or even hostile.

As militant Negroes press more vigorously for a great leap forward in integrated education, however, their support for the "Blue Ribbon" school administration with its emphasis on the unitary nature of both school and community may rapidly turn to hostile demonstrations. Conversely, other sectors of the community perceive the Negro demands for de facto integration as coming at the expense of educational values. Small-householder demands for economy in public services are made at the expense of the culturally deprived Negroes. A city is not a unitary community in education, and fewer and fewer people any longer accept the old mythology.

The main point of the discussion so far has been that urban public school systems are isolated from and insulated against the main centers of political power and decision in the city. However useful this autonomy may have been in the past, it no longer protects the schools from deeply controversial community issues, especially those which rest on matters of race and religion. But isolation of the schools is not only disfunctional in terms of public support for general education; it prevents the schools from contributing to the over-all development of the city.

Today's metropolis is beset by a wide range of deeply rooted difficulties. Its governmental structures are riotously fragmented. Its fiscal arrangements are virtually medieval. Its physical plant is deteriorating, its traffic is strangling its commercial centers, its neighborhoods are losing identity, and its various subcultures, no longer content with the ghetto, demand the acknowledgment from each other that they are equals.

All of these generic urban problems are reflected in the schools. But with the partial exception of race relations the schools have been unwilling to attempt directly to attack these problems. "We have enough to do, to teach the individual child the basic skills," is the traditional argument, and one cannot but be sympathetic to it. And the autonomy provided by the governmental structure and reinforced by educational ideology has made it possible to keep the school system aloof from all the issues except race.

Yet a case can and should be made for integration of the schools with the community for the mutual benefits that may be derived. Take, for example, the question of neighborhood planning. It has become increasingly clear in recent years that if urban life is to be tolerable there must develop a network of neighborhoods with local facilities and institutions, physically cohesive, rather than divided by numerous arterial streets, and hopefully generating among the residents some identification with the locale. There is little expectation that mobility will cease, but its untoward effects may be reduced if a community grid of viable neighborhoods exists, through which people can move, always finding a stable setting.

If this vision seems a bit utopian, it is well to realize that much of current federal urban renewal and antipoverty money is now being spent in this direction, and many cities are attempting to move toward this kind of community network. The point here is that the schools must play a vital role in such a program. The school is obviously a prime choice for a neighborhood anchoring facility. An elementary school generally has playground equipment indoors and out; it has rooms that can be used for a wide variety of public meetings; it has a name and an identity that are immediately recognized by large numbers of the area residents. Properly located and broadly utilized, the neighborhood school might be the prime instrument in achieving neighborhood stability and integration. Yet there is little evidence that schoolmen have given this kind of question much attention. In locating a new school they have talked about convenience and need of mere numbers of children. They have searched for available sites with an eye to short-run economy, and they have not discussed the effects of the location on noneducational values of the community.

Again, the exception is race. On this matter, forced by militant Negroes, school boards in many cities have been compelled to reorganize school boundaries and sometimes relocate new schools so as to break through ghettolike housing patterns and achieve de facto integration in the schools. School boards and administrators have generally resisted these demands on the ground that extensive bussing or other means which took children out of their neighborhoods would impede the educational process. Negroes replied that segregated education was inherently so inferior that drastic means were required which would *first* attack segregation as a precondition of effective learning.

A similar example occurred recently when the school board of a large city turned down a program of free breakfasts, to be paid for by nonschool money but served in school facilities. They based their decision on the principle that "their function was education, not welfare." They were unimpressed by the evidence that many children who seemed to be slow learners were, in fact, only hungry.

These illustrations suggest that educators have been conventionally narrow in their efforts to maintain the priority of traditional educational skills over other social values. Obviously the school affects both categories, and obviously the schoolmen must contemplate both very carefully if they are to act in a manner designed to promote the community's well-being in the largest sense of that term. The legal and political autonomy of the schools, however, has encouraged the educators to ignore the other social values. Even in the case of segregation, the schools have been pretty unresponsive, except to the argument that segregation harmed traditionally defined education. There has been little disposition by schoolmen to promote racial integration through the school system simply because it was a good thing.

The traditional educator's defense of neighborhood schools

has nothing to do with the neighborhood as a social entity. It is simply a convenient way of defining a set of physical limits for elementary-school district size. Accordingly, though educators have long used the word and have recently tried to defend the concept against the integrationists, they really have had no concept to defend. But they should have. The neighborhood school should be vitally linked, by location and broad community use, with every other phase of neighborhood life. A school should be located so as to maximize its usefulness in recreation, adult and youth groups, traffic flow planning and open space development, to mention only a few. It is false economy to strip the school facility of its nonclassroom elements if the school is indeed to be a facility for the total community.

I am well aware that many schools are used for many purposes which go far beyond conventional "three R" education. Board members and educators in many communities are anxious to play an active role in the broader regeneration of their cities. But institutional autonomy, too often still combined with ideological separatism, results in great inefficiencies and lost opportunities. The schools are built, the broader programs are delayed, and another generation of city dwellers is the poorer.

I have spoken so far primarily of the physical facilities of the school and the central role they could play in neighborhood reconstruction. Surely the personnel of the urban school systems also constitute a much underutilized urban resource. Obviously, I am not proposing that overworked teachers simply be given more responsibilities. Rather, I am suggesting that it is folly to allow large numbers of highly trained people to fend for themselves in the summer, or, in the winter, waste their skills on clerical trivia, while other urban agencies search desperately for a reasonably literate staff. The present use of physical education teachers in city-sponsored summer recreation programs is a happy example of what might be more widely attempted if there were closer institutional connections between the schools and other community services.

We are led to the conclusion that an effective and comprehensive assault on the crucial urban problem of how to get social integration and stability requires genuine and thoroughgoing coordination of the school system with other community agencies. Logically, this means the restoration of effective mayoral or council control over the schools. Independent school boards, in law or in fact, are incompatible with long-range, detailed coordination of facility and program. Site location and development, broad budgetary policy, plant use and many aspects of personnel recruitment and employment can quite properly be determined by the regular elected city officials. Educators in this case would compete with other public services for support from the city fathers. The latter, in turn, could allocate resources much more freely, bringing them to bear on *problems* rather than necessarily assigning them to administrative units as is required by the present institutional fragmentation.

The community development agencies organized to administer the poverty program are examples, though perhaps not yet very good ones, of a problem-centered administration making use of diverse agencies and skills in what will hopefully become a coordinated, multifaceted program. Educators are part of these programs, but as they begin to receive their own funds from new federal aid programs we may expect a reassertion of autonomy for the schools. The community development agencies are ad hoc and not always effective yet, even though they illustrate the necessity for new institutional forms to develop innovative programs of coordinated action in the education and welfare fields.

There are dangers, of course, in the reorganization I propose. Inept city leadership may at present be bypassed by a separately elected and competent school board. Educators have been protected from much political hanky-panky by their institutional autonomy. But in today's city, incompetent or corrupt city officials will hasten general urban collapse anyway. The schools will suffer if there is economic decay or physical blight or racial tension in the community, regardless of what the educators themselves or their autonomous board may do. Moreover, it is not apparent that schoolmen handle contemporary urban crises more wisely than do other public officials, as witness the continuing educational chaos in Chicago and New York.

Finally, in this regard, there is the budget. Unless the whole complex of urban public agencies can be mobilized together, there is a very good prospect that urban tax funds will soon be hopelessly inadequate. Solutions to local fiscal problems require imaginative effort and hard persuasion if any kind of community consensus on fiscal support of public services is to be achieved. Without consensus, the various city agencies are quite likely to cut each other to pieces in competitive drives for the reluctant property tax dollar. State and federal aid may conceivably prop up each urban program separately, but such aid is a very problematic reed to lean upon.

The educator may wonder what would happen to his professional identity as educator if he were to lose his institutional autonomy. One answer is that if education is genuinely a profession, it can be practiced, as law and medicine are, in many institutional settings. Moreover, it can be associated with a variety of goals and programs in addition to those inherent in the profession itself. The particular administrative structure relating the school and the community need have nothing to do with the integrity of the educator as a professional. Indeed, perhaps it is high time that his professionalism was tested by putting him in daily contact, sometimes as superior, sometimes as subordinate, always as competitor and colleague, with other professionals in the urban community.

I have so far talked only about institutional reorganization within the core city. In the metropolitan region, too, the school system could become the cutting edge of an effort to enlarge the opportunities to solve urban problems by rational action. Quite clearly, the matter of schools has been very near the center of contemporary metropolitan disputation and fragmentation. City dwellers flee to suburbs, rich suburbs refuse to collaborate with poor suburbs, while both shun the core city and its problems, and largely because of schools. The yearning for middle-class educational styles may not explain the proliferation of suburbia, but the defense of their local school systems surely keeps suburbanites from agreeing to break down their governmental barriers against each other and the city. Suburban schools are frequently less "reorganized" than rural districts, for example, and, if metropolitan cooperation for purposes of, say, arterial traffic is proposed, many suburbanites will oppose it, fearing that it may be the first step down the path leading to metropolitanizing the schools. Only at the junior- or community-college level has there been effective metropolitan action on education, and here there were seldom any established programs to create resistance to the new organizational forms.

Not only are most suburban citizens unwilling to contemplate metropolitan public schools; so also are most schoolmen, especially those in the suburban districts. Quite understandably, they do not relish the prospect of merging their relatively prosperous and uncomplicated suburban systems, harried though each one of them might be at any particular time, in a great metropolitan mass system, much of which would consist of lower-income core-city residents.

We have reached the time, however, when we must seriously explore "metropolitanized" schools. For one thing, local school finances will grow increasingly inadequate until steps are taken to use substantially the whole metropolis as a taxing base. If, at least, all commercial and industrial property in the metropolis were taxed at a uniform rate, the proceeds to be distributed to communities on the basis of population, it would be a major step toward better financing of the needy districts and also toward reducing intermunicipal competition for industry using tax incentives as bait.

A second reason for a metropolitan school system is that it is essential for genuine racial integration. Except perhaps for a few of the very largest cities, the core city does not offer a sufficient range of population types or life styles to make integration of the city schools an effective cutting edge for integration generally. One can, for example, already integrate the District of Columbia schools thoroughly and have a quite meaningless result because most white children are outside the District boundaries. It seems clear that this will become true in more and more large cities, to the detriment of the education of both the deprived Negro children and the protected white children.

Third, core city schools have especially vexing problems with such matters as recruiting and holding teachers, and their main competitors are the plush suburbs. Protected and wealthy suburban schools may well be a luxury the metropolis can no longer afford. A single personnel system would permit the best teachers to be assigned to the most challenging spots, many of which are in the slums, *and to be paid accordingly.*

A gifted teacher in a slum district is worth far more to the community than one in a comfortable middle-class setting where the children will learn regardless of what the teacher does. It is high time that the pay scales reflect this worth. That it does not is partly a reflection of teacher groups' depression-oriented thinking, combined with their petty craft-unionism, which insists on equal pay for equal status, where status is defined in terms of seniority and formal training. These factors operate within each school system, but no system much wants to risk upsetting them for fear that other competing systems will snatch away their teachers. If, however, there were one major metropolitan school system, diversity in pay and duties could be introduced with less fear. The dissatisfied teacher would have to leave the area rather than just the local community system. For cities of less than a million in population, such a reorganization would appear essential if educational quality and flexibility are to be attained in the urban setting. The largest systems present problems of scale that probably require different types of solutions, perhaps breaking up the school system into smaller pieces in order to reassert effective public control and coordination.

The observant reader may by now be a bit perplexed by the several different and apparently divergent proposals presented. Whereas earlier the virtues of urban neighborhood schools were stressed, and subsequently it was urged that core-city schools be placed under the control of the regular elected city officials, the most recent argument strongly implies turning all the urban and suburban schools over to some kind of metropolitan authority. I should like, in concluding this paper, to suggest some restructuring of present systems and some ways and means to help these changes come to pass.

First, let me urge the importance of providing diversity of program, encouraging experimentation and maintaining direct parental involvement with local schools within the metropolis. None of the remarks, heretofore or subsequently, should be construed as urging abolition of local schools and the creation of giant economy size systems operating uniformly throughout each metropolitan area. Such systems might equalize financial burdens and opportunities among the several metropolitan parts, but they would stifle intrametropolitan competition and tend to keep education at an acceptable minimum level rather than encourage the development of distinctive programs.

Reorganization of the educational structure should encourage each community to compete for favor as a place to live through the quality of its schools and/or its tax rate on residential property. If each community shares the entire area's commercial and industrial property taxes and commercially or work-derived taxes based on sales and income in proportion to its population, there would be incentive for a municipality to spend more for services in order to attract more residents since thereby a larger proportion of the metropolitan revenues would accrue. Each community would be encouraged both to tax itself and to spend the money on imaginative programs. A community that chose low-density residential zoning would lose out compared to a high-density community in getting a share of commercial and industrial revenues for want of population, but neither would be advantaged directly by the specific location decisions of business and industry.

The suggestion is, therefore, that a metropolitan taxing authority be superimposed on all the existing governmental structure of the urban community with the exclusive power to assess property and levy, collect, and distribute all local taxes on industrial and commercial property, sales, inventories, gross receipts, and incomes. The distribution of funds would be made to existing spending units according to population. Obviously, such a change would have far broader impact than simply on education. What is proposed here, however, is that the issues in urban education particularly require vigorous moves in this direction. And we must lead with that need rather than hang back on it as metropolitan reformers heretofore have done.

A second main type of metropolitan action for quality urban education relates to the earlier discussion of personnel. A metropolitan system of teacher recruitment and assignment, possibly coupled with teacher training programs associated with a metropolitan community-college system, would greatly strengthen this vital part of the educational effort. In addition, however, the local schools of each community should be integrated into the appropriate local public personnel system to realize efficiences in the utilization of nonacademic personnel and in nonacademic uses of the educators themselves.

Thus despite the creation of a number of metropolitan agencies affecting education directly or indirectly, we may still adhere to the position that the schools of each community ought to become integral parts of the whole governmental system of that community. Where there is such hopeless Balkanization of suburbs as to lose all correspondence between city and school district, other arrangements would be necessary. Generally, however, geographical identities are close enough to cause only minor adjustment problems. The content of the school programs, the provision of physical facilities, nonacademic personnel, taxing of residential property, and budgeting of all locally expended monies would be within the province of the locally elected, general-purpose mayors and councils of each municipality.

Finally, at the metropolitan level, there might be established experimental programs, drawing teachers and students from the whole area to deal with special problems. Slow learners, drop-outs, scientific geniuses, incipient performing artists and other special cases might profitably be brought to this level for intensive work. Above all, the limited "metropolitanization" of the schools here proposed should encourage flexibility and innovation, a restructuring of teacher incentives and rewards, and a substantial broadening of the local base for meeting such thorny questions as race and money.

There are, of course, some alternatives that are functional equivalents for at least part of the reforms suggested here. Increased state and federal aid has a financial impact not unlike the proposal here. One difference is that most state aid formulas emphasize equalization among school systems at minimum levels of support and do very little to encourage innovation or excellence. Moreover, federal legislation has made no attempt to redefine the local jurisdictional boundaries in the field of education. Federal aid to schools has so far been given under special-purpose formulas, such as for federally impacted areas or poverty, which do not begin to provide the full combination of benefits and incentives desired.

Nevertheless, it is through state and federal aid that the greatest prospect for effective reorganization of urban public education lies. At the federal level there are the beginnings of serious attempts to achieve coordination between the new school aid program and the poverty program. Implicit in this development is the view that the schools are to be thought of as part of a community's total resources, to be used in whatever ways are most effective in solving urban problems. In a number of policy areas, federal money is now being distributed to local communities on the condition that certain kinds of reorganization take place at the local level. Urban renewal, open space, poverty, and (particularly significant for its insistence on creating *metropolitan* planning structures) highways are all programs where such conditions have been imposed. State aid, too, has often required local school reorganization in order for a district to be eligible for money. Thus local consensus on the matter of metropolitan action is not invariably a prerequisite to action. State and federal programs can and increasingly do make it too expensive not to reorganize. The task is to apply this general tendency to the specifics of public education. If we can, it may become possible to think with real optimism about the future quality of urban life.

References

Only a few political scientists have examined the public schools. The New York City system is discussed in Wallace Sayre and Herbert Kaufman, *Governing New York City* (New York: Russell Sage Foundation, 1960); New Haven schools are treated in Robert A. Dahl, *Who Governs?* (New Haven: Yale University Press, 1961); the school systems of St. Louis, Kansas City, Chicago, and Detroit are considered, primarily as they are related to the state politics, in Nicholas A. Masters, Robert H. Salisbury, and Thomas H. Eliot, *State Politics and the Public Schools* (New York: Alfred A. Knopf, 1964). A recent and comprehensive examination of a major big-city system is Robert J. Havighurst, *The Public Schools of Chicago* (Chicago: The Board of Education of the City of Chicago, 1964). Of course, a major statement which calls attention to the special and difficult problems of the core-city schools is James B. Conant, *Slums and Suburbs* (New York: McGraw-Hill, 1961). A number of Conant's other works are also highly relevant to the problems discussed in this paper.

CHAPTER SIXTEEN

THE REINSTITUTIONALIZATION OF SOCIAL WELFARE

Ralph E. Pumphrey

The quality of American urban life is now seriously degraded by the narrow goals and historic patchwork of social welfare services. Social welfare should be reoriented toward the universal and predictable crises which threaten normal American citizens and their normal personal development. Professor Pumphrey outlines the steps needed to give American social welfare this universal orientation.

Social welfare today is laden with program disparities, inadequacies and prohibitions. Although less visible to the casual observer than the traffic jams that occur at poorly planned interchanges, the shortcomings in social welfare seriously diminish the quality of urban living. What is needed is an over-all strategy that will guide our collective efforts into more constructive and effective channels.

In any metropolitan area the objectives of the multitudinous social welfare activities reflect such varied concerns that many are nearly incompatible. They employ the talents of highly trained people from a wide variety of professions, but in some programs both the public and the administrators show a superb Jacksonian disdain for professional qualifications. While some services in any given metropolitan area are administered

Ralph E. Pumphrey is a Professor at the George Warren Brown School of Social Work, Washington University, and editor with Muriel W. Pumphrey of *The Heritage of American Social Work* (1961).

by state or national agencies, many of the most important are organized and financed by the smallest local governmental and voluntary units with little or no regard to the standards and practices of their neighbors. Services are not always available to persons in similar circumstances in all parts of a metropolitan area, and few indeed are the ones that are uniformly available in all parts of the country.

What we have is the outgrowth of generations, sometimes centuries, of organizational and program development with a minimum of consultation and joint planning among the organizations. For the most part, the programs are geared to meet the immediate needs of persons struck down by illness or misfortune. Sometimes this sort of help is all the natural recuperative processes of body and personality need. But often this is not enough. For example, the victim of a "cerebral accident" needs care and treatment to get the cardiovascular system to function again at an acceptable level. Too often this is where care stops, without the additional retraining of nerves and muscles that restores mobility. There are many other preventive and restorative aids that are within our knowledge but not our usual practice.

One type of situation around which a strategy for the development of social welfare services might be built is that of personal and social crises. From birth to death the normal individual experiences innumerable crises. Many, such as birth itself, major illnesses, and the threat of death, happen to everybody. Others, such as being born in a large family with an inadequate income, leaving school for economic reasons, and recurring unemployment, are less frequent, but still predictable episodes fraught with uncertainty and the threat of actual harm to individual development. Similarly, communities are subject to periods of stress and strain that can be damaging to their collective existences as well as to their individual members.

Weathering such experiences successfully helps an individual to mature and to deal more effectively with later challenges as they occur. Failure, and especially repeated failure, often results in immaturity or in handicapping conditions that make it difficult or impossible for a person to progress through life normally. As Ben Franklin recognized long ago,[1] when society takes supportive measures to ensure that an individual comes through one situation successfully, it reduces or eliminates the need for other supportive services at later periods. If we were to use this understanding as the basis for developing a strategy of social welfare, the planning of a metropolitan program would be directed toward clusters of crisis-producing situations that threaten normal citizens and normal personal development. In the present state of American governmental organization many of the policy decisions and much of the administration would have to take place at state or federal levels, but the collective voice of the metropolitan areas in interpreting needs and strategies would be vital in reaching those policy decisions.

Ill Health

Since reliable bodily performance is essential to a normal life and to opportunities for personal achievement, any illness, and particularly any severe illness, constitutes a threat of great magnitude. In the concept of responsibility that we have derived from the days of the Elizabethan Poor Law, the individual must make his own arrangements for medical care, with public provision entering at the latest possible date and in the least possible amount. Within a crisis-oriented strategy, society would seek to insure that every person would have immediate access to medical care when he becomes ill.

Unfortunately, such access is not an automatic by-product of our steadily improving knowledge and techniques in medicine. Medical knowledge is available only in those places where the physicians having the knowledge and skill are found. It is accessible only to those patients the physicians are willing to serve. At present, in spite of all past efforts to improve distribution, the availability of medical care is still uneven. In

[1] *Continuation of the Account of the Pennsylvania Hospital . . . to the Fifth of May, 1761* (Philadelphia, Pa.: B. Franklin and D. Hall, 1761) pp. 113–114.

addition, the vital statistics of almost any city reveal a wide disparity of accessibility. Legislation must hasten universal plans either for publicly financed medical care services or for prepayment health insurance.

However, such curative care is essentially a secondary approach to health problems. The primary approach should be to maintain an array of precautionary and preventive services. These services should help all people through the normal vicissitudes of life with the minimum of damaging experience. In the process, they should detect at an early period the need for specific remedial measures, rather than allow conditions to develop to damaging proportions without attention. Examples of such precautionary and preventive services that are now unavailable or inaccessible to large segments of the population are the following: premarital examinations; prenatal and well-baby clinics; pediatric supervision for the preschool child; full dental care for children and adults (not merely extractions); periodic physical examinations, including consultation on problems of the climacteric; homemaker services in case of illness; and delivery of meals to homes of persons who are otherwise able to care for themselves.

Social Adjustment

Under the most favorable circumstances society can offer, many people will still sometimes find it hard to make personal adjustments — for example, when taking on a new job, getting married, having a baby, moving to a strange community, losing a wife, husband, or child. A variety of services such as personal counseling and educational and vocational guidance should be available to help people detect and deal with such problems early. For maximum accessibility such services must be located at strategic places in the community: in schools, churches, and places of employment, as well as at busy commercial or traffic centers where a person might "drop in" in a more or less anonymous way. Examples of such services and settings now exist, sometimes under governmental, sometimes under voluntary sponsorship, but the total of what is being done gives only a glimpse of the potential value of a full-scale metropolitan program.

A city can also promote social adjustment by encouraging persons of all ages to greater personal self-development. We make much of our commitment to public education. Since we rely primarily on local and state implementation of this policy, however, we have allowed wide disparities to arise within and among metropolises. Museums, art, craft, and technical schools, and park and recreation facilities are marked by even more serious disparities in availability and accessibility. There is urgent need for metropolitan reassessment of this whole area of public responsibility and for improvement of performance in it.

Inadequate Income

Nothing is more threatening to an individual's health and social adjustment than a prolonged failure of income. At some time in life nearly everyone experiences a "pinch" — income or financial resources which are insufficient for the needs or desires of the moment. Usually this is a temporary condition, or it is not so serious but that it can be adjusted to without endangering nutrition, health, or social relations. However, prolonged or chronic financial need with accompanying substandard living arrangements can have a devastating effect on the morale, the health, the educational achievement, and the occupational potential of individuals and the communities in which they live.

Our present method of dealing with income failure involves a maze of insurance and assistance programs. Because these are so specialized and many of them require elaborate procedures of investigation of eligibility, they are cumbersome and expensive to administer. These same features mean that many citizens whose needs are real cannot be helped because their qualifications do not match those established for the programs. It is like matching square pegs to round holes.

The social insurance programs that have been developed

during the past half century—workmen's compensation as well as unemployment, retirement, disability, and others—are each highly specialized. By simplifying the determination of eligibility and standardizing benefits, however, their costs of administration have been greatly reduced. At the same time, the contractual type of relationship used in them lends an "honorable" status to the beneficiary who is not associated with public assistance.

These insurance programs can be enlarged and improved in many ways, but they will remain piecemeal approaches to income loss. Lack of income, irrespective of the occasion, must be generally understood as a crisis-precipitating situation of such seriousness as to require a universal set of preventive and remedial measures. Otherwise the public will continue to see the insurance and assistance programs as forms of charity to the improvident which drain the public treasury rather than as socially constructive measures that enable individuals to realize their potentials, while enabling the metropolises in which they live to enlarge their human resources.

Several current proposals would fill in some of the gaps in existing programs. Adolescents should be paid for staying in school; we should follow the Canadian example of providing governmental allowances for all children, thus somewhat equalizing the benefits now enjoyed by the well-to-do through tax exemptions. Helpful as these proposals would be, they would reach only limited segments of the population, largely determined by age.

Another current type of proposal is that poor people with few, if any, qualifications but lack of income, should receive cash income through the operation of some form of a "reverse income tax." This offers universality and ease of administration. Its greatest drawback would be in its perpetuation of a form of "means test." Since this test would be applied mechanically and without the harassing investigations associated with most public assistance, this drawback might not be too serious. However, it does suggest the need to look for a device that would be even more universal.

Such a truly universal device for income maintenance would be a system of wage payments to every individual having less than a prescribed minimum income. These wage payments would be made for the performance of socially useful tasks appropriate to the age and sex of the recipient. Many of these would normally be performed in the home, as in the case of the preschool child going through the learning and development expected at that period of life, or his mother, as she cares for him. Others, such as school attendance or job hunting, would take place outside the home. Persons who went beyond normal life tasks to engage in various community activities might be eligible for additional compensation. Incentives to self-development and to self-care for those who might otherwise be dependent could be incorporated. By integrating the plan with a set of individual wage records from birth to death, both income tax and wage payments could be serviced by a single set of records.

Such a system of wage payments would greatly modify the need for social insurance, public assistance programs, and such services as medical care for the indigent as we now know them. For instance, today in a three-generation indigent family we may well be using most of the following programs: Old Age and Survivor's Insurance, Old Age Assistance, Unemployment Insurance, Assistance to Families with Dependent Children, General Assistance, and free medical care in a municipal hospital. Under the wage payment system, the grandfather, who is an ambulatory invalid, might receive pay for self-care, while his wife could receive pay as a homemaker. The son, who is unemployed, might receive a base pay related to his efforts to secure employment, possibly augmented by increments on account of participation in a retraining program and his leadership in a neighborhood recreation activity. His wife would receive homemaker's pay based on the number of children, possibly augmented in recognition of any special care required by her father-in-law. Each child would receive pay that might be graduated according to age or school grade. Payments to any individual would be terminated whenever payroll reports for income tax purposes indicated income above the established cutoff level. Payments to any individual would also be challenged whenever there was an indication of failure to perform expected tasks, as in case of a school report of truancy. With this sort of assured income, not only would most public assistance cease to be needed, families would be helped to use their strengths instead of being constantly weakened through deprivation, and the nature and volume of demands for free medical care would almost certainly be drastically altered.

Handicapping Conditions

Arrangements appropriate for normal persons will not meet the needs of those whose income-producing capacities are reduced by physical, mental, social, or emotional handicaps. Great personal frustration to the individual, and economic loss to the community, could be avoided by eliminating the arbitrary exclusion of handicapped persons from those productive activities which they are capable of performing to everybody's satisfaction. Until recently, orthopedic and a few other physical difficulties were the only ones for which there were positive rehabilitation programs. Substantial but spotty efforts are beginning to be directed toward mental retardation and technological unemployment. For persons who have suffered mental illness, alcoholism, or imprisonment, to mention only a few other categories of handicap, there is seldom more than token rehabilitative treatment available.

The design of a metropolitan program for this segment of the population should begin with a recognition that to diagnose a handicapping condition is to predict a long series of crises for that person. If transformed into policy, such recognition would permit strategies to deal with crises in advance, or at least as soon as they arise. Standards for the utilization of handicapped persons could be developed. Increased attention could be given to the evaluation of disabilities, to the application of therapeutic measures for the restoration of lost capacities, to the appropriate assignment or reassignment of tasks, and to the promotion of public acceptance of a productive role for persons of limited abilities. A broad, publicly financed program of sheltered employment for handicapped persons might be extended to include persons displaced from industry. The work habits, skills, and morale of marginally employable persons could thereby be maintained at the same time that the existence of such a group would be kept before the public.

For the relatively small number of children whose families are unsuitable for child rearing, there will likewise be need for special services and institutions for protection, care, and encouragement. The preventive value of such services for this special type of handicapped person can be measured only by the success of each child in meeting later strains without requiring excessive supportive or controlling services.

Elderly and other persons who cannot today be seen as economically productive are subject to chronic and overwhelming frustration. They and those around them seldom exercise any substantial measure of their real capacities. Occupying chairs or cots in homes or boarding houses or nursing homes, they have been relegated to a sense of helplessness and hopelessness. By cultivation of self-care, they could obtain substantial personal satisfaction while at the same time they would lessen the demands upon available manpower for housekeeping and nursing services. By encouraging aged and chronic invalids to engage in activities of benefit to others, the satisfactions of achievement once more might come within their grasp. Some might even find that their handicaps were not so severe as had been thought, and, given proper outlets, they might join the productive group again.

Whatever the degree and probable duration of a handicapping condition, it is essential to promote positive social attitudes toward the victims. If society assumes or decrees that they are incapable of further productive activity, it probably will be so. On the other hand, to demand immediate resumption of full activities may prevent effective recuperation. The institutional arrangements available to all people must be prepared to help society give the encouragement and support needed by the handicapped during their periods of recovery.

The General Program

Within such a social welfare framework, it is evident that the over-all emphasis must be a positive one in the direction of higher standards of normal opportunities and performance. This major thrust would support and be supported by other thrusts that would offer opportunities to all persons to develop their capacities for excellence and, at the same time, would keep the handicapped as much as possible within the main stream of society.

Interference with opportunities for self-development by poverty, race, and the unequal distribution of educational, health, and other facilities must be minimized. At the same time, a strategy based on an orientation to crises would recognize that at all times any individual is subject to threats and blows which can be permanently detrimental to self-development. Primary defenses should be mass measures designed to eliminate or minimize threatening situations before the individual is affected. However, given a failure of preventive measures, chances of a citizen's survival undamaged from an actual threat or blow will be greatly increased by a full metropolitan array of immediately available facilities to support the individual's defensive and recuperative powers, and to provide curative and restorative services.

Research and Policy Decisions

To bring social welfare activities of a metropolis to such a minimum adequate standard will require intensive research activities far beyond anything heretofore devoted to the social, behavioral, or biological sciences, with the possible exception of medicine. Outcomes of such research might be

1. The establishment of realistic norms of expectation for personal performance.
2. Understanding of motivation, so that individuals might be freed to undertake the personal effort involved in high achievement.
3. Techniques for care and rehabilitation of many forms of handicapping conditions, not merely the physical ones.
4. Development of new ways to utilize the productive capacities and energies of people.

The conversion of research findings into operational measures will, of course, require policy decisions on many issues at many levels. Several types of issues can be anticipated readily:

1. The extent and boundaries of mandatory performance to be required of individuals, administrative units, or both.
2. The extent to which the individual would be encouraged or enabled to obtain goods and services in the open market, as against the provision by society of the goods and services themselves.
3. Short-range as against long-range objectives.
4. The location of administrative and fiscal authority.

Larger Jurisdictional Units

In determining the location of authority, there is much to be said for the use of larger jurisdictional units for administration and/or standard setting. Present reliance on a myriad of small, outmoded local units, whether voluntary or governmental, functioning as social welfare agencies with a minimum of effective supervision, results in a denial of adequacy, equality, and universality of treatment. With more supervision and program assistance, larger units could combat the harmful effects of parochialism. There is no clear indication from past experience that larger jurisdictions have been more detrimental to experimentation or less adaptable than smaller ones. This does not rule out categorically either local or state-sized units, but it does say that the relative utility of the smaller units needs to be carefully weighed before they are adopted or continued. In general, the appropriateness of any administrative unit could be judged by these criteria:

1. It is practical to put services on a professional basis.
2. They can be made subject to enforceable uniform standards of administration and service.
3. They have an equal minimum access to the resources of the total economy of the nation, and are not entirely tied to the fluctuating economic resources of a single community or area.

Social Invention

The reinstitutionalization of social welfare will have to be, above all, a process of application of social invention. But this will require a change in social attitudes toward that which is new. The acclaim and financial rewards accorded inventors in business, industry, and some professions have not been available in the public sector of social organization. Creative ideas are formulated constantly; some, such as the living wage and workmen's compensation, have been adopted. A neighborhood legal service is a hopeful invention emerging from the war on poverty. But without personal recognition and financial rewards few social inventors can afford the promotional effort needed to put their ideas across.

There are indications that the climate of the times may be becoming more favorable to social change. If this is so, we may hope that within the not-too-distant future it might be possible to make real progress toward goals which now seem utopian. This will be particularly true if it is recognized that much of what we already have is good and will remain useful. Using what we have as a platform we can produce new ideas and new ways of using old tools. Will society accept them for trial, and recognize the value it receives?

References

A comprehensive view of existing social welfare programs and problems can be obtained from the more than one hundred topical articles and the statistical supplement in the *Encyclopedia of Social Work* (New York: National Association of Social Workers, 1965). Several volumes of assembled critical and analytical studies, comments, and proposals are available, of which *Poverty in America,* edited by Ferman, Kornbluh, and Haber, with an introduction by Michael Harrington (Ann Arbor: University of Michigan Press, 1965), is one of the most useful. An incisive view of the role of social welfare in the development of individuals, communities, and nations is Elizabeth Wickenden, *Social Welfare in a Changing World* (Washington, D.C.: U.S. Department of Health, Education, and Welfare, Welfare Administration, 1965). An analytical review of crisis theory literature is found in Kent Miller and Ira Iscoe, "The Concept of Crisis: Current Status and Mental Health Implications," *Human Organization, xxii* (Fall, 1963) 195–201. Twenty-nine articles on crisis theory, common crisis situations, clinical applications, and measurement are collected in *Crisis Intervention*, Howard J. Parad (ed.) (New York: Family Service Association of America, 1965).

INDEX

Abercrombie, Patrick, 198
Aerospace industries, 65
Affluence, 82, 158
Aged, the, 15, 16, 293
  government concern with, 26
  in labor market, 82, 100
  and projected federal expenditure, 63
  and retirement communities, 177
  wealthy, 158
Agricultural policy, 13, 34, 75
  and exodus to city, 170
  and federal grant-in-aid program, 51
  in Great Britain, 198
  and projected federal spending, 63
Agriculture, U.S. Department of, 26
  as rural affairs agency, 67
Aid to Dependent Children, 291
Airports, 51
  federal aid to, 72
Alberti, Leon Battista, 166
Amenities, urban, 163–177
  cultural, 165, 169
  and future labor force, 176
  geography of, 168
  in Great Britain, 201
  and new town idea, 213, 225
  physical, 165, 169–170
  and private capital, 181–182
  of "Riviera" regions, 168–170
  and service workers, 175
  and white-collar workers, 174
American Federation of Teachers (AFT), 270
"Americanism," 148–151, 154–155
  and suburbia, 155–157
American Society (Williams), 150
Amish, 152
Anomic society, 108, 109
Appalachia Bill, 33–34. *See also* War on Poverty
Apparel industry, 132–134
Architect, 9, 10, 179, 184–186
  lack of experimenting by, 58
  and urban renewal, 57
Argentina, 194
Asia, 169
Asocial behavior, 4, 7
  and unemployables, 19
Atmospheric basins, 38
Automation, 20, 24, 137
  and job enlargement, 90, 101
  and job fragmentation, 101
  and quality, 136
  and service sector, 175
  and white-collar labor, 174

Bargaining, 35
Baudelaire, Charles, 166
Beautification program, federal, 26
Berger, Bennett, 143, 184
Bettelheim, Bruno, 153
Birth rate, 138. *See also* Population, general increase in
Blauner, Robert, 86, 90
Blight, 36, 165–166
  and age distribution of housing, 237
Bond issues, 250–251, 254. *See also* Fiscal policy
Boston, Massachusetts, 252. *See also* West End Study
Brown, George, 202
Buchanan, Colin D., 195
Budget surpluses, federal, *see* Fiscal policy
Bureaucracy, 25–26, 42
  and cost-efficiency, 25
  and federal requirements for local planning, 39
  public-school, 265–266
  vested interests of local, 31–33
Bureau of Public Roads, U.S., 39
Burke, Kenneth, 153

Bussing, of school children, 41, 275
in St. Louis, 249, 251
and socioeconomic mixing, 239
See also Schools, integration of

California, 34
and defense industries, 66
population rise in, 167–168
as "Riviera" region, 168, 169, 176
San Francisco, 40, 195
Canals, 68
Capital investment, public, 28
Caucasus, 176
Census Bureau, U.S., 9
and metropolitan information center, 39
Charity, 13. *See also* Welfare policy
Chicago, Illinois, 30, 125–126, 278
Lake Meadows project, 182
Child-guidance clinics, 261
Children, needy, 14–16, 275
alienated, and elementary school, 259–261
drop-outs, 261–264
education of, 246–257
preschool, 257–259
stimulus deprivation of, 257
Cincinnati, Ohio, 253
City, 163–177, 183, 193–197, *passim*
advantage of for seasonal worker, 134–135
allocations problems of, 44
appeal of for migrant, 124–125
and consumer-market judgments, 136
diversified services of, 43–44
economic functions of, 128, 229–231
federal programs, effects of, 127–128
growth, long-term planning for, 198
historical trends, U.S., 45–46, 49, 164
inflow of migrants, 126–127, 137–140
inhabitants' preferences for, 241
interdependence of service sector, 175
and legal system, 208–226
loss of leadership of, 49–51
lowest status population of, 83. *See also* Slums
and manufacturing sites, 174
national network of, 46–48, 52–53
need for federal experimental institutions in, 57–59, 190
need for national policy for, 23–42
optimum size, 199
physical structure of, 10–11, 44, 46, 179–180, 273
policy making for, *see* Policy making, urban
and programs for physical planning, 183–186
and private investment, 181–183, 197
and public investment, 180–181
and public management, 229–244
reorganization of local government in, 53, 56–57, 59
shifts and variations of network, 46–47
small-scale environment in, 49–52
social and economic strength of, 194, 235–236
spatial pattern of, 235–237
and specialized employment, 129–132
special-purpose districts of, 57. *See also* Core cities
Civil defense, 51
Civil rights, 165, 238, 247, 257
Civil service, 50, 58
federal, and national public works, 53–54
federal supervision of state and local, 52, 53, 59
Class differences, 40–41, 183
and urban planning, 159–160
and valid identity, 105
and work orientations, 88–93
Climate, 168. *See also* "Riviera" regions
Cobb, Henry, 181
Cold War, 54, 64
Colorado, 176
Commerce, U.S. Department of, 38
and metropolitan information center, 39
Communications
and federal responsibility, 53
and pressure for success, 109–110
Community
agencies, and education, 256–257
class conflicts, 35
development and federal spending, 65
enclosed, 151
facilities, 4, 211
mixed-income, 236–237. *See also* New town communities
planning, federal requirements for, 39
power structure, 31–32, 35
services, 10, 35, 44, 50, 164, 182, 187–188. *See also* Public services
unitary, and education, 271–272
Community Action Programs, 258, 265, 277
in New York, 264

Computers, 131
Congress of Industrial Organizations (CIO), 24
Congress, U.S., 29, 37
Conservation, 40, 52, 75, 183
in Great Britain, 195
and green belts, 198
and U.S. federal grants-in-aid programs, 51
Construction, 21
commercial, 196
federal experimentation in, 58
home, 32, 236
public, 53
redundant, 185, 186
urban, 52, 183
Core cities, 49
conversion of, 206
exclusion of vehicular traffic from, 195–196, 200, 201
in Great Britain, 195–197
institutional reorganization in, 268–278
multilevel transportation in, 196
and regional planning policy, 194
renewal of, 236. *See also* Urban renewal
schools of, 237–238, 280–281
Council of Economic Advisors, 14, 38
Council of Mayors, 32
Council for Mid-Wales, 202
Council for the Preservation of Rural England, 195
Crestwood Heights (Seely et al.), 145
Crimean "Riviera," 176
Culturally disadvantaged, 7, 16, 247, 251, 257
and alienated elementary school child, 259–261
and parochial schools, 252
and preschool child, 257-259
Culture, 7, 44, 158
and city's poor, 54
and cultural deprivation, 82
and rural migrant, 94
See also Pluralism, cultural

Data banks, *see* Information centers, metropolitan
Davis, Allison, 118–119, 122
Davis, Wylie H., 249
Day-care centers, 258. *See also* Children, preschool
Decision-making, metropolitan, *see* Policy-making, urban
Defense programs, *see* National defense
Defense, U.S. Department of, 131
Desalinization, 68
Design, urban, 165–166, 179, 185
Detroit, Michigan, 242
Deutsch, Martin, 259
Dewey, John, 153
Disarmament, 64
Disaster relief, 51
Discrimination, 12, 99–104
and cultural patterns, 161–162
and full employment, 100
in hiring practices, 100
and increased unemployment, 138
and job situation, 84
in labor market, 19
and occupational and social mobility, 92–93
rural, 124
urban, 124
District of Columbia, 280
Domestic policy, federal, 50–59
"Downstream effects," 182–183
Durkheim, Emile, 109, 157
Dyckman, John, 182

Economic growth, 3–4, 17–22, 75
and budget surplus, federal, 15
and creation of labor scarcity, 18–21, 22
and federal influence, 31
and unemployment, 82
Economic Opportunity Act, 262
Education, 16, 24, 29, 52, 75, 170, 187, 246–267
and academically gifted, 247
and community resources, 255
compensatory, 253–254
federal expenditure (1965–1975), 65
and federal grants-in-aid program, 51
in Great Britain, 201
of immigrants, 44, 149
in new town program, 213
nonacademic functions of, 246, 250
for the poor, 11-12. *See also* Children, needy
preschool, 257-259
and public expenditure, 69
and retraining programs, 38
special programs in, 250, 262
and social position, 8, 9, 235–240
and social sciences, 57
urban orientation, 50
and urban politics, 268–284
and urban price structure, 232, 250

Education (*continued*)
and white-collar worker, 173
vocational, 262. *See also* Vocational training
Education Act of 1965, 58, 254–255
and culturally disadvantaged child, 261
Educational parks, 239
Education, U.S. Office of, 69
"Effectiveness of Metropolitan Planning," (M.I.T.-Harvard Joint Center for Urban Studies), 201
Eisenhower, Dwight D., 17, 18
Electronics, 65
Employer, 124
choice of urban, 125–126
expectations of, 85–86
and Negro style of life, 122
Employment, 3, 267
counseling, 247
and "drop-out," 261–262
full, 20, 100–101, 165
in Great Britain, 203–204, 207
and metropolitan information centers, 39
and rise in GNP, 18–22
in service sector, 175
sheltered for handicapped, 293
specialization of urban, 129–131
stability, and fiscal policy, 61, 70–71
in urban government, 130–131
in urban manufacturing, 131–132
urban, and rural migration, 137–140
Employment Opportunity Act, 262
Employment Security Administration, 51
Engineers, 9, 10
Engineers, U.S. Corps of, 54
England, see Great Britain
Equal Opportunity Act, 220, 235
Erikson, Eric H., 106
Europe, 169. *See also* "Riviera" regions
European Economic Community (E.E.C.), 207
European Free Trade Association (E.F.T.A.), 207
Expenditure, federal, see Fiscal policy, federal

Farm parity program, 127, 171
Federal Housing Administration (F.H.A.), 32, 33, 128, 220–221
Federal Manpower Development and Training Act, 262
Federal Reserve Board, 32
Federal Trade Commission, 54
Feinstein, Harold, 112
Fire departments, urban, 50
Fiscal policy, 61–77, 273
and aid, state and local, 70–75, 234
and allocation of public resources, 75–77
and conditional grants, 71–72
and core area education, 237–238, 278
and direct federal expenditures, 71
and federal budget trends, 62–63, 77
and federal expenditure, 15, 63–66, 67
federal-state-local relationship, 68–70
and federal tax reduction, 73–75, 234
shifts in emphasis, 65–66
and surpluses, 15, 68, 70, 72, 74, 234
and tax credits, 73
and tax sharing, 73, 74
and total federal revenues, 66–67
and unconditional grants, 72–73
Florida, 168, 169
Everglades, 176
France, 168
Greater Paris, 169
Mediterranean seashore, 169
urban renewal planning in, 201–202
Franklin, Benjamin, 287
Fried, Marc, 154, 191
Friedmann, Georges, 90–91
Friends of the Lakes, 195
Funds, allocation of public, 75–77. *See also* Fiscal policy

Galbraith, J. Kenneth, 62, 243
Gans, Herbert, 112, 160–161
Levittown study, 145
Garden Cities of To-morrow (Howard) 195
Georgia, 74
Ghettos, 148–149, 162, 266
core area, 239. *See also* Slums
and Jews, 152
Goldman, Ray, 182
Gottmann, Jean, 183
Government, local, 9
consolidation of, 12
and uniform standards, 8–12
See also Policy-making, urban
Grants-in-aid, federal, 43, 49, 52, 72, 75
and Great Depression, 51

Grants-in-aid (*continued*)
and local fiscal difficulties, 69
and new town programs, 217
projected expansion of, 70
staffing of, 51
Great Britain, 14, 169
and channel tunnel to France, 206
farmer in, 171
Gross National Product, 207
Labour Party, 207
local government commission, 200–201, 213–215, 218–219
Ministry of Housing and Local Government, 200, 213–215
regional planning in, 193–208. *See also* New towns; Green belt towns
South East Study, 203–208
Great Depression (1930's), 49, 50
Great Society, 65, 165
and social change, 99
Green belt towns, 58
in Great Britain, 194, 195, 197–199, 204, 205
Gross National Product, 17–18, 63, 64, 207, 230
projected (1965–1975), 64
and total federal revenue, 66–67
Guest, Robert H., 86
Gulf Coast, U.S., 34

Haar, Charles M., 203
Hailsham Report, 202
Hammond, Indiana, 30
Handicapped, 14, 16
education for, 250, 260–261
in the labor market, 82, 100, 293
and social policy, 292–294
stable incomes for, 15
Haryou Act, 263
Haussmann, Baron Georges Eugène, 166
Health, 247, 287–288
curative care, 287–288
and federal grants-in-aid, 51
preventative services, 288
Health, Education, and Welfare, U.S. Department of, 38
Heller, Walter, 72
Henry, Jules, 114
Highways, 5, 35, 37, 75, 283
and federal grants-in-aid, 51, 56, 63, 70
and federal interstate program, 28, 45, 54, 224
federal requirements for local planning, 39, 181
and inner city–outer ring commercial sites, 32
intercity routes, 54
and population displacement, 210, 213
and state leadership, 38
Hospitals, 35, 201
city, 50
dual role of urban, 44
and the poor, 55
state responsibility for, 50
Housing, 4, 8, 16, 164, 210, 235, 267
age distribution of, 237
codes, 54
construction, suburban, 69, 128
federal grants for, 72
and the law, 209
and locational choice, 27
in London, 204–205
low-cost for the poor, 14–15, 28, 210, 220, 222, 237
mixed-market, 223
and new town communities, 213, 215, 218, 220, 225
restrictive covenants for, 4, 127, 219
segregation, 4–8, 99–100, 220
in slums, 17, 210
suburban, federal experiments in, *see* Green belt towns
U.S. policy for, 13, 37
Housing and Home Finance Agency (HHFA), 32, 34, 39
Housing and Urban Development, U.S. Department of, 37
Howard, Ebenezer, 195, 199–200
Human resources, 38, 230
accounting systems for, 39
and policy-making, 28–29, 31
Hunt, H. L., 158

Identity, 105–123
in anomic society, 108
and career success, 109, 110–111, 121
and depersonalization, 107
and equalitarianism, 111
and "good American life," 110, 121
lower-class, 111–123
and nonconformity, 108, 111, 112
and normal achievement, 106
personal, defined, 106–107
and work role, 108–109, 111, 121–123

Immigration, 4, 46, 83, 126, 140, 149
 and city schools, 44
 and ghettos, 148
Income, 7, 53, 69, 165, 234, 286
 distribution, alteration in, 14, 65, 232
 equalization of, 72
 and federal fiscal policy, 61, 70
 guaranteed minimum, 48, 54–56, 59, 291–292
 low, and urban renewal, 210
 nonagricultural, 165
 and social policy, 289–292
Industrial location, 38, 174, 235
 factors governing decisions for, 27–28
 federal decisions in, 27–28
 in Great Britain, 201
 and new town programs, 225
 for seasonal industries, 134–135, 137
 suburbanization of, 49
 urban, 131–133, 137
Industrial processes, *see* Technology
Inflation, 21, 234
 and time-lag in development, 212
Information centers, metropolitan, 39
 in California, 66
 for policy-making, 240–244
Inner city, 6–7, 8
 FHA policy for construction in, 32
 and outer ring, 32
 See also Core cities
Integration, school, *see* School, integration of
Interior, U.S. Department of, 54
International affairs, 52, 64
International Business Machines Corp. (IBM), 175
Interstate Commerce Commission, 54
Interstate compacts, 39
 and urban government reorganization, 57
Italy, 168, 176

Jacobs, Jane, 160–161, 195
Japan, 194
Jefferson, Thomas, 72
Jews, 152, 153
Jobs
 access to, 209
 fragmentation of, 101
 opportunities for, 7, 16, 24, 90, 100, 169, 209
 performance in, lower-class, 117–123
 placement in, 28
 stability in, 85
Job Corps, see Office of Economic Opportunity
Job Opportunities in Neighborhoods, New York City (JOIN), 263
Johnson, Lyndon B., 18, 21, 22, 163–164
Joint Center for Urban Studies (M.I.T.-Harvard), 201
Junkyards, 165
Juvenile delinquency, 112

Kennedy, John F., 18, 21, 22
Kindergarten, 259. *See also* Children, preschool
Kinship, 86
Korean War, 64, 70
Ktsanes, Thomas, 146

Labor, 18–21, 123, 173–176
 farm, 173
 and location choice, 175
 and metropolitan information system, 39
 and national policy, 26, 38
 and Negro identity, 117–118
 organization of, 24
 seasonal, 134–135
 and service industries, 175
 specialization, 129–131
 and technology, 82, 90
 unskilled, 89, 127, 137
 urban, 124–140
 white-collar, 173
Labor, U.S. Department of, 38
Lake Michigan, 30
Land development, 38, 41, 231, 235
 and federal organization, 56
 and new town idea, 213, 219, 223
 private, and public control, 212
Landscape, 168, 198–199. *See also* Blight
Leisure time, 170
 and white-collar labor, 174
 See also Amenities
Levittown
 institutional facilities of, 148
 New Jersey (Gans's study), 145
 New York (Dobriner-Liell study), 145
Letchworth, England, 199
Libraries, 35, 236
Lindemann, Erich, 102
London, 196
 Barbican project, 196
 County Council, 197

London (*continued*)
employment growth rate in, 203–204
Greater London Council (1965–), 201, 205
green belt, 199
Royal Commission, 201

McKinley, William, 131
Manufacturing
advantages of city for, 134–135
employment in, 131–132, 173–174
federal role in growth of, 33
and housing requirements, 174
productivity advance of, 137
Medicare, 14. *See also* Social insurance
Megalopolis, 34, 163, 167–177
defined, 169
density of, 167–168
employment in, 174
recreational facilities of, 170
world popularity of, 169
Mental health, 185
in California, 66
government concern with, 26
and the school, 247
Merit goods, 29–30
subsidization of, 233
and urban price structure, 232–233
Merritt Parkway, Connecticut, 54
Merton, Robert, 109
Metropolis, *see* City
Middle class, 6, 184, 233
cultural patterns of, 159, 161
and level of aspiration, 110–111
and Negro occupational role, 116
suburbanization of, 49, 144
and U.S. housing policy, 13
Migrants, 34, 37
anxiety of, 85
British, 205
choices of, 99, 102
rural, 84–104, 138, 167
service workers, 28
shift in orientation of, 84–85, 139
and transition crises, 97, 102
and unemployment assistance, 103
urban industrial, 83, 93n, 125–126
volume of, 126–127
white, 168–169
See also Negro
Minimum-wage legislation, 13
Minority, ethnic, 6
and ghetto, 148–149
subculture, 149, 151
and urban schools, 246–247
Missouri, 250. *See also* St. Louis
Mobility, 170, 177
occupational, 83
social, 83–84
Mobilization for Youth, 263
Morris, William, 195
Mortgage insurance, 5, 181
and nonsegregated housing, 220
Mumford, Lewis, 195
Museums, 232–233, 289. *See also* Culture

National defense, 29, 30, 75, 77
federal concentration of, 52
and projected federal spending, 63–65
National Education Association (NEA), 270
National Opinion Research Center, University of Chicago, 145
National Parks and Access to the Countryside legislation, Great Britain, 195
National Resources Planning Board, 23
National resources, *see* Conservation
Negro, 4, 6, 24, 34, 183
and ascribed status, 114
culture patterns of, 113–116, 154, 161
and discrimination, 99–100, 138
effect of World War II upon, 127
and federal policy, 12
and ghetto organization, 162
in labor market, 92–93
"language," 113
mobility of, 93n, 139
music and dancing, 113
political apathy of, 13–14
and problem of identity, 108, 112–123
religion, 113
and reputation in peer group, 113
Revolution, organization and funding of, 26
school orientation of, 117
and self-awareness, 113–114
and social progress, 15, 272–273
transition crises of, 97–98
unemployment, 19, 138
and urban school, 248–249, 266–267, 275
work orientation of, 117
Neighborhoods, 186–191, 273
defined, 187

Neighborhoods (*continued*)
and federal research money, 190–191
and forced displacement, 210
planning, and schools, 274–276. *See also* Schools, neighborhood
public services for, 191
and residential environment, 188–190
New Deal (1933–1935), 52
New town communities, 199–200, 204, 209–210, 212–226, 236
Act, 42, 195, 196, 199, 206
advantages of British system, 215–216
aims of, 224–226
amenities for, 213
for America, 217–226
automobile regulation in, 195–196, 200
and centralization of authority, 200–201, 213–215, 216
Commission, Great Britain, 200–201, 213–215
defined, 212–213
and federal commitment, 217–221
fixed population of, 199
flexibility of, 216
history of, 213–215
housing for, 220
initiative for development of, 216, 220, 222
and master plan, 214
public-private partnership in, 222–225
scale, control of, 216, 225
and state legislation, 218–219
and timing, 215–216, 222
and urban setting, 220–221
New York City, 24, 195, 266, 269–270
changes in structure of, 47
community action programs, 263
education and public services in, 56
and integration, 266, 278
Port Authority, 33
study of commuter movements in, 41
New York Life Insurance Company, 182
Netherlands, 169
Randstadt Holland, 169
1949 Housing Act, 32
Nonconformity, 108, 111–112
Northeast U.S., *see* Megalopolis
Norway, 11
Nursery schools, 258
teacher training for, 258–259
See also Children, preschool
Old-age pensions, 14. *See also* Social insurance
Office of Economic Opportunity, 258
Job Corps, 264
Office building, 196
Ohio, 168, 253
Old Age Assistance, 291
Old Age Survivor's Insurance, 63, 75, 291
Open space, 42, 201, 283
and federal highway program, 45
and federal regulation, 48
and green belt, Great Britain, 198
See also Conservation
Operation Head Start, 26, 257
federal support level for, 258
See also Culturally disadvantaged
Outer ring, 32
FHA policy for construction in, 32
See also Suburbs
Outgoing Life, The (Whyte), 145
Overspill, population, 38, 194, 197, 201
in London, 206
Owen, Robert, 195
Oxford City Plan, Great Britain, 195

Panic of 1837, 74
Parks, 5, 8, 10, 35, 55, 236, 289
See also Recreational facilities
Parochial schools, 251
changing policies of, 252–257
as college preparatory schools, 253
financial problems of, 252
growth of (1950–1960), 252
Parsons, Talcott, 116–117
Pei, I. M., 181
Pennsylvania Turnpike, 54
Playground facilities, 8, 10, 55
in slums, 233
See also Recreational facilities
Pluralism, cultural, 184
and ghettos, 148
and planning, 157–162
and suburbia, 148–151, 154
See also Americanism
Police, urban, 44, 50, 164, 187–188
Policy-making, urban, 8–22, 23, 25
and allocation of public funds, 75–77
apparatus for, 40
bureaucratic competition in, 35, 39
constraints to federal, 43–59
coordination in, 31–36
division of power in, 210–212
and "externalities," 31

Policy-making (*continued*)
federal, 3, 8, 11, 21, 22, 28, 36–42, 190–191, 211
financing for, 15–16, 27–28
in Great Britain, 200–203
and human resources, 28–29, 31
and image of solidarity, 157–159
and information, 240–244
inventory for, 179–191
legal structure for, 209–226
at local level, 3, 11, 22, 26, 35–36, 39, 190–191, 211
and local sovereignty, 25
manpower, 37
and merit goods, 29–30
and over-all planning, 216
and overspill, 38, 194, 197, 201
and "policies plan," 39
private, 25
public control of, 27
and public goods, 29
and research capability, 240
social, 15, 28–29, 31, 157–164, 285–296
spatial units of, 25
at state level, 38
uniform standards in, 8–12, 36–42
and U.S. economy, 17–22, 31
Pollution, air and water, 30, 38, 165
in California, 66
and federal regulation, 48
and federal responsibility, 53
and "policies plan," 40
Poor, the, 54, 246
commuting patterns of, 210
and economic and social policy, U.S., 13–16
in Great Britain, 197
and housing, 14–15, 28, 54, 210
and minimum personal income, 54
and public service prices, 233–234
and residential developments, 159
and transition crises, 103–104
U.S. image of, 157
See also Underclass
Population, 6
of American metropolises, 47
concentration, and political pressure, 171–172, 248–249
density, urban, 165, 170, 193–194, 246
displacement, 210, 213
general increase in, 5, 169
growth, U.S., 17–18
in Great Britain, 205, 207
and mixed industry, 229
national distribution of, 37, 170–171
and political-economic balance, 171–172
rural, 171
and unemployment, 20
Postal Service, U.S., 29
Postindustrial society, 24–25
Poverty, 3–8, 247, 283
government concern with, 26
and labor scarcity, 19–20
and number of children, 14
and U.S. economic growth, 17–22
See also War on Poverty
Power services,
federal minimum standards for, 48
and federal responsibility, 53
Prejudice, 4–5, 16. *See also* Discrimination
Preschools, 257–259
and pediatric supervision, 288
President's Economic Council, *see* Council of Economic Advisors
Prices, 21, 184
and promotional pricing, 233
urban structure for, 231–235
Procurements, governmental, 65
Public health, 52
Public housing, 5, 75, 219, 237
architectural blandness of, 58
custodial aspect of, 41
federal investment in, 34, 63, 65
and the poor, 55
Public goods, 29–30, 232
and "user charges," 233–234
Public sector, U.S. economy, 65–66, 232
and decision-making, 240
entrepreneurship in, 243–244
and resarch capability, 241–242
salaries of experts in, 242–243
Public services, 10, 273
local, 237–240
price-setting for, 231–234
Public works, 44, 49, 50, 179
and commercial regulation, federal, 53–54, 59
and creative civil service, 50
and federal grants-in-aid, 51
in Great Britain, 201
and suburbanization, 69

Quaternary activities, 175, 177

Race relations, 165
  and new town housing, 213, 220
Railways, 204
Rainwater, Lee, 154, 161
Real estate, services to, see Community services
Reapportionment, legislative, 38, 171
Recreational facilities, 55, 289
  free, public, 233
  of Megalopolis, 170
  and new town idea, 213
  public demand for, 183
  of "Riviera" regions, 169
  urban, and the law, 209
  for white-collar labor, 174
  See also Playground facilities
Regional development, 33–34
  and economic growth rate, 202
  and government organization, 200–208, 224
  in Great Britain, 193–208
  and green belt towns, 197–199
  and local government autonomy, 211
  and public-private partnership, 222–225
  and two-tier control, 219
  See also New town communities
Regional manpower board, 39
Rehabilitiation, 41
  and handicapped, 292–294, 295
  vocational, and federal grants-in-aid, 51
Reissman, Leonard, 146
Reith study, 199
Relief, 7
  federal programs of, 127
  and Great Depression, 50–51
  See also Welfare policy
Relocation, 210, 215
Rent subsidies, 237
Research and development, 243
  in California, 66
  federal expenditures for, 67–68
Resources, public, 61–77, 179, 230
Retailing, 32
"Riviera" regions, 163, 168–177
  defined, 169, 176
  world popularity of, 169
Roads, 201
  radial, 200, 204
  state responsibility for, 50
Rockingham, Lord Charles, 195
Ruskin, John, 195
Russia, 194
St. Louis, Missouri, 56, 188–189
  bicentennial conference, Washington University, 163, 165
  de facto segregation and schools, 248–249
  financing of schools in, 250–251
  Greer's study of, 145
  Kinloch, 182–183
  parochial school education in, 252–253
  Pruitt-Igoe housing project, 112
Salisbury, Robert H., 191
Salt, Sir Titus, 195
Sapir, Edward, 115
Saturday Review, 85
Schools, 4, 15, 35, 164, 286
  autonomy of big-city, 269–273, 276
  construction, 249
  core area, 237–238, 280–281
  and culturally disadvantaged, 247–267
  and education of immigrants, 44
  and federal aid, 251, 254, 263–264, 283
  and financing problems, 249–251, 254, 279, 282–283
  and generic urban problems, 273
  improvements and the law, 209
  integration, 41, 246, 249, 265–267, 269, 272–277, 279–280
  limiting functions of, 255–256
  "metropolitanized," 279–281, 283
  and minority groups, 246
  neighborhood, 260, 273–278, 281
  nongraded primary, 259
  parochial, *see* Parochial schools
  political fragmentation of, 235, 270–284
  program diversification in, 281
  segregation, 7, 275
  in slums, 5, 8, 16, 19, 235–240, 280–281
  and socioeconomic segregation, 235–240
  spatial planning for, 239–240
  specialized, 239–240. *See also* Vocational training
  suburban, 9, 279
  and state responsibility, 50, 283
Scotland, 202
Seasonal workers, 135
Segregation, 3-4, 101
  cultural, 5
  economic, 210
  ethnic, 5, 210

Segregation (*continued*)
of the poor, 17
racial, 5, 210
religious, 5
residential, 4–8, 99–100, 248–249
school, 7, 266
sexual, 161
socioeconomic, 235
Seniority, 84
in urban school system, 270–271
Service industries, 24
and megalopolis, 175
and quality judgment, 136–137
urban, 130, 136, 137
Seward, William, 77
Sewerage, 35, 182
Shaplin, Judson T., 191
Shopping centers, 10
in Great Britain, 196, 201
Slums, 5–11, 16, 46, 165, 235–236
creation of, 127
in Great Britain, 196–197, 205
and housing improvements, 16
"image" of, 157
increase in, 6, 7
and low-status migrant, 94
relationship patterns of, 95
and "slummindedness," 16
transitional function of, 94–98
Sochi, U.S.S.R., 176
Social insurance, 289–290
and means test, 290
See also Welfare policy
Social Security, 13, 56
expansion of, 68
and federal expenditures (1965–1975), 65
and health facilities, 14
Solidarity, cultural, 157–162
South East Study, England, 202, 203–208
Southwest, U.S., 33
and white migrants, 168
Space exploration, 52, 65, 67
Status
and job hierarchy, 84, 88
of Negro, 92–93, 114
and opportunities, 91
and parental occupational achievement, 88–89, 92
transition in, 95–98
and work, 81–82, 90
Stone, Gregory, 106
Streets, 8
city responsibility for, 50
See also Highways; Roads
Subcultures, 149, 151–154, 273
Amish, 152
aristocratic, 152, 158
and ghetto Jews, 152
instability of, 152
vulnerability of, 153
See also Negro, cultural patterns of
Suburbs, 6, 143–162, 164, 167, 183, 248
building in, 32, 128, 144
and city, relationship, 25, 32, 145
cultural character of, 145
and cultural pluralism, 148–151
effects of on suburbanite, 143–144
in Great Britain, 197, 201
industrial, 49
and local expenditures, 69
myth of, 146–148, 154–157
and nonwhites, 41
planning and construction in, 58, 183
political orientation of, 146
and reapportionment, 38
recent surveys on, 145
religious orientation of, 146
residential, 49
of St. Louis, 251
schools in, 9, 279–280
sociability patterns of, 146
transient attitudes, 146
and urban parochial school, 253
Supercity systems, 24. *See also* Megalopolis
Supreme Court, U.S., 7
and integrated schools, 249
and reapportionment, 38
Survey Research Center, University of Michigan, 145
Sweden, 14
economic and population growth in, 18
regional labor market boards in, 38
Switzerland, 169

Taconic Parkway, New York, 54
Taxes, 15, 181, 232
credits, 73
and economic growth, U.S., 18
and federal fiscal planning, 38, 64, 69–71
local, and schools, 250, 254, 265
and municipal reorganization, 57
opposition to increased federal, 70
reduction, federal, 73–75, 234
regressive and the poor, 13, 290
and social insurance, 14, 289–292
-sharing, 73, 74

Taxes (*continued*)
at state and local level, 68–69
and suburbanized middle class, 49
and uniform standards for policy, 8–10
Teachers, 7, 246
in core city, 280
for culturally disadvantaged, 260–261, 265–267
and equal pay fallacy, 238, 280
and extra pay provisions, 238, 254, 280, 283
male, 238–239
parochial school, 252
professional organizations of, 270, 280
-pupil ratio, 254, 265
recruitment, 282
in slum schools, 9, 16, 238
Technology, 82
and alienation of worker, 90
and amenities, 176–177
social organizations of, 90, 101
Texas, 168
"Riviera" quality of, 176
Thomas, William I., 156
Thompson, Wilbur R., 184, 186
Toothill Report, 202
Toronto, Clark's study of, 145
Town and Country Planning Association, 195
Town cluster, 199, 200
and Britain's South East Report, 206
Town Development Act (1952), Great Britain, 206
Trade Unions, 13
Traffic, core city, 195–196, 200, 201, 273
Transportation, 12, 35, 37, 41, 75, 164, 194, 243–244
and American mobility, 167
and British new town policy, 199–200
and British regional development, 201
in California, 66
in core city, 196
employment in, 173
federal aid to, 72
federal regulatory standards for, 48
and federal responsibility, 53
low-cost mass, 233
and New York Port Authority, 33
planning, 56, 224
and "policies plan," 40
and suburbanization, 69, 164
supersonic, 68
Tyler, Ralph, 255

Underclass, 6, 13
and discrimination, 99–100, 101
and expressive life style, 112–123
and identity, 111–117
and job attitudes, 117–123
and job opportunity, 100
and means test, 103
occupational upgrading of, 91–92, 101
political apathy of, 14
transition crises of, 97–98
Underemployment, 4, 19–20, 82
and handicapped worker, 293
and underclass, 100
Unemployment, 16–22, 247, 286
and birth rate, 138
compensation, 75, 135, 290, 291
and cultural deprivation, 82
discrimination, 138–139
disguised, 20, 21
and economic expansion, 82
and Great Depression, 50–51
hard-core, 19
and migrant, 84, 124, 138–140
among nonwhites, 19, 138
of school drop-out, 261–264
stable level of, 18–19
structural, 20
by technological displacement, 137
among teenagers, 19
and underclass, 100
and the unemployable, 19
and urban specialization, 124, 137
United States Government, departments of, *see* names of specific departments
Urban policy, national, 23–42
constraints to, 43–59
federal strategy for, 52–53
Urban renewal, 5, 98, 181, 283
agency authority for, 218–221
and division of government powers, 211, 216–217, 222–225
and equalization of city, 235–236
and fashions in architecture, 57
and federal grants-in-aid, 51, 72
in Great Britain, 196–197, 201
as Negro clearance program, 41
and neighborhood planning, 274
and 1949 Housing Act, 32
and population displacement, 210, 213
and private developers, 219
and public investment policy, 183

Urban Renewal Administration, 57
Urbanization, 6, 165
and population concentration, 172
Utilities, 50
employment in, 173
and suburbanization, 69
urban, 231

Veblen, Thorstein, 153
Veterans Administration, 32, 128
Veterans' pensions, 63
Vietnam, 26, 64
Vocational training, 247, 250, 253, 288
and potential school drop-out, 262
Vocational Training Act, 262
Voting, 13–14
and middle-class suburbanization, 49

Wales, 194, 202
Walker, Charles R., 86
War on Poverty, 8–17, 41, 58, 165, 248, 277
and economic growth, 18–22
and local initiative, 57
and national policy, 22, 38
and schools, 255
and social welfare services, 45
Washington (state), 168
Waterways, 38, 77
Water supply, 164, 201
commissions, 44
Weidenbaum, Murray L., 234
Welfare policy, 11, 34, 36, 52, 75, 101–104, 246
administrative units, 295–296
and children's allowances, 290
and class differences, 159–160
crisis-oriented, 102–104, 286–289
custodial aspect of, 41
and federal fiscal policy (1965–1975), 65
and federal grants-in-aid, 51
and federal regulation, 48
in Great Britain, 201
and handicapped, 292–294
and ill health, 287, 288
lack of coordination in, 28–29, 285–286
and occupational mobility, 102
population-oriented, 102
"pricing" of, 233–234
protective, 293–294
and social adjustment, 288–289
and social attitudes, 296
and social policy, 285–296
suburban, 25
urban, 25, 35, 124
and urban wealthy, 158
Weller, Jack, 85
Welwyn Garden City, England, 199
West Coast, U.S., 33
West End Study (Boston), 82, 84
aspiration of worker of, 92
occupational level of workers of, 92
relationship patterns of, 96
Wheaton, W. L. C., 35
Whyte, William Foote, 154
Whyte, William H., 144, 145, 146
Wilmington, Delaware, Tilly study, 145
Williams, Robin, 150
Women, 291
in labor market, 82, 100
in urban employment, 135, 137
Wordsworth, William, 195
Work, 81–104
and aspiration, 92, 108–112
blue-collar, 90
as a career, 87, 99
and community-peer relationships, 95, 118
expectations, 85–86, 90
and identity, 105, 109, 119–123
as job, 85–86, 98
for Negro, 117–123
as occupation, 87
orientation, 85–88, 92, 98, 117
potentialities, 82
routine, 87
rural conceptions of, 84
security in, 85
and social participation, 87
and social position, 88-93
and social transitions, 91
as a task, 86
and transition of rural migrant, 94–98, 102
Working-Class Suburb: A Study of Auto Workers in Suburbia (Berger), 143
World War I, 49
veterans' pensions, 68
World War II, 54, 65, 69, 126

Yalta, 176

Zoning, 5, 36, 44, 212, 216
conflicts in, 211
and shift in values, 181
and slums, 128